Praise for *Why We Hate the Oil Companies*

"Provocative, insightful, stimulating....See the alternative view of an insider! Share his outrage."

—Ram Charan, bestselling coauthor of *Execution* and author of *What the CEO Wants You to Know*

"I have been interested in energy issues since high school and have read extensively on energy-related subjects. This is, by far, the most coherent, thoughtful, practical, and compelling book I have ever read on energy technology and policy issues."

—Mike Critelli, Chairman of Dossia Service Corporation, Retired Chairman and CEO, Pitney Bowes

"*Why We Hate the Oil Companies* is riveting. I keep quoting it to people. Reading it is like having a wise uncle in the energy industry (and an environmental advocate to boot) who takes you aside and tells you, in straight language, exactly what's wrong and right with the current American system. Candor, insight, and urgency at John Hofmeister's level are so rare that, before this book arrived, I'd forgotten they existed."

—Art Kleiner, Editor-in-Chief, *strategy+business*

"[Hofmeister] takes a broad view of what we need to do to craft a successful energy strategy for our nation and has firsthand knowledge of why our past policies have failed to prepare us for twenty-first century challenges."

—Robert S. Walker, Former Chairman of the Science Committee of the U.S. House of Representatives, Chairman of the Hydrogen and Fuel Cell Technical Advisory Committee of the U.S. Department of Energy

"As President of Shell Oil, [Hofmeister] addressed future energy and environmental security, challenging the industry to increase awareness of the energy issues. Now, [he] is reaching out to educate Americans about energy and solutions to ensure that preserving the environment is a top priority for public policy. John knows his 'business' and will help citizens and policy makers alike change the way we view our responsibility to the future."

—Gretchen M. Bataille, President, University of North Texas

"Entertaining and irreverent, skewering nicely all participants in energy supplies, demand, and policies and is founded on a deep understanding of the economics, technologies, and politics that drive the system. Fulfills a very important role in educating a broad readership in the critical issues of the national energy system and proposing pragmatic solutions with flair and candor. For the sake of the nation, I very much hope it attracts the high level of attention that it deserves."

—Christopher E. Ross, Vice President, Charles River Associates and coauthor of *Terra Incognita— A Navigation Aid for Energy Leaders*

WHY WE HATE THE OIL COMPANIES

STRAIGHT TALK FROM AN ENERGY INSIDER

JOHN HOFMEISTER

palgrave
macmillan

WHY WE HATE THE OIL COMPANIES
Copyright © John Hofmeister, 2010.

First published in 2010 by
PALGRAVE MACMILLAN®
in the United States—a division of St. Martin's Press LLC,
175 Fifth Avenue, New York, NY 10010.

Where this book is distributed in the UK, Europe, and the rest of the world,
this is by Palgrave Macmillan, a division of Macmillan Publishers Limited,
registered in England, company number 785998, of Houndmills,
Basingstoke, Hampshire RG21 6XS.

Palgrave Macmillan is the global academic imprint of the above companies
and has companies and representatives throughout the world.

Palgrave® and Macmillan® are registered trademarks in the United States,
the United Kingdom, Europe and other countries.

ISBN: 978–0–230–10208–8

Library of Congress Cataloging-in-Publication Data

Hofmeister, John.
    Why we hate the oil companies : straight talk from an energy insider /
John Hofmeister.
      p. cm.
    ISBN 978–0–230–10208–8
      1. Petroleum industry and trade—Political aspects—United States.
   2. Petroleum industry and trade—United States. I. Title.

HD9565.H64 2010
338.2′72820973—dc22   2009052385

A catalogue record of the book is available from the British Library.

Design by Newgen Imaging Systems (P) Ltd., Chennai, India

First edition: June 2010

10 9 8 7 6 5 4 3 2 1

Printed in the United States of America.

CONTENTS

Introduction   1

1 **The Future Is More, Not Less**   11
   A postindustrial information-based economy demands
   more energy, not less. Surprised?

2 **Energy Independence? Keep Dreaming**   23
   Energy independence should not be a goal—it should be a
   by-product of effective policies.

3 **There Is an Energy Shortage, but There Is No**
   Shortage of Energy   33
   We will never run out of energy, unless we choose
   wrong policies or fail to implement right policies.

4 **Inconvenient or Not, the Truth Is that Climate**
   Change Is Not the Issue   61
   Let's quit debating global warming and manage
   gaseous wastes as we do other trash.

5 **Beware the Reckless Right and Ludicrous Left**   75
   Put in charge of energy, the right wing will destroy
   the earth; the left wing will destroy our society.

6 **Forget the Free Market**   95
   Let's quit pretending. Energy access, production, storage,
   distribution, and sales have been regulated for decades.

7 **The Industry Is Parochial. Surprised?**   113
   The energy industry cannot solve our energy
   crisis. I should know.

8 **Oil and Gas: Unlovable and Unavoidable.**
   Utilities: Ditto!   125
   The oil and gas industry, locked in its paradigm, is
   unlovable but essential. So quit complaining
   and get used to it.

9   Conservation Starts with Land Use Management   **143**
*If we are unwilling as a nation to address urban and
rural planning in more significant ways, let's quit
pretending we're serious about energy efficiency.*

10   Energy and Politics: Oil and Water   **159**
*There is a basic conflict between "energy time," which
is defined by decades, and "political time," which is
defined by two- and four-year cycles.*

11   Our Government Is Broken   **175**
*When addressing energy and the environment, the federal
government is paralyzed by partisanship and stymied by
dysfunction. "Political time" makes it worse.*

12   Here's How We Fix It!   **193**
*We need an intervention to put the nation on the
right course to deliver energy security and
environmental protection.*

13   Every Voice Counts   **209**
*Governments will create independent regulatory bodies to
govern energy security and the environment only if
grassroots citizens demand them.*

14   Where Do We Go from Here?   **219**
*Independent regulatory leadership could launch nations
toward multi-decade journeys of unprecedented economic
and environmental renewal. Its absence will take many
nations, in particular the United States, to an
unprecedented energy abyss.*

Acknowledgments   238

Notes   241

Bibliography   243

Index   246

INTRODUCTION

Americans have long had a love-hate relationship with the oil industry. Myself included.

Although I spent the last third of my corporate career working for Royal Dutch Shell, one of the world's largest international oil companies, and the final three years as president of its U.S. subsidiary, Shell Oil Company, my perceptions of the industry were shaped long before I first stepped through the doors of Shell's elegantly understated European headquarters back in September 1997.

I started paying attention to energy policy the year Richard Nixon turned out the Christmas lights. It was 1973, and I had just started working as a management trainee at General Electric's lighting headquarters in Nela Park, near Cleveland, Ohio. On October 20, Saudi Arabia, supported by other Arab states, cut off all oil supplies to the United States as retaliation for U.S. funding of Israel in the latest Arab-Israeli conflict. To conserve energy during the embargo, Nixon asked Americans to turn off their Christmas lights. GE, of course, was in the holiday light bulb business. At the company's campus where I worked, our Christmas lighting display was a local historic landmark. Generations of Cleveland-area families looked forward to an annual drive-through of the displays. GE made the symbolic gesture of turning off the lights to comply with the president's request, but the real impact was that we had to lay off hundreds of local employees in a matter of months because of the drop in business caused by that government policy decision. Just down the road from Nela Park was the Gulf station on Euclid Avenue where I filled up my stripped-down 1972 Chevy Nova. During the embargo, the station owner wore a pistol on each hip because customers were fighting over places in the gas lines and he wanted order, not chaos. Over the next 25 years, as I moved into management and executive positions at companies that were large consumers of energy, oil shocks and surpluses played havoc with business planning, and I continued to manage uncertainty around energy costs. During my 15 years at GE, we were continually buffeted by the energy waves, as prices spiked and fell and alternative forms of energy rose in favor then quickly ebbed. In 1979, when an Arab oil cutback sent U.S. gasoline prices soaring, then-president Jimmy Carter announced a huge push to create synthetic crude oil from coal and oil shale deposits in the Rocky Mountains. He projected 2.5 million barrels of production by 1990. Three years later, oil prices had fallen, and on May 2, 1982, a day remembered in Colorado as Black Sunday, Exxon shut down its synthetic crude operation, eliminating thousands of jobs on the remote western slope of the Rockies. Over the next several years of my career I was at Nortel, a global telecommunications technology company, and AlliedSignal, a large aerospace, automotive, and engineered materials company that later acquired Honeywell and took its name. Both companies were large energy consumers that benefited from a period of mostly low oil prices. However, when the first Gulf War took place in 1992, I was at AlliedSignal's aerospace business, and the airline industry lost more profit that year than it had made in its entire history, due to the high cost of fuel and loss of customers. We shed some 20,000 employees in the restructurings that followed.

After 24 years on the consumer side of oil, I joined Shell. I had worked in companies that paid for the consequences of energy policies—or the lack of policy—and I wanted to see if it was possible to make a difference on the energy producer side. I did not have the traditional petroleum engineering or geophysics background of an energy executive—my degrees were in political science—but I had strong global business strategic and leadership experience, a diverse background in marketing, manufacturing, and human resources, gained at top *Fortune* magazine–rated companies, and I believed that sometimes an outsider can provide a fresh perspective and accomplish more—or so I hoped.

What I found at Shell was a company that pushes the frontiers of technology, employs many of the smartest people on Earth, enables economic growth and development around the world, increasingly appreciates and responds to sustainable development needs, and provides solid shareholder returns. Yet it is a company in one of the most hated industries in the United States, an industry that consistently ranks at the bottom in reputation polls.[1]

That animosity came to a head after Hurricanes Katrina and Rita hit the Gulf Coast in the late summer of 2005, just months after I became president of Shell Oil Company. Prices had been climbing for the past three years, but the serious supply disruptions caused by the storms sent prices skyrocketing. I started receiving hate mail, including a drawing showing me hanging in effigy. Not exactly what I expected when I took the job.

In June 2006, Jim Mulva, chairman of ConocoPhillips, Dave O'Reilly, chairman of Chevron, and I appeared together on *Meet the Press,* where host Tim Russert began by confronting us with a set of negative poll numbers and asking us, "Why is that?"[2]

■ ■ ■ ■

One of the two most humbling moments in my tenure as president of Shell Oil Company was having to raise my hand alongside four other energy executives and swear to tell "the truth, the whole truth, and nothing but the truth" before the Senate Judiciary Committee hearing on oil prices in the late winter of 2006. Customarily, those testifying before Senate committees are not sworn in because it is against the law to lie to Congress. And Congress is not a courtroom. The requirement that we swear in—in unison—was, first and foremost, a staged media photo opportunity but also was indicative of the presumption on the part of legislators that, given the opportunity, we would choose not to tell the truth. The anemic explanation by Arlen Specter, the Republican senator from Pennsylvania who chaired the committee and who has since switched to the Democratic Party, that he trusted us (but not enough to waive the swearing-in shenanigan), was simple bad faith, disguising acrimony.

The second most humbling moment was realizing—despite my personal commitment and efforts, along with that of my leadership team at Shell Oil, the parent company executives and board of directors, and tens of thousands of colleagues at Shell—our complete and utter failure to communicate the critical importance of energy security to the nation's political leadership during my tenure. Despite trying, including making some two dozen or more trips per year to Washington, DC, I essentially failed to persuade our political leaders of energy's relationship to national security, the implications of misguided energy policy for the U.S. economy, and the toll high energy prices due to sup- ply constraints take on our citizens. My failure to do so was also the nation's failure to develop national energy and environmen- tal policy that works over the short, medium, and long term to benefit citizens from all walks of life. As a result, we are now facing a future of energy haves and have-nots in our pluralistic, democratic society.

But then again, what else could you expect from the industry that brought you such shining moments as the Standard Oil Trust at the end of the nineteenth century, which controlled upward of 85 percent of the market and is still used as a case study for unethical monopolization of a market; the spill from an offshore well near Santa Barbara in 1969 that washed nearly 6,000 bar- rels of oil onto a 35-mile stretch of Southern California beaches; the 1989 *Exxon Valdez* spill, when an oil tanker ran aground off the coast of Alaska, spreading a sheen of oil across 11 mil- lion square miles of ocean; and the scandal at natural gas mar- keter Enron, which collapsed into bankruptcy in 2001, when it was discovered that its many billions in revenues and profits were built on a deliberately designed structure of accounting fraud? My former company is also not without blame. The 2004 re-categorization of proven oil reserves was well reported.

Yet even when the industry has not been perceived as behav ing badly, energy companies have let their reputations fall into disrepair by consistently failing to tell their stories to the public. Some have not even tried; others have filtered their communi- cation through such obfuscation that it came across as disin- formation; still others have been unwilling to present a human face that people can relate to. Instead of being accessible to the media, many energy companies choose to buy advertising space to tell a guarded version of the truth. Instead of educating consumers on the real risks and real costs of energy, they choose to sponsor cultural and educational television programs. Instead of being on-site to respond to a crisis, they send the lawyers. Instead of patiently and repeatedly explaining their enormous revenue, profit, and investment numbers in layman's terms, they use investor relations–speak. This leaves the impression that they believe people are too stupid to understand them, so there is no point in explaining. I actually heard one executive from another company say, "Why waste money to communicate with people who don't like us? If they don't want our products, there are plenty of others who do."

The result is lack of understanding and vilification of oil and other energy companies, which just adds to the problem and frustrates the pursuit of energy solutions. There is a perception, for example, that oil companies have more control of the market than they do and that they deliberately create crises in order to move their own agendas forward. On multiple occasions I was asked what role Shell played in promoting the Iraq war and how much Shell stood to gain from future access to oil in that country as a result. Shell played *no* role in promoting the war in Iraq; decisions to go to war are made by governments, not by oil companies. The fact that people believe otherwise is symptomatic of the reputation problem oil companies have.

■   ■   ■   ■   ■

If the oil companies have the answers to the energy crisis—and in some cases they do—who will believe them now? Would you accept the fox's plan for a chicken coop? When Big Oil is the enemy, all solutions it presents are suspect. When energy companies speak, hearts and minds have been taught to shut down.

Yet energy is the basis of much of our economy and quality of life. Ignorance about energy leads in one direction: bad public policy that ultimately hurts all energy consumers. Ignorance also leads to the abundance of energy misinformation and disinformation that has become rampant across our society and a favorite tool of political leaders running for office.

If lack of communication helped create the problem, I believe openness and transparency must be a major part of the solution. We need education that enables people to ask the right questions of the various players—energy companies, politicians, and other interest groups—to get better answers. Such answers must move past industry techno-speak. Preventing the public's full understanding by hiding behind industrial jargon serves no one's interest. Humanizing information is most effective, to give it a real face and an authentic personality.

I began working toward that goal at Shell Oil in 2006 with a face-to-face outreach effort. I personally crisscrossed the country, visiting 50 important cities, together with about five Shell managers per city—some 250 leaders in all—to meet with business leaders, community leaders, government representatives, the general public, and our own wholesalers and retailers. In those cities, we listened in stand-up town hall–style meetings to what our stakeholders had to say and spoke in a range of venues providing our perspective on energy issues. We engaged and we learned. It was sometimes humbling but always energizing. Real people in genuine dialogue on matters of substance to daily and national life found common ground on which they shared mutual concerns and spoke frankly about possible solutions. I thank every one of my former colleagues and the 15,000 or so fellow citizens who came to meet with us for their involvement. Two takeaways that I carry to this day: Americans are smart when they have the facts, and they are pragmatic about what to do when they understand the circumstances.

On one level, the program was a success. It separated Shell from the industry pack and moved our national favorability ratings from third and fourth place to first place among our industry peers. But that only made us the least hated in a still-hated industry. (Other companies, including ConocoPhillips and Chevron, and the American Petroleum Institute on behalf of the industry, quickly followed with outreach programs of their own. Later, ExxonMobil developed its own image campaign.)

Elected officials (and those hoping to get elected) continue to vilify Big Oil and get applause for it every time. While this is frustrating, it is not surprising. You can't erase decades of insensitivity and vast and widening gaps of misunderstanding with two or three years of outreach and reputation building, especially when cash is pouring out of consumer pockets to buy gas and into oil company treasuries, funding record profits at the companies that are accused of overcharging for their products.

I retired from Shell in June 2008, persuaded that the answers do not lie with the oil companies alone or with any of the other energy special interest groups—coal producers, utilities, transmission companies—and that they do not lie with partisan elected officials, who have their own short-cycle agendas. I started Citizens for Affordable Energy, Inc. (www.citizensforaffordable-energy.org), to do something about providing those answers. It is a not-for-profit education-based effort to help grassroots Americans learn about energy and environmental solutions in the layman's language they speak and in the neighborhoods where they live. The most recent promises for green jobs, clean energy, and energy independence coming from the current administration ring as hollow for what issues they do not address as did the promises of politicians past. The answers also do not lie with other special interests that promote their own selfish, narrow environmental solutions—from "carbon is bad for us" to "carbon is good for us" agendas. The answers lie instead in the collective will of the American people—and people around the world—to become informed and take appropriate actions.

Maybe that sounds naive, but I remember what Americans did to bring about an end to segregation and, around the same time, the Vietnam War. I remember not only the marches and the sit-ins, but ultimately the fact that an increasing majority of people from throughout society finally said "Enough is enough" to their elected officials and made their voices heard through the electoral process to get people into power with the mandate to bring about change. Grassroots movements in other democracies have had similar impact.

We have the same power now to fix our energy and environmental problems, which I believe are on the same national, social, economic, and political scales as segregation and unnecessary war. We have endured at least four decades of failure to address energy and environmental systems in the United States. We are starting our fifth. The promises of the current administration, like those of its predecessors, are inadequate to the requirements of the future, despite their appeal, and will not meet the nation's needs. This book explains what we need to know and describes what we can do collectively to change the energy and environmental system in this and every country forever, regardless of the perspectives of energy companies, special interests, and today's partisan, electorally focused government leaders.

·   ·   ·   ·   ·

The truth is that affordable energy is essential for American economic growth. It is essential for our national security and position in world leadership. And it is necessary to maintain our quality of life. It is also important for citizens around the world who desire to maintain or pursue similar levels of comfortable living, especially the billions of people who cannot access any energy but fire. Affordable energy and environmental sustainability are challenges that require our urgent attention. Our nation was founded on a commitment to develop and protect a society in which economic and social justice and equality under the law are provided to all citizens. We cannot deliver on that commitment in the twenty-first century if we become a country of energy haves and have-nots. To deliver our promise to ourselves, we must have *affordable* energy, which is possible from pragmatic, nonpartisan solutions built on short-, medium-, and long-term plans that balance the wide range of interests of all stakeholders. As a society, we cannot promote policies that reward just a few or make energy too expensive for all but a few.

These are not the words of a Cassandra crying out a litany of prophecies. These are the words of a deeply worried business leader who has seen firsthand the parochialism of the energy industry and its uncanny ability to look out for its own interests and to make money without regard to political party in power or social impact. As a former energy executive, I have had access to reports and analyses of the world's energy supplies and technology, and I listen in horror to the wishful and unrealistic thinking of the anti-hydrocarbon and anti-nuclear elements in this country. I am a well-read and studied political scientist who sees movement throughout the developed and developing world where countries will take care of themselves regardless of what happens in and to the United States. Other countries will not regret America's energy problems. As a lifelong environmentally conscientious person, I am convinced of the need to control gaseous wastes and ensure the future quality of land, water, and the atmosphere. I am a deeply worried American citizen who has confronted and argued unsuccessfully with leaders of both political parties for solutions at the highest levels of national public policy making. I am an American taxpayer who has watched hard-earned tax dollars consumed by voracious federal government structural and procedural dysfunction. In addition, I am a father and grandfather who sees the future of his children and grandchildren at risk because of the impact of energy issues on our economy, competitiveness, and national security and the failure of the government and other key groups to come to grips with what is needed. The negative relationship between energy producers and energy consumers, provoked and coddled by partisan politicians, has gone on too long and costs too much. It is time to confront this problem and move forward to solutions that will benefit us all, now and forever, here in the United States and around the world. *Why We Hate the Oil Companies: Straight Talk from an Energy Insider* was written to do just that.

THE FUTURE IS MORE, NOT LESS

A postindustrial information-based economy demands
more energy, not less. Surprised?

On a mild January day in 2007, I sat across the breakfast table from several senior Microsoft executives at a Seattle hotel not far from their headquarters in Redmond, Washington. "Our business plans say we need to build at least six new information centers across the Northwest to support our Internet and other growth plans," they told me. "We need new electricity equivalent to the output of a 350-megawatt power plant to support them. But we don't know where we're going to get that much new electricity in Washington or Oregon. Hydropower has peaked, there's not enough natural gas, coal-burning plants cannot be built here for now, wind is too erratic, and no nuclear plants are on the horizon in the time frame of our business growth. Do you have any suggestions about where electricity is going to come from in the future?"

They were hoping that, as an energy executive, I could give them some new ideas and long-range thinking. But, in fact, they had given me a new perspective on the scope of our energy challenge. They explained that information centers are intensely electrified operations, requiring power not just for racks and racks of computers and switches but also for heating, cooling, and dehumidifying to create the proper environment for the sensitive electronics. Looking at the exist-ing power infrastructure in the region, it was clear they would come up short.

The huge worry on the table that morning was whether, to meet near-term growth, Microsoft would have to go offshore with its information centers to take advantage of greater energy growth outside the United States. The executives were aware that competitors were doing it, but they hoped they would not have to. What was clear to me after this meeting was this: in the digital age, we are more power-hungry than ever. Our economic growth depends more than ever on electrons.

■   ■   ■   ■   ■

The landscape across America looks different from what it was when my career began in the early 1970s: there are fewer for-ests of belching smokestacks, sending up the exhaust from the energy consumed by massive steel and textile mills, foundries, and consumer goods manufacturing plants. What is left of the smokestack operations of our industrial economy are now far more likely to be on the other side of the globe, in India and China and other low-wage countries.

Instead of these energy-devouring smokestack behemoths, we have millions and millions of electronic devices in electricity-intensive, mountain range–like structures of shining clean office buildings, in home offices, on kitchen counters, mounted on our dashboards, carried in our pockets, and clipped to our ears. Rather than a few giant industrial lions consuming our energy, it is being eaten away by millions of tiny digital gnats. Our human capital is purposefully engaged more with intellectual manipula-tion of information than with brawn or manual dexterity. The future of economic growth via our applied human intelligence is a future of unlimited potential—provided we have the electrons to make it possible.

Total energy use in the United States has tripled in the last six decades. When you look at how that energy is being used, the shift is clear. In 1949, industrial manufacturing consumed nearly half of the energy used in this country. In 2007, industrial manufacturing accounted for less than a third of the total energy used. While the percentage of energy that went toward transportation rose slightly, the biggest increases were in residential and commercial use. Commercial use has quintupled since 1949, and much of that growth can be traced directly to the increased use of computers and all of the associated servers, printers, modems, routers, and other data devices that devour electrons, often on a 24/7 basis.

Our lives are increasingly electronic in every imaginable way. From the microwaves that heat our Lean Cuisine dinners to the cell phones that keep us connected with voice and text; from the home computers and high-definition televisions and game systems that populate our homes to the massive digital networks without which corporations and government would come to a crashing halt; from the movies showing in the megaplexes to the brightly illuminated live sports events broadcast via satellite around the globe; from magnetic resonance imaging technology to digital thermometers; from home security alarms to national security technology; from the global positioning systems in our cars to the iPods in our pockets—we have it all because electrons make it possible.

Hurricane Ike, in September 2008, brought this point home vividly to Houston, America's fourth largest city. The energy capital of the world was virtually powerless in the aftermath of the storm. More than 90 percent of the city lost power. Business came to a standstill. The mayor imposed a curfew to keep cars off the streets at night because there were few working streetlights or traffic signals. There were lines for emergency ice and water supplies, but there were also lines at the few locations with power where electronics-starved residents could plug in their laptops and charge their depleted cell phones. It took two weeks for power to be restored to 75 percent of the city, and during that period many Houstonians lived in a world with no air conditioning, no TV, no lights, no refrigerators, no movies, no Internet, scarce gasoline, water interruptions, and sporadic phone communication. Millions of people did without all that, just because the electrons went missing.

Ironically, the power plants were functioning at that time; it was the distribution system that went down, primarily due to tree damage to power lines. Less than 1 percent of power line poles were impacted, yet most of the city's residents were without power. The response to this outage is a plan for the future that will result in even more need for electrons. Houston is creating a smart grid that utilizes additional electrons to flip switches and self-heal huge swaths of the electricity network around the downed lines, as well as more distributed generation in neighborhoods. The goal: fewer people will lose power and recovery will be swifter for those who do.

■   ■   ■   ■   ■

For Microsoft on that January morning, a shortage of electrons was limiting its ability to grow. The company's information-age model was predicated on an ever-increasing supply of electrons at a scale that would support robust growth. Washington State's regional energy resources—or rather the *anticipated* lack of future electricity resources—created a business constraint. We talked about the potential growth of wind and solar power that morning, but these technologies were not—and are not—up to the scale of the task Microsoft was outlining. In consequence, despite its preference to expand domestically, the company was forced to look around the globe to see where the electricity infrastructure would support its needs.

Unfortunately, too many companies are facing the same challenge, due not only to availability of electrons but also to the volatility of other energy prices, such as oil products and natural gas. Since 2005, more than 50 percent of U.S. fertilizer manufacturing has moved offshore to find cheaper sources of natural gas, which is used to produce ammonia, a primary ingredient in fertilizer. While chemical plant construction is booming in China, India, and the Middle East, the United States is rapidly losing much of its chemical manufacturing base because of cost increases for feedstock, primarily oil and natural gas. Many people believe that we are losing our manufacturing jobs because of high wages. In the larger picture, costs and availability of energy are factors as well.

Just as we are realizing the increased need for new affordable energy, we are also putting political constraints on our ability to produce it on the scale required. It is very difficult to obtain permits for new coal-fired power plants, nuclear plants, liquefied natural gas regasification plants, offshore drilling, new transmission lines, pipelines, switching stations, refineries, gas plants— you name it. Even wind farms are hard to site, especially when they might affect the view of "important" people who live part time on Nantucket and other scenic locales.

NIMBYism (not-in-my-backyard efforts to stop infrastructure from being built), often fomented by plaintiff law firms looking for business, seriously threatens the availability of new energy to support a growing economy. Litigants are looking out for their individual interests at the expense of the wider community's interests. How, in the twenty-first century, can we persist in denying ourselves the energy that we need to sustain our economic growth and quality of life?

Opposition comes in many forms, not just lawsuits from NIMBYists. Anti-coal, anti-nuclear, and anti–liquefied natural gas interests try to stop mega-projects, and even smaller infrastructure investments, for different reasons. They often cite fear-invoking claims of security issues, terrorist threats, or threats to clean air and water. Meanwhile, failure to expand our electricity supply drives prices up, putting fixed- and low-income people at ever higher risk of being unable to afford electricity and businesses, small and large, at risk of shrinking, moving, or closing. Who is really being helped by this determination to stop new infrastructure?

■　■　■　■

Energy fuels not just our electronics but also our lifestyle. Our personal pride and joy often sits in our driveways. A first car is a rite of passage; future cars are a necessity; and it is an emotional wrench when we take away a senior citizen's car keys for his or her own safety. Personal mobility is as much a way of life in America as personal electronics. We can't do without either. While the percentage of energy that has gone toward transportation has remained somewhat stable over the last six decades, in raw numbers U.S. gasoline consumption has nearly quadrupled while the population has slightly more than doubled. That means we are using nearly 75 percent more gasoline per person—per man, woman, and child—now than we were in 1949. (This upward trend has been fairly consistent over the last 60 years, with the most significant drop in the late 1970s, when higher oil prices and U.S. automaker quality issues combined to pave the way for an influx of smaller cars from Japan.)

Driving is part of our national character, from the days of the advertising slogan "See the U.S.A. in your Chevrolet" to today's drive-through culture for everything from bank transactions to lattes. The only decline in energy consumption in recent memory came at the expense of economic growth and was due to the severe global recession that started during 2008 and extended through most of 2009. Resuming economic growth in this country, and globally, will return us to the same underlying problems of scarcity and higher costs for energy supplies. Keep a neck brace close by—whiplash from fast-rising prices can hurt.

We are in a precarious balance today. Just as Hurricane Ike knocked out power to Houston, it also disrupted fuel supplies. Gulf Coast petroleum refineries that supply the southeastern to Middle Atlantic states, from Texas to Maryland, were shut down twice in quick succession for Hurricanes Gustav and Ike, whose one-two punch was eerily similar to the Katrina/Rita combination in 2005. Oil product and gasoline production feeding into the Plantation and Colonial pipelines that transport fuel to this region was interrupted for weeks. Having experienced Katrina and Rita as president of Shell Oil Company, I could see what was coming next. The Monday following Ike's landfall, I was in a meeting with the *Washington Times* editorial board. I pointed out that in order to maintain a calm and orderly market in nearly a quarter of the country, now was the time for governors in those states to impose an odd-even rationing system based on license plate numbers for gasoline and other fuels. Without this step, I predicted, there would be long gas station lines and frustrated citizens. The problem would be temporary, and by anticipating it and acting quickly, it would be possible to get through it with minimal discomfort: deferring purchases by just one day.

The next day, the *Washington Times* front-page headline read, "Former Oil Exec: Gas Rationing Needed."[1] The response was immediate and negative—the White House and the American Petroleum Institute, an industry trade association, both denied any problem existed. Virtually no one supported the rationing concept. Within two weeks, national media were reporting gas lines and outages. As drivers waited in long lines to top off their fuel tanks, a local Atlanta petroleum company owner went so far as to recommend that the governor of Georgia cancel the weekend's Georgia-Alabama football game to conserve fuel. Radio talk-show hosts were deluged with callers who reported station outages, phoned in updates on tank truck deliveries, and told individual horror stories about waking up at 2:00 a.m. to buy gas when there would be no lines, only to discover lines wherever they went. The anger and frustration led many people to blame Big Oil—the major oil brands—for both shortages and higher prices. The shortage was temporary, and the media coverage was even more abbreviated, especially on a national scale, as the crash of the financial markets pushed stories of post-Ike issues of the Gulf Coast to the back pages. But the people who feared for their ability to get to work or school were reminded of the vulnerability of both supply and affordability.

Every outage reminds us how critical fuel is to the way we live.

■   ■   ■   ■   ■

The comparatively low cost and plentiful supply of energy throughout the 1990s and the first years of the twenty-first century helped drive a low unemployment rate and a lifestyle of larger cars, commuting to larger houses, located farther from downtown employment centers or industrial areas. These suburban McMansions not only require heating and cooling of more cubic feet but also become the repository for more electron-fed devices, from countless light bulbs to brighten the high-ceilinged spaces to multiple flat-screen televisions, sound systems, and computer systems, to heated swimming pools with automatic filtration systems and three-car garages with automatic door openers (and, of course, three cars inside). Cheap energy built America, and it was cheap because it was plentiful.

This boom of prosperity meant that, until recently, we were spending more money to live better than ever before—which translated to consuming more total energy than ever before, both gasoline and electric power. To many, the spiral—available energy, to lifestyle improvements, to more energy demand—felt like an upward path, until we began to push against the constraints of energy supply and recognize that our fossil-fueled lives were threatening our environment and thus our long-term quality of life. Sustainability may be an overused term, but it is very apt: how do we sustain our forward progress without compromising the ability of future generations to enjoy the same quality of life?

There are about 250 million cars and trucks on the road in the United States. More than 99 percent run on liquid fuel powering an internal combustion or diesel engine. Today's fleet will most likely continue in use for much of the next 20 years—the life span of current vehicles.

When we are not driving, we are flying, more often and farther afield. Despite a 60 percent decrease in fuel use per passenger in the last 35 years, U.S. airlines consumed 81 percent more fuel in 2008 than in 1977, and the percentage of that total attributed to international travel increased 50 percent. Growth in aviation fuel use has slowed since 2000 in developed countries, but most of the decline is due to flatter growth in passengers and passenger miles; fuel efficiency improvements have stalled at 1 percent per year. Developing countries are seeing increased fuel growth.

When we are not flying, we are cruising. In 2008 more than 10.2 million people in America took a cruise trip. However, cruise ships accounted for only a small percentage of the tens of billions of gallons of fuel used in the maritime sector. Where did most of it go? To marine shipping: 2.3 billion metric tons of cargo, including a 13 percent increase in petroleum imports over the past five years. In other words, we are spending fuel to obtain fuel.

■ ■ ■ ■ ■

In Europe, the same digital-driven electricity demand is evident as, since 1990, electricity consumption has increased at nearly triple the rate of overall energy consumption. The European Union is ahead of the United States in responding to the environmental consequences of this increased demand: new taxes on gasoline, natural gas, and electricity; an emphasis on nuclear energy (Europe now produces more than 40 percent of the world's nuclear power); emissions-reduction regulations; and funding of expanded research on low-carbon fuels have all been put in place with a goal of increasing energy security and reducing emissions.

In the world's emerging economies, especially China and India, we are watching the spiral of energy development repeat itself. But with massive populations, the ability to rapidly adopt technology that already exists elsewhere, and the desire to catch up with European and American standards of living, this spiral is accelerated and enlarged exponentially. In China, per-capita consumption of energy has more than doubled since 1980—yet a Chinese person still uses an average of just over one-sixth the energy that an American uses every day. In India, per-capita consumption has nearly tripled in the same time frame—but the average Indian's energy use still lags behind where China's populace was in 1980. Even at these very modest per-capita levels, the huge populations in both China and India means total energy consumption of the two countries combined is equivalent to more than 90 percent of the energy used in the United States.

And let us not leave out the approximately 1.5 billion people on Earth who have no access to electricity at all. As the future unfolds, these people will demand their rightful share of the planet's energy potential, fueling continued energy consumption growth at ever-greater demand levels in the decades to come. No continent can tolerate twenty-first-century social inequities of energy haves versus have-nots. There are limits to relative deprivation, and society must step up to alleviate it.

Global growth in demand for automobiles is another contributor to spiraling energy use worldwide. The 250 million cars and trucks on the road in the United States constitute one-quarter of the billion cars on the planet—a number that is expected to double in the next 20 years.[2] Most of that growth will be outside North America, as more and more families in developing countries strive to realize their dream of owning their first car. And more than 96 percent of those cars in the next decade or longer will be powered by liquid-fueled internal combustion engines, which for the present are the most affordable power source.

The implication is clear: as developing regions continue to expand their economies and raise their standards of living, the demand for energy will continue to spiral upward, both for electricity and liquid fuel. Energy conservation and energy efficiency efforts will play a role in moderating that growth somewhat, but the underlying trends of a growing worldwide population and rising standards of living mean that we cannot delude ourselves into thinking we can "save" our way to energy prosperity. The increasing number of people who want—and should not be denied—access to electrons and mobility are an unstoppable force of modern society.

This constantly increasing demand for energy is a challenge to both our ability to deliver energy supply and our environmental sustainability. The most prolific and readily accessible sources of energy right now are still carbon based: oil, coal, and natural gas. The scale of energy demand cannot be fully met in the near future by cleaner alternatives, such as wind and solar power or biofuels. While we scale up these alternatives over the next several decades, we must also put significant effort into developing the pathways by which more carbon-based energy can be produced and consumed in cleaner, more sustainable ways.

It may be politically popular to promote primarily renewables and alternatives as the next wave of energy supplies. But, plain and simple, renewables and alternatives are not going to get the job done. There is not enough wind and sunlight in the right places for long enough to supply base-load energy, the energy we need every day, to meet future demand growth, let alone peak demand periods. Until we make major advances in solar technology via nanotechnology, until we unwind the myths that prevent investment in nuclear power, until we embrace hydrogen fuel cell technology as an alternative to internal combustion engines, we must develop new and more hydrocarbon sources of energy over the next 20, 30, and even 50 years. And yes, we must also address the carbon management implications of more hydrocarbon fuel consumption at the same time. Gaseous waste, like physical and liquid waste, must be controlled, managed, and reduced in order for humans to continue to live safely and healthfully on this planet.

Some environmental advocates have been promoting the idea that the United States can move to carbon-free electricity production within the next decade. This no-more-carbon-in-10-years crowd may have laudable motives and intense commitment to the environmental cause. But considering the vast and growing demand for energy, and the dependence on energy of more and more of the world's population for economic well-being and a comfortable lifestyle, it is clear that future energy consumption will include both more hydrocarbons and more of every other source of energy. This is inevitable over the next several decades because there are simply not sufficient renewable energy sources and technologies at affordable prices to displace hydrocarbons.

What is possible later in terms of transitioning to carbon-free energy sources is very exciting and highly probable. But let us be honest: it will require persistence, investment, continued use of reliable and transition to new technologies for a long time to come. In the meantime, no one wants to be without energy, nor should it become an expensive privilege of the very wealthy. For that reason, we have to balance how and when we move from the old to the new in ways that support a clean environment and social justice at the same time.

Transforming our energy economy and its environmental consequences is the major domestic and international issue of our time. Energy is the basis of global economic success, growth, and sustenance. Not only is it unrealistic to expect energy demand to lessen, it is also unrealistic to believe that the United States can declare energy independence and achieve its energy goals without depending on outside sources.

2

ENERGY INDEPENDENCE? KEEP DREAMING

Energy independence should not be a goal—it should be a by-product of effective policies.

I remember where I was when I heard about the fall of the Berlin Wall in November 1989. I was in Raleigh, North Carolina, watching events unfold on television. I had tears in my eyes as I felt the excitement and joy of the celebration and saw Berliners greet Berliners, streaming through the newly opened wall. The images of young East Berliners, driving their Trabants, being given bananas and oranges—produce that they had only read about—by welcoming West Berliners, will always remain poignant.

The Berlin Wall was built at the height of Cold War tensions to do nothing more than make a political point. However, it stood for years, symbolizing the outlook on the future from two very different perspectives. People lost their lives crossing over the wall. Eventually, electronic images of life in the West demonstrated the wall's futility. People in East Berlin who had been told over and over from the end of the War onward that their lives were far better than those of the people of West Berlin could see the folly and untruths, not just hear about them. When smart people saw through the mythical nature of the wall, they did something about it. They got practical.

I remember the events running up to the wall's demise—candlelight demonstrations in Leipzig and elsewhere, as the government of the German Democratic Republic did all the wrong things, powerless to stop the dynamics of social change. "They just don't get it," I realized. False statements and promises by politicians cannot long endure the scrutiny and honesty that people crave.

But politicians have been building walls—real and virtual—for thousands of years. The Berlin Wall. The Iron Curtain. The Maginot Line. The Mason-Dixon Line. The Great Wall of China. Walls seem to be a way of drawing lines in the sand to represent important positions. The world's newest physical wall, being built along the border between Mexico and the United States, is nothing more than a line in the sand (literally, since it is in the great southwestern desert of the United States) to make a political point. To think it will last is to believe in fairy tales. It too will be discredited and disowned by people who move from political rhetoric to practical reality.

In a world where borders are increasingly invisible, where cars built and driven in the United States are designed in Japan and cars designed in the United States are on the roads in China and Australia, where carbon dioxide and other emissions from power plants in Guangdong, China, can affect the atmosphere and skies in Omaha, Nebraska, borders mean little. Where two of the top three suppliers of oil and gas to the United States are our neighbors Canada and Mexico, drawing a metaphorical line in the sand or building an imaginary wall and espousing "energy independence" in this country seems pointless at best and self-defeating at worst.

■　■　■　■　■

Energy that is transportable will be transported. Electricity over grids, oil and gas in pipelines, oil in crude oil carriers, biofuels in barges and tankers, liquefied natural gas in carriers, uranium in trucks and rail cars, coal in trucks, trains, barges, and ships—energy is tradable and transportable. Why wouldn't we want to trade and move energy to markets where it is needed from the places where it is sourced? What is it about "energy independence" that keeps this mantra in the political rhetoric of political campaign after campaign? As we'll see below, this idea lacks substance. The more energy independence has been promised, the less it has been delivered. As we experience yet one more round of efforts at energy independence, we should understand our national experience with this mythical line in the sand.

There's no doubt in my mind that President Nixon's call for energy independence back in November 1973 was seriously intended. He saw the gas lines provoked by the Arab oil embargo. He could read the polling numbers as the anger of the American people grew. People on his staff undoubtedly were aware of the increasing numbers of incidents—fistfights, line breaking, and might-makes-right behaviors—at service stations across the country. As fall gave way to winter that year, Nixon knew time was running out to do something big to change the game: the way oil is produced and consumed in America. He had the best information available about the then-known U.S. reserves, the prospects for Alaska oil production, and the need for a massive and long pipeline across the Arctic region. He also had a sense from the industry about what could be done by when. Most of all, he had a credibility dilemma called Watergate that was growing by the day and debilitating his administration. The Arab oil embargo was a nuisance that he did not need.

Directed primarily at the United States and the Netherlands for their perceived support of Israel at the expense of Arab peoples, the oil embargo of 1973 disrupted the movement of oil, certainly, even though it did not significantly reduce the amount of oil being produced. Trading and shipping channels were impacted in the short term. What actually drove the U.S. shortages, however, was the nationwide phenomenon of people topping off their tanks out of fear of running out of gas.

Some U.S. deliveries were deferred. But ultimately, oil moves around the world through a trading system that balances supply with demand, and ultimately, oil would get to the United States regardless of the embargo. However, the impatience of the American people and the need for a full tank in the face of

feared shortages made sure that we were short. (This is generally the case after hurricanes as well. When supplies are at risk,
Americans rush to nearby gas stations to make sure they are not
caught with an empty tank. Their actions, multiplied by millions
of individual decisions, ensure that stations run out, if there is
no intervention, such as odd-even rationing, to balance demand
with supply.)

The call for American energy independence was first made
more than 35 years ago. At that time, we imported about one-
third of our oil from other nations. After three and a half decades
of repeated commitments by presidents, presidential candidates,
and countless elected and appointed officials of both major parties at federal and state levels, after dozens of energy bills over
the intervening years, through recessions and periods of heady
economic growth and prosperity, by 2008 we imported two-
thirds of our oil from other nations. Our reliance on foreign oil
increased, not decreased. How's that for performance?

With the "pain at the pump" caused by tight oil supplies and
high demand from 2005 to mid-2008 fresh in our minds, it is
no wonder that candidates for elected office in 2008, from both
parties, banged their drums repeatedly and loudly with the same
rants over energy independence that we've heard for decades.
The rhetoric has gone so far that presidential candidate Barack
Obama, both during the campaign and after his victory, promised that by 2016, the American people will no longer need to
import oil from the Middle East or from Venezuela. Whether it
turns out that way, of course, remains to be seen. But it won't
really matter because 2016 will be the last year of Obama's
potential two-term presidency and will be too late to hold him
accountable. He can't run again. (What happens in 2016 also
won't matter if he is not reelected in 2012.)

The point is this: political speeches, no matter how well
intended, are not public policy. Commitments by candidates
are subject to executive, legislative, and judicial branch governing, legislating, and adjudicating. No candidate, no elected or
appointed official, can deliver on promises without the support
of the entire government sustained over time. The crucial phrase
is "sustained over time." Americans hold candidates accountable

every two, four, and six years. Political career continuity is difficult enough; political policy continuity is even more difficult. It's been impossible over these past three-plus decades, during which time we have had five Republican and three Democratic presidents. Congress meanwhile has changed majorities multiple times both in the Senate and the House, meaning that policy proposals and committee chairs have turned over multiple times. The U.S. courts have seen dozens of federal judges come and go, appointed by Republican presidents and Democratic presidents, and their rulings on energy cases (as on other issues) have reflected their respective interpretations of law, sometimes based on strict construction and sometimes essentially legislating from the bench.

There has been, in other words, no meaningful continuity of political leadership for sufficient sustained periods of time to deliver on the many, many promises of energy independence. Is anything different this time around? Will President Obama govern more than one or two terms? No. Will the current Democratic majority keep its hold on Congress more than two or four years? Too soon to tell. Will new federal judges be appointed over the next four and eight years? Yes. So has anything changed?

If 8 presidents and 18 Congresses and many dozens of federal judges over the past 35 years can't make energy independence a reality, what is it that keeps prompting candidates to promise it?

Well, even I have to admit: it sounds good! What message carries more bravado and more assertive masculinity than "energy independence"? It says, "We can tell the rest of the world to go to hell." There's something earthy, powerful, atavistic, and pugilistic, even legitimately xenophobic, about saying it. It speaks for all Americans regardless of gender, ethnicity, or age. It creates an image of national solidarity and the idea of a final one-upsmanship over the Organization of Petroleum Exporting Countries, more familiarly known as OPEC. This organization is an international cartel that works cooperatively to set production quotas on crude oil so that the price is "managed." In times of tight supplies, its members may cooperate to produce more oil to reduce prices. In times of low prices, they may restrict supplies to raise prices. They also may do neither. As the members control approximately one-third of global oil production, the cooperative efforts of OPEC have an impact on oil price and availability, whenever they choose, complicating and frustrating the supply and price of gasoline for Americans. Yet as mythical as the notion of U.S. energy independence may be, we always let politicians get away with this promise. But in terms of what actually happens after candidates win, frankly, they may as well stand on the beach, flap their arms up and down, and tell the waves to stop.

Postelection, energy independence is quickly taken out of the hands of the winner and is worked on by executive branch staff, congressional staff, committee chairs of extraordinary seniority—and therefore power—and committee members from various geographic regions and states—each of which has different needs and wants. Also chiming in are special interests from every part of the energy and environmental industries as well as other related parties, such as manufacturers, consumers, labor, farmers, and associations from virtually every other industry (since energy touches everyone). All these viewpoints have to be heard and accommodated and the serious international relations issues have to be sorted out, and then suddenly it's time for the next election.

By that time, priorities and issues have changed, and members and candidates do what they have always done best: they run for office, and all bets are off until the outcome of the vote is known. Two years is an eternity for a House member during which his or her political life can prosper or collapse. But two years in energy time is a blink of an eye. Not much can change in such a short period, other than prices.

■   ■   ■   ■   ■

From a political, practical, market, resources and technological standpoint, based on the plans that are in place or under consideration, we won't be energy independent over the terms of the next several presidents—not because we don't want to be, but because we simply can't be. The energy system is so invested in what it is that it cannot materially change in the term(s) of any president. We can be considerably less dependent over the next 10 to 20 years if we make some hard choices, but we won't be independent. And we're not yet on course to make material changes.

Effective policies, however, can move the balance in our favor. How?

Let's start with liquid fuels. Americans use between 20 and 21 million barrels of oil per day. That translates into 10,000 gallons per second. Currently we produce domestically about 7 million barrels per day, roughly one-third of our own consumption. (During the recession, we used somewhat less, but we were also producing less as a combined result of hurricane issues, oil field decline, and a credit-crunch-driven drop in investment in new oil and gas opportunities.) So about 13 to 14 million barrels are imported every day.

If the industry were permitted to drill both offshore and on federal lands, we could significantly increase our domestic production. However, drilling offshore has been prohibited in over 85 percent of the U.S. outer continental shelf for the past 30 years by both presidential and congressional moratoria, and drilling on federal lands has been prohibited by federal regulation. How much would these sources increase domestic production? Based on my own analysis and discussion with many experts, by implementing a sustained, committed, capitalized effort to seriously increase domestic drilling off Alaska's coast, the West Coast, the eastern Gulf of Mexico, and the East Coast, along with more access on federal lands, I believe we could reverse the ongoing decline in domestic production and raise it to about 10 million barrels per day, where it was in 1970, over the next 10 to 15 years. This level of activity can be achieved in an environmentally sustainable way. New technology and improved processes over the past three decades have increased both safety and reliability. We could maintain that production for another decade or two, during which time, based on every scenario that has so far been put forward, we will continue to need oil products.

In addition, we can keep working on two more fronts: efficiency and alternative liquid fuels, mainly non–corn-based biofuels. By continuing to raise the mile-per-gallon efficiency of our vehicles over the next 10 to 20 years, we could reduce demand for oil by at least 1 if not 2 million barrels per day. The combination of increased production and reduced demand is the equivalent of producing approximately 12 million barrels per day domestically. Biofuels are projected to move from about 10 billion gallons in 2008 to 36 billion gallons (equal to 2.3 million barrels per day) by 2022. If we can substitute domestically produced biofuels (including a significant percentage produced from cellulose, algae, and other nonfood sources) at this level, we reach the equivalent of, say, 15 million barrels of domestic oil per day.

At the same time, demand is expected to grow as our population increases, so more miles will be driven. We may well be consuming 22 to 23 million barrels per day by around 2020 or 2025. So if we drill more, become more efficient, and produce more biofuels, we could get to 15 million barrels equivalent of domestic production against demand of some 23 million, which gets us back to where we were in 1973. We would still need to import one-third of our oil supply from other nations. But isn't that much better than two-thirds? Our national security would be greater, our impact on global crude oil prices would be beneficial because we're producing two-thirds of what we consume, our biofuels industry would be the biggest in the world, and all the jobs, traditional and new, that would be created over the next two decades in the energy industry would be a fantastic boost to our collective economic well-being.

■   ■   ■   ■   ■

Why aren't we headed down the path I just described? It's too pragmatic. There is no political cheese there. It is not popular to speak for a rational drilling program. Many politically powerful voices across America say that since we cannot drill our way to independence, we should not grant any additional drilling rights on our land or coasts. These voices point to millions of acres of current leases not being drilled as justification for not granting more acres. In fact, the leased acres not being drilled are vacant for one of two reasons: tests (which cannot be conducted until the lease is acquired) have shown there is insufficient oil to drill; or the plans and engineering programs to drill are under development. If there is oil or gas on the lease in commercial quantities and there are capital and human resources available to get the work done, no competent oil executive would not drill where he or she can. Drilling is what oil companies do. Their shareholders demand it of them. And the costs of inaction are high: the oil companies have paid up front for the leases and make additional annual payments to the government for the 10-year duration of the lease. If the leases are not developed in that time, they are generally rebid, and some other company goes to work on them.

To mislead the American people with politically twisted mistruths and politician-crafted explanations, e.g. "...companies are not drilling, they're waiting for the price to rise," on what is being said or not said is fair politics well within the rules of political campaigning. It is, however, a practical disservice to the people who do not have sufficient industry knowledge to catch on to the mistruths directly. Even armed with facts, it is hard to challenge candidates. I have done so. I can tell you, it is generally a one-way, one-time conversation. Political candidates do not like to be confronted by persons who may know more than they do about certain topics. They don't like to be caught out; their staffs like it even less. Consequently, they develop "messages" that have enough political polish on them that misinformation or disinformation, and even lack of information, sounds like knowledge and therefore can get them to election day. This practice is not restricted to candidates from one party, either.

It is so politically incorrect to argue for more drilling that many have given up. I should know; I testified in Congress on six occasions between 2005 and 2008, during the last pain-at-the-pump period. I also tried to talk with presidential candidates from both parties during the run-up to the 2008 election. Some listened carefully; some were not interested. Basically, oil and gas, as necessary as they are, are not politically popular:

they offer nothing new, and they are stereotyped by all the dirty connotations attached to carbon-based fuels.

Disconcerting? Yes. Impractical? Yes. Likely to continue? Yes, until we're so short of supply that prices are well past $4 per gallon and low- and fixed-income citizens are beside themselves. Then we might begrudgingly throw the industry some additional drilling rights, possibly in areas so far offshore, so distant from existing infrastructure that the industry will not see a commercially viable way to go after the prospects. The problem will then be thrown back on the industry with the message: "We gave you opportunities; why didn't you develop them?" It could be a lot different if pragmatism became more mainstream in energy matters. That is what we need to work on. If the American people are provided the facts rather than perpetuating myths, we could produce more and more and more of our own energy supplies to meet our demand.

If we do that and keep at it, year after year, decade after decade, without political distractions and populist demagoguery on two- or four-year cycles, we can become less energy dependent. Over a sustained period of time, without machismo short-term promises, like energy independence from wind, solar, bio-fuels and green jobs, we can evolve the energy system of this country. Success will mean that at some time in the future, energy independence actually happens. It will not come all of a sudden. It will happen in the United States and at the same time and in many of the same ways in many other countries around the world. Energy independence will come from developing the short-, medium-, and long-term plans that address every aspect of energy. It will not come from a political agenda that promises what cannot be delivered or sustained when the political wind shifts. Politics and energy, like oil and water, do not mix. Why haven't we learned that by now? Thirty-five years of energy independence rhetoric and political commitment have gotten us nowhere. We're more dependent than ever. It's time to go down a different path.

THERE IS AN ENERGY SHORTAGE, BUT THERE IS NO SHORTAGE OF ENERGY

We will never run out of energy, unless we choose wrong policies or fail to implement right policies.

When I listen to people say they fear the world is running out of energy, my mind flashes back to the Shell Eco-Marathon event I attended in April 2007 at a NASCAR track in Fontana, California, just outside Los Angeles.

It was a beautiful cloudless day, the sun so intense that we had gathered under a tent to avoid its rays. Hundreds of bright and creative high school and college students had brought their fuel-efficient vehicles to the track for this miles-per-gallon contest. As the speaker explained the rules of the Eco-Marathon, the winds were so strong that the snapping of the tent flaps drowned out his amplified voice. Meanwhile, elsewhere on the track, NASCAR wannabes—people who love NASCAR racing so much that they were paying hundreds of dollars per person to run authentic cars around the track—were racing, their super-charged engines blasting away the high-octane fuel they were burning, heedless of the low miles per gallon they were getting. Had the sound waves been convertible into physical energy, those cars would have been airborne.

It occurred to me that we were holding this event just an hour's drive from the La Brea Tar Pits, the most visible reminder of the rich oil reserves of the Los Angeles Basin, where 17 million barrels of oil are still produced every year. On that afternoon, we were surrounded by almost everything we need for a future of abundant and affordable transportation energy: fossil fuels, wind, sun, and human creativity.

Watching the winning team from California Polytechnic State University complete the course in its vehicle, the Curb Hopper, with a fuel economy of 1,902.7 miles per gallon, I thought: There is no shortage of energy and there never has to be one. We never have to run out of oil and gas; we simply won't need as much of it when we embrace sound strategies for the future.

The same principles I saw at work on mobility energy that day also apply to electricity. The bottom line is that we already have what could be an endless supply of energy for electric power generation and for transportation fuels. What we are short on is a coherent, pragmatic energy policy. We see this lack of coherence play out in periodic price spikes, supply shortages, infrastructure breakdowns, and threats of repeated disruptions if we don't conserve energy. Our present course is a politically driven zigzag path that will bring blackouts, brownouts, and lines at the pumps within the next decade. In a land of plenty, we will be short of the energy we need. When it happens, the situation will take years to correct. This is the future we are headed for, but it doesn't have to be that way.

■   ■   ■   ■   ■

It's not that today's ideas are bad; there's nothing wrong with so-called clean, green, renewable energy. The challenge is that there is not enough of that kind of energy and there won't be for decades to come. By emphasizing what is new and preaching hostility toward what is old, we fail to invest in what is needed.

The laments of the fossil fuel suppliers are not just the shrieks for survival of the last dinosaurs. They are genuine warnings that the death of their fuels is also the death of the U.S. economy, security, and quality of life. Likewise, those who stymie nuclear energy development more for political than scientific reasons (I'll come back to this complex issue later in the chapter) are driving nails into the coffin of sustainable, carbon-free power of an intensity unmatched by any other known source. Partisan politics has failed to provide for future energy security for nearly four decades. By the end of the fifth decade, we all will pay the price, unless we adopt a coherent short-, medium-, and long-range plan now.

Let me make a potentially controversial point that may offend a lot of people: There is no such thing as "clean energy" as we know energy today. Anyone who claims a clean energy pathway is suspect. They are not telling the whole story. From coal to oil to natural gas to nuclear to wind to solar to biofuels to hydropower, geothermal, and hydrogen, we deceive ourselves by declaring specific forms of energy "clean." There are certainly relative differences in degree, but every form of energy known to humans requires destruction and/or modification of molecules, landscapes, water supplies, or wildlife. Every form of energy has an impact on the environment. Clean energy is a relative, not an absolute, term.

■ ■ ■ ■ ■

I've learned something about energy by making it. In 1996, my wife and I purchased Lime Valley Mill in Lancaster County, Pennsylvania, a former gristmill on the Pequea Creek. It was a sight to behold at the time, a literal junkyard of discarded wood, metal, and glass scrap, old equipment, and parts inside and out. The roof leaked; daylight showed through where walls were made of wood; mortar was crumbling from stone walls. Downstairs, where the millrace came through the basement, the cement floor was covered by three feet of caked and gooey mud. In the race itself, two turbines were barely visible. The wall of water outside was held back by thick, ancient wooden beams.

We bought the mill to reconnect part of Lancaster County's history, because we also purchased the mill house, barn, and farm property across the street. We put an historic property back together. I also was attracted by the power of water as energy.

On the first floor, above the race and turbines, was a World War II–era vertical 50-horsepower submarine electric motor, its shaft attached by a 60-foot-by-8-inch belt to the main turbine's power shaft. The motor had been reverse-wired to operate as a generator. When water poured through the race, the turbine rotated the belt and the generator produced electricity that went directly into the Pennsylvania Power and Light Company grid. Imagine that: my wife and I, owners of a power-generating plant that could produce clean hydropower for the people of Lancaster County!

For several years we tried our hand at generating power. Occasionally we had enough water to keep the mill generating. And when we did, wow! It was an amazing experience to feel the energy of a mass of water falling some 14 feet to supply a turbine to turn a generator. It made me appreciate even more the power generation at Hoover Dam, where more than 10,000 cubic feet of water per second fall 500 feet to generate 4 billion kilowatts per hour.

Sadly, we lost the head, the top section, of our 150-year-old dam in 2003 when three trees tried to wash over it during a flood. It is unlikely in these times and in the spirit of reharmonizing the natural course of the Pequea that the dam will ever be rebuilt. But our mill was one small example of a power source that has been around forever. It helped industrialize, feed, and clothe a young nation. Even today, some 5 percent of America's energy comes from water.

Can we really supply all the electricity to meet our growing demand? Yes, if we properly pursue the options available. Diversity of sources is the essence of our future energy security. Coal, gas, nuclear, wind, sun, water, hydrogen, and geothermal—all of these sources have a role in our electricity future, if properly managed and balanced.

ENERGY SOURCES FOR ELECTRIC POWER

Coal

Let's start with coal. Nearly half of the electricity in the United States comes from coal-burning generating plants. Believe it or

not, we burn through a train car–load of coal every three sec-
onds, 20 car–loads per minute, 1,200 per hour. That's a lot of
coal! It is plentiful and cheap, and there is more than enough
at current consumption rates to go on for another 100-plus
years. The United States has more coal than any other country.
Unfortunately, burning so much coal also causes serious environmental problems in terms of gaseous and particulate waste.
Coal produces 82 percent of the carbon dioxide emissions from
electricity production—nearly 2 billion metric tons equivalent of
carbon dioxide per year. With this track record, is it any wonder that the climate-change fearmongers chant "No more coal"
with little regard for the scale of the economic repercussions and
supply problems that would arise if they succeeded, or for the
social and economic consequences of what closing coal plants
would mean to communities and society as a whole? Without
coal-fired electricity production, accompanied by a comprehensive national plan for future energy supplies that might diminish
coal use or transition coal use to clean coal technology (described
below), our society would simply fall apart. Coal produces about
half of our electricity; we can't just turn it off. In an electron
society, we couldn't run our hospitals, banks, companies, house-
holds, governments, schools, and public safety without it. For
these reasons, it is naive and dangerous simply to argue for no
more coal.

I'm a proponent of the continued use of this important natural resource not only for its energy, but also for its hundreds
of additional applications in other products that benefit society. (Think aspirin, which is synthesized from a coal derivative.
Paint, soap, and nylon also use coal by-products.) But there is
such animosity toward coal in the United States that opponents
have taken to discounting technology that enables its use with
virtually no particulate or gaseous emissions.

Integrated gas combined cycle (IGCC) technology, a primary
source of "clean coal" energy, which gasifies coal rather than
burns it, takes place within a self-contained gasifier, enabling
the capture and safe management of emissions and particulates before they leave the vessel. IGCC is a vast environmental improvement over burning pulverized coal and exhausting

fumes and solids up a tall chimney into the sky. Gasified coal with added oxygen produces synthetic gas (equivalent in energy value to natural gas), which is then burned in a turbine to produce electricity. Shell and other companies have been developing and implementing gasification technology around the world for years. Except for the United States, there are markets eager to utilize such cleaner coal technology for both energy security and affordability. If we attach carbon capture and sequestration technology to coal gasification, we can produce electricity from coal with virtually no carbon dioxide or particulate emissions.

Coal production is also often criticized for the destruction caused by surface mining, but other countries have figured out how to reclaim mined land. I've personally walked on renewed landscapes in Queensland, Australia, where creative laws and regulations have restored a productive biosphere and wildlife on top of former surface mines.

We've been sequestering carbon dioxide—pumping it into formations beneath the earth—for years in West Texas without environmental consequences. Other countries are investing in major carbon sequestration projects to prove the technology. Americans need to do more than talk about carbon sequestration. Moving forward requires updated regulatory oversight and rules that enable use of best technology, from mining to reclaiming and gasifying to sequestering. Encouraging tax, depreciation, and rate-setting schedules that take advantage of the increased productivity of gasified coal can lead to cleaner, affordable electricity and sustain an essential American industry. The rest of the world is going to do it. Why shouldn't the United States?

Will we allow the politics of "now" to overrule the requirements of tomorrow? With anticipated carbon management restrictions that impact pulverized coal plants (the technology in current use), the more than 600 such plants, whose average age exceeds 38 years, will be reduced within the decade. As our energy demand grows, the only way to supply it using coal is with cleaner coal technology. If we don't start implementing this technology now, it will be too late to avoid serious electricity supply disruptions.

Natural Gas

There is a lot of natural gas in the United States. Many are familiar with the Pickens Plan, an effort promoted by oil and gas billionaire entrepreneur T. Boone Pickens to make Americans aware of the abundance of natural gas beneath our nation's lands and continental shelf and to use it, along with wind, to substitute for other energy sources. Natural gas is a fossil fuel that emits about one-half the carbon dioxide of coal to generate an equal amount of energy, measured in Btu's (British thermal units). Therefore, it is much cleaner than traditional pulverized coal burning (although gasified coal with carbon capture and sequestration is actually cleaner than gas).

Worldwide, there are more than 6.2 quadrillion cubic feet of natural gas reserves, enough to meet the world's needs for 58 years at current rates. In recent years, new horizontal drilling technology with the use of hydraulic fracturing along the length of the well has evolved to open up hundreds and perhaps thousands of trillions of cubic feet of new reserves of natural gas that have been locked for millennia in rock formations underneath several U.S. states in different regions of the country. Natural gas is versatile as well. In addition to producing electricity through combined cycle turbine technology, natural gas fuels homes, stoves, hot water heaters, factories, and food processing plants. As Pickens promotes, it could even be used as fuel in internal combustion engines. Critics of the new drilling technology—people who are often against any future fossil fuel expansion—are moving to establish national rather than state regulations to govern the drilling process, its use of chemicals to release the gas molecules more readily, and its impact on subterranean water. Depending on the regulatory process, either we will have abundant future supplies of affordable, clean natural gas, or we won't.

Nuclear Power

Then there is nuclear power, which could be a major source of carbon-free electricity forever. William Tucker, in his book

Terrestrial Energy, points out that nuclear fuel produces 2 million times more energy per equivalent fuel unit than fossil fuel.[1] Large coal-powered electricity plants receive train deliveries of up to 100 rail cars several times per week. Nuclear plants receive a nuclear fuel delivery of one tractor trailer truck every 12 to 18 months. No one has ever died in the United States as a result of nuclear energy plant operations or accidents. Yet, since March 28, 1979, when a combination of equipment malfunctions, design-related problems, and worker errors led to a partial meltdown of the reactor core of one unit at the Three Mile Island nuclear plant in Pennsylvania, we have stopped building nuclear plants. We have essentially allowed myths and misunderstanding, such as the notion that commercial nuclear fuel can be used for nuclear weapons, to terrorize our citizenry into believing that nuclear energy production is too high risk to expand into the future. We've tolerated existing facilities but made it all but impossible to build new ones, despite the redesign of nuclear plant control rooms and improved training and increased professionalism of operators.

In addition, we've only pretended to establish public policy to deal with nuclear waste at a national level. After 20 years of approved legislation and $20 billion of taxpayer expenditures to build and outfit Yucca Mountain in Nevada as a site to store spent nuclear fuel, the Obama administration has unilaterally decided to abandon the policy and the waste storage project in favor of a supposed safer, more reliable solution. That better answer: "TBD" (to be determined). When it was announced that Yucca Mountain would no longer be funded by the Department of Energy, the secretary of energy, Stephen Chu, promised the establishment of a panel to identify new safe and reliable storage approaches. Months later, the status of the panel and nuclear storage remains "TBD." Why was Yucca Mountain canceled after decades of development? I can only conclude that the cancellation was out of deference to Senator Harry Reid (D-NV), Senate majority leader, who opposes the project in his home state. Congress is unwilling to push back on the decision. Essentially, a nation of some 300 million citizens in need of energy security and affordability, including the safe storage of nuclear waste so that more nuclear plants might be constructed, after spending $20 billion of taxpayer money, is being held hostage to the 2010 reelection prospects of an incumbent senator in one of the nation's least populated states. In political terms, this is called "throwing Senator Reid a bone, regardless of the national interest."

France generates roughly 80 percent of its electricity from nuclear plants, reprocesses its nuclear waste for reuse to reduce the need to store spent fuel (resulting in a 95 percent reduction in waste compared to the United States), and has never had a nuclear incident that threatened its people or communities. Of the three dozen nuclear plant construction projects around the world today, not one is in the United States. If we continue our current course, we may not build a new nuclear plant in this country in the next decade. Federal loan guarantees are a timid response to the national need for more new nuclear plants. Meanwhile, existing plants are running up against their licensing limits (plants are initially licensed for 40 years). Unless these licenses are extended, plants will be taken out of service just when we need them most, as we reduce the number of existing coal plants due to anticipated carbon management restrictions. We could have plenty of clean, affordable nuclear energy—except we don't.

Wind Power

We also have a lot of wind. But it is sporadic, variable, and regional. It doesn't blow everywhere and doesn't blow all the time. Energy needs to be ubiquitous to be efficient. Nonetheless, there is good reason to develop wind energy where we can and to export electricity from regional wind farms to other areas of the country. Wind technology is well established, based on turbine and generator technologies that have been around for a century. Wind energy, however, is kinesthetic energy, which means it is not nearly as efficient as energy from fossil or nuclear fuels, even if there is an everlasting supply generated by the rotation of Earth and the natural warming and cooling of day and night. Despite wind power's limitations, we should develop it as fully as we can. But let's be clear: The more wind we rely on, the more Earth's landscape will be disrupted and potentially abused by massive wind farms and the more birds will be mashed by the windmill blades. And the more wind energy we produce, the more backup base-load energy, such as natural gas, must be built so that wind variability does not wreak havoc with transmission systems and interfere with reliability of supplies. For some period of time as well, taxpayer subsidies will be required to enable wind farms to be built.

For real impact on energy security, we need not thousands of wind turbines but hundreds of thousands. Are we prepared for that? Many questions remain unanswered: Are landowners ready to give over use of their land to endless horizons of rotating blades, creating potential visual disruptions in the remote, unpopulated regions where they live? Will naturalists and environmentalists support what the National Audubon Society once referred to as "condor Cuisinarts"[2] to be built in vast numbers on the most wind-prolific sites, with the accompanying land excavation, maintenance tracks, disrupted water flow, and wildlife and plant life destruction? Will large offshore wind farms be acceptable to citizens and government when issues of national defense, alternative use, and natural preservation arise? More significantly, will landowners, rural and urban municipalities, counties, and states collaborate with one another to build intra- and interstate transmission lines across vast swaths of the United States, moving east or west from the wind-rich Rocky Mountains and Appalachians to consumers a thousand miles or more distant? Will the inefficiency of current technology transmission lines be addressed so that the amount of electricity lost in transmission does not exceed the amount ultimately delivered? Currently wind electricity is perhaps among the least affordable forms of new energy due to transmission losses. Why aren't we demanding that turbines, blades, and the equipment used on America's wind farms be manufactured in this country, instead of imported? The real question is this: Will we as a society accept the landscape disruptions and the inconvenience—possible power-grid irregularities, including blackouts that shut down televisions and computers without notice—that wind energy promises in return for its low-carbon profile? We face some tough choices, and we need to understand the implications if we are to make them.

Solar Energy

Of course, there is the sun. Solar energy is sound science up to a theoretical point. The technology has been around for decades. But the costs are too high and the efficiency too low, right now, for broad adoption and expansion. It was a difficult call in 2005 for Shell to sell its solar panel manufacturing and marketing business just when the nation was suffering from hurricane-induced oil and gas shortages and had turned its attention to alternatives and renewables as never before. But it was a good decision. Shell's business was based on silicon wafer panels, the most common solar technology in use today. But silicon wafer panels are to the solar industry what cast-iron skillets are to the modern kitchen: heavy, thick, inefficient devices that are rapidly being made obsolete by advances in thin film and nanotechnology research. I would argue that solar technology is in its infancy. Like any new product, its costs are high, its learning curve is steep, and there are multiple generations of improvement in store for future years.

Silicon is sand-heated, purified, then turned into thick, heavy round ingots. Then it is reheated to molten temperatures, sliced into wafers, and manufactured onto flat panels. The energy consumed to make and heat the ingots multiple times must be weighed against how much electricity the manufactured wafers can produce. The energy balance is not impressive. Silicon wafers are fragile yet, when assembled on a panel, quite heavy compared to the next-generation-technology thin-film panels. Current technology is maybe 8 to 15 percent efficient (versus fossil fuels in the 40 to 50 percent efficiency range). Nanotechnology research breakthroughs suggest that much higher efficiencies are possible, say 20 to 30 percent or higher. Shouldn't we wait a few more years or even a decade or so to build out the future of solar energy rather than deficit-spend our way to inefficiency in using current solar power technology? Who wins with the promotion and construction of publicly subsidized obsolete solar technology? Venture capitalists and political adventurers may come out ahead in the short term, but consumers and taxpayers, who heavily subsidize solar electricity, will have to bear the burden over the medium term.

An alternative type of solar power, solar thermal technology, uses mirrored panels to reflect sunlight and heat a liquid, such as oil, to power steam turbines to produce electricity. It works—expensively. Unlike photovoltaic electric panels, which only work under direct sunlight, solar thermal technology can store heat to provide electricity when the sun is not available. But is it clean? With respect to emissions, it is. With respect to land use management, it is anything but. Vast acreage is needed to build out solar thermal facilities of a size that matters. The facilities transform land in ways that make it unusable for any other purpose and remove it from its natural state for as long as the facilities remain. They affect wildlife and plant life. Most of all, they affect local water supplies. Water to produce the steam to make the electricity is the essential energy carrier. But where are solar thermal plants being built? In deserts, of course, where sunlight is ample but water is scarce. Given the water challenges of the nation's Southwest, is solar thermal electricity production a sustainable choice? The answer is no if the expectation is that it will replace fossil or nuclear electricity generation in these regions, or if the intent is to export the energy to other regions. Solar thermal is not proposed for the well-watered regions of the country where most of our citizens live. Why? It's obvious. Clouds bring the rain and block the sun. In addition, there are too many people and not enough vacant land.

So let's invest in research. Let's see what can be done. But let's not commit huge public expenditures to subsidize vast production and construction of today's soon-to-be-obsolete technology before we know more than what we know now.

Hydropower

I mentioned my own experience with the mill dam, otherwise known as hydropower. Currently hydropower, including the Hoover Dam in Nevada and the Grand Coulee Dam in Washington State, accounts for about 5 percent of total U.S. electricity generation. It is a renewable, low-carbon option. However, hydropower requires very specific geographic characteristics—a lot of water, flowing or falling with great force. The best sites for hydropower plants are already being tapped. While some other sites meet the geographic requirements, the benefits of power generation are offset by the negative effects on river navigation and ecosystems, not the least of which is the well-reported issue of salmon migration, which is hindered by river dams. Frankly, there is little opportunity to expand hydropower other than improving the efficiency of existing sites. Some support wave energy as an alternative form of hydropower. There are efforts underway to promote pilot projects. It is too soon to tell whether they are viable.

Geothermal Energy

What about geothermal energy? Cynics say it offers great promise and always will. Geothermal energy comes from mining Earth's core heat and using water to produce steam to generate electricity. There are potential resources across the country, with the most cost-effective sites in the western states. These sites require less drilling because the hot rocks are relatively close to the surface. There are several downsides, though: the high required water supply (just as in solar thermal), potential seismic risk, and long distances from markets. But geothermal energy is a huge energy trove—one we may choose to develop more fully as a natural resource someday. Currently, the costs and risks are deemed too high by investors, utilities, and even the U.S. Department of Energy, which recently canceled an experimental drilling project in California.

Stationary Hydrogen Fuel Cells

There is also a future for stationary hydrogen fuel cells. Hydrogen fuel cell technology works for stationary power production as it does for mobility needs (detailed later in this chapter). As we learn more about how to produce and harness hydrogen, especially from the electrolysis of water using low- or no-carbon electricity, fuel cells can produce clean, distributed electricity virtually anywhere, on or off the grid. There are enormous product development opportunities to replace carbon-based energy uses with carbon-free hydrogen. As one example, small, light hydrogen cartridges can replace heavier batteries that power personal computers.

The Issue of Subsidies

In comparing various resources for electricity, it is important to consider government subsidies that currently enable their development. Because energy resources are hard to develop, highly risky to exploit, and filled with innumerable uncertainties for long periods of time, the U.S. government has rightly chosen to jump-start various efforts in the interests of the nation. Over time, however, subsidies should be withdrawn as commercial development unfolds. That is essentially what has happened with subsidies for fossil fuels and nuclear energy; taxpayer subsidies in these areas today are more symbolic than real.

Natural gas receives a subsidy in the form of tax depreciation allowances and government-funded research to the tune of about $0.25 per megawatt hour of electricity produced. Coal receives $0.44; hydroelectricity, $0.67; and nuclear power, $1.59. According to the U.S. Energy Information Administration, in early 2008—even before the effect of the 2009 stimulus package and 2010 budget framework, which emphasize more public support for wind and solar—the corresponding subsidies were $24.34 per megawatt hour for solar energy and $23.37 for wind.[3] The new renewable forms of energy are subsidized at extraordinary levels to promote the technology. Such subsidies are obviously unsustainable. And it is safe to say that without them there would not be wind or solar energy in our future.

When we look at the sum total of what we know about our natural resources and the technologies that are either available now or will be developed in the future, and add to that the advances taking place on the demand side in terms of efficient use of energy, it is fair to describe our electricity supplies as inexhaustible—unless we fail to agree on the public policies that support sound development of these supplies.

Unfortunately, the lack of coherent public policy has been and continues to be a barrier to future affordability and availability.

Given the course that we as a nation are on, we will be short of electricity within the decade. Constraints on coal, natural gas, and nuclear energy cannot possibly be offset by new wind and solar energy supplies. Essentially we're cutting back on 93 percent of today's energy supply, sitting still with 5 percent (hydropower), and expanding on the 2 percent base of renewables. The math from this public policy doesn't align the future of supply with the future of demand for a growing population.

So far, we've been discussing energy sources for electric power. But what about energy for transportation: do we have enough energy to preserve our mobile lifestyle?

ENERGY FOR TRANSPORTATION

I have been enamored of the internal combustion engine since the summer when I was 11 years old and was allowed to drive a dusty orange 1950-ish hand-clutch, 30-something horsepower Allis-Chalmers tractor, pulling a double set of tobacco-laden wagons from field to barn on our landlord's farm just south of New Holland, Pennsylvania.

Blame it on the invention of the wheel. We're stuck on transportation. Again, if we implement the right policies, we can maintain the mobility that is so essential to our society. And once more, that is a big if.

Fossil Fuels

Notwithstanding the theorists who claim that the world's oil supplies have peaked, or will soon do so, and the environmental extremists, we're not yet at the twilight of fossil fuels for transportation. Despite the incredible amounts of oil we have consumed, there is more still available than we have used and more than we will ever need. As we often said during my years in the oil business, "The Stone Age did not end for the lack of rocks; the Oil Age will not end for the lack of oil."

Current estimates are that there are more than 1.3 trillion barrels of conventional liquid oil reserves in the world—enough supply for both mobile and stationary energy uses for the next 35 years at current consumption rates. And new oil exploration based on advances in technology continues to confound conventional wisdom about the extent of the potential supply. In Brazil, for example, a new field more than 500 miles long has been discovered offshore in formations made visible through new advances in seismic technology.

Unconventional oil resources—those not in liquid form—add to the total. A Rand Corporation study estimated that there are 1.5 to 1.8 trillion barrels of oil trapped in the shale formations of the Rocky Mountains, more than doubling the world's known oil supply. Add to that more than a trillion barrels in Canadian and Venezuelan oil sands, and it is clear that Earth's oil bounty is indeed huge.

As they say in late-night television pitches: "But wait, there's more." Enhanced oil recovery, made possible by carbon capture and sequestration technology, could lead us back to old oil fields, where as much as 60 to 70 percent of the original oil still remains in the ground and could be developed to greatly increase our known oil reserves. Don't be misled by the disinformation promoted by anti-oil advocates suggesting that since the United States has only 3 percent of the world's proven oil reserves, it is not worth trying to increase domestic oil production. They are not counting probable reserves, new technology, and unconventional resources in the hundreds of billions and trillion of barrels.

The resources are there. The question is: do we *want* to continue to use these fossil fuels at current—or increasing—rates until they are eventually exhausted? The answer, unequivocally, is no. The economic, social, and environmental costs of such an approach are becoming ever clearer and ever higher.

While there is no such thing as clean energy, fossil fuels are the dirtiest form of energy. It's a given within the oil industry, for example, that if you see, touch, taste, or smell the product you are producing, you're probably in trouble. Petroleum is extracted, processed, shipped, and used in closed systems. Any break in the system creates a problem. And even when systems run perfectly, burning fossil fuels emit both particulates and carbon dioxide.

Relying forever on such a troubling source of energy, when we can do better, is too much risk.

But let's be clear: we are not ready to abandon fossil fuels for transportation yet. There are 250 million vehicles on the road in the United States today, most of which will be around for the next 15 to 20 years. It is likely that the vast majority of cars and trucks built in the next 20 years will continue to rely on fossil fuels at least for long-distance driving, and those cars in turn will have a life span of 15 to 20 years. Thus, we will be dependent on fossil fuels for transportation well into the late 2030s and 2040s. Some people may not want to acknowledge this reality and may wish for a different one. Some people may also wish for world peace and the end of hunger; and bullfrogs may wish they had wings. Reality is what reality is. Besides the large U.S. auto and truck fleet, the global road fleet will likely grow to about 2 billion cars. The vast majority will rely on fossil fuels for long-distance mobility. As long as the internal combustion engine is used to power vehicles and/or to generate electricity in battery vehicles, we're largely dependent on fossil fuels for transportation energy.

Biofuels

How viable are biofuels—ethanol and other fuels made from corn, grasses, algae, and other organic matter? They can certainly play a role as a liquid source of energy for the internal combustion engine. There are sound reasons for investing in biofuels research and development. We should not be naive, however, about the costs, barriers, and obstacles to commercial biofuels production. Nor should we overestimate their potential. Biofuels are not about to replace classic fossil fuels as the primary source of engine power in the lifetime of anyone alive today. In fact, before we develop the capability for biofuels to replace fossil fuels, internal combustion engines will mostly disappear, and with them the need for massive quantities of biofuels.

Biofuels are a useful domestic extension of the supply of liquid fuels. They reduce the carbon effect of the overall fuel supply, but they do emit carbon dioxide. The theory is that the amount of carbon dioxide absorbed by the living plant is about equal to or slightly greater than the amount emitted when the plant is burned as liquid fuel in an engine. The net carbon dioxide impact is generally lower than that of petroleum-based fuels, although when the carbon fuels expended in planting, cultivating, fertilizing, and harvesting are accounted for, we're hard-pressed to quantify whether biofuels are significantly more environmentally sound than hydrocarbons.

An additional issue for biofuels is their inherently lower British thermal unit (Btu) content compared to gasoline. If a biofuel, such as ethanol, is 20 to 25 percent weaker than its gasoline equivalent, more ethanol is burned to achieve the same amount of motive power, contributing to the challenge of achieving environmental improvement.

Notwithstanding the uncertainties, there is good reason to invest in biofuels research to explore what biochemistry can add to future energy supplies. If we can find a way to produce biofuels as cost effectively as, in the quantities of, and with environmental improvements over hydrocarbons, we'd be fools not to pursue the possibilities.

But not every biofuels pursuit is a good idea.

For example, corn ethanol is a bad idea—unless you are a corn farmer or a politician who wants to look "green." In a world that can't solve the problem of hunger, food for fuel is a bad concept for society. To make matters worse, absent a public subsidy (currently $0.45 per gallon), it's unlikely that corn ethanol can be commercially viable, unless we use public policy to ratchet up the price of crude oil by making it more scarce, which is artificial inflation by government of a natural resource commodity.

In addition, like any intensively grown crop, corn production has environmental negatives that aren't included in the carbon dioxide comparison with hydrocarbons. Intensive agriculture, especially in the U.S. plains states, means that nitrogen fertilizers are used extensively. The runoff from these fertilized fields contributes to loss of oxygen in our rivers, lakes, and especially the Mississippi River system and ultimately the Gulf of Mexico. Few Americans realize that the Gulf of Mexico has a large and growing "dead zone," a large tract of lifeless ocean. It came about with the introduction of modern chemical fertilizers and is growing at an unprecedented rate of about 20 percent per year, according to the National Oceanic and Atmospheric Administration.

Along with its other disadvantages, corn ethanol cannot be transported by pipeline. As an alcohol, ethanol dilutes with water, which pipelines are prone to attract due to natural condensation that occurs along the route as temperatures change. Ethanol must be carried by truck or rail car, the most inefficient transportation methods imaginable.

Despite these issues, there are still those who insist that we should require E-85 ethanol (an 85 percent ethanol/15 percent gasoline blend) as a future fuel for America's cars by public decree. The George W. Bush administration recommended, and Congress passed, a mandate of 36 billion gallons per year of biofuels by 2022, of which 15 billion gallons should be corn ethanol. We currently produce about 10 billion gallons, most of which is blended into gasoline at levels up to 10 percent, a level that standard automobile engines can tolerate.

At the E-85 level, corn ethanol requires a flex-fuel engine (which about 10 percent of U.S. cars now have), and a new and different gas station infrastructure for storage and pumping, which somebody (think consumers) has to pay for. All things considered, corn ethanol is a bad idea for everyone but the corn farmers.

When I got wind that President Bush was going to call for such a huge ethanol mandate, premised on corn, in his 2006 State of the Union speech, I got on the phone to people I knew in Washington, DC, to ask why and to find out whether he could be dissuaded. I guess I had worked up a pretty strong head of steam. When I finally got to Clay Sell, deputy secretary of energy, just prior to the president's speech, he did his best to calm me down. He told me that he knew exactly what I was saying and that I shouldn't think for a minute that he hadn't said the same things at the White House. He calmed me down when he told me frankly that logic was not at work in this matter. That says a lot about our energy policy.

Fortunately, there are other potential sources for biofuels, such as cellulose, switchgrass, and even algae. But let's be clear. While a thousand flowers may bloom, not all of them are potential candidates for sourcing vast quantities of commercially affordable biofuels. Here's why.

Biochemical reactions in biofuels processing are far less well understood than the chemical reactions that take place with hydrocarbon processing. (Of course, we've been refining oil for more than a century.) Depending on the type of biochemical processes, we are still at the early discovery stages. We can produce, for example, cellulosic ethanol (from the cellulose in woody plant matter) in a laboratory, using enzymes. We can even engineer superenzymes to make the energy production happen faster. But outside the laboratory, when you start to scale production in larger quantities, you introduce not only the plant biomass (corn fodder, switchgrass, or sorghum grass) and the enzymes into the manufacturing process, you also add large amounts of insects, field mice, the odd dead rabbit or bird that could not escape the harvesting machine, along with bird droppings, other animal wastes, dust, dirt, rocks, and whatever else might be picked up with the harvest. The enzymes don't know what to do with these contaminating materials and the batch of ethanol is compromised, even ruined. When Shell began its market test of E-85 ethanol in Chicago in 2007, obtaining consistent quality ethanol was a major challenge. The laboratory is not a manufacturing plant. Achieving large-scale production of non-corn ethanol is a long way off.

Other sources of biofuels, such as algae, are receiving increased attention. Headlines trumpeted ExxonMobil's 2009 announcement of a $600 million commitment to algae research. Algae plants have the fattiest carbon molecule structure known to humans. I can attest to this, having seen the molecular drawings in a Shell laboratory. But they also have a long way to go to become fuel contenders. Looking more closely behind the ExxonMobil announcement, you can get a sense of timing. The big headline number represents a multiyear program, perhaps five or six years of research, similar to the $500 million number that BP announced regarding biofuels research at the University of California at Berkeley and the University of Illinois several years ago—over a 10-year span. By comparison, these same companies spend between $20 and $25 *billion* per year on capital investments in their core business, hydrocarbons. Spending more does not push the development rope forward faster. What these companies are working on is not just science; it is applied science that must function on a vast scale. It will require a lot of trial and error to succeed.

For all the political and media attention it has been given, the biofuels journey will be long and frustrating, and no one knows yet what success might look like. We should pursue it, however. It's the nature of technical curiosity to pursue the unknown to find out what we can and to apply the findings productively in society. But there is one caveat: public laws and regulations, whether mandatory biofuels or mandated miles per gallon, as precise as they may be and as well intended as they should be, do not determine outcomes that are dependent on the laws of nature.

The journey to produce material quantities of commercially affordable biofuels for personal transportation will take so long that by the time we get there, we will be shifting to an alternate power system, relegating the internal combustion engine to the museum of automotive history. That doesn't mean there won't be a role in the meantime; nor does it mean that we won't use large quantities of biodiesel in the future, especially for long-haul and off-road commercial purposes. It also doesn't mean that we won't see biofuels evolve into aviation fuel products and potentially substitute for some petrochemical applications. So let's do the research and see where it takes us. But let's not hold our breath waiting for a biofuels silver bullet for personal transportation. We won't need it.

Hybrid and Electric Engines

We can't discuss transportation fuels without also addressing electricity as a power source for transportation. The role of hybrid and electric engines is significant. The best way to increase miles per gallon per vehicle is to introduce hybrid systems and electrification into the personal transportation fleet of vehicles. Doing so takes some of the burden of mobility off the 20-percent-efficient internal combustion engine. We are most likely on a path to more advanced hybrids and electric cars for a time, but it is a slow road with a number of unanswered questions.

The 2009 report of the Boston Consulting Group (BCG) on the "comeback of the electric car" describes the new technology pathway. It reviews the spectrum of higher mile-per-gallon vehicles as follows: advances in the internal combustion engine, such as direct injection and power train improvements, to move it beyond the 20-percent-efficiency barrier of the current model; next, the mild hybrid, similar to those on the road since 2001; then a full hybrid, which is propelled only by electricity at low speeds; followed by a plug-in hybrid; on to a range-extender hybrid (the flip side of the full hybrid, it runs on battery power almost exclusively, with an internal combustion engine to recharge the battery); to the fully electric battery-powered vehicle.

BCG predicts that under the best conditions, we're likely to see the range of hybrids, plug-in hybrids, and electric cars achieve at best a roughly 20 to 22 percent market penetration by the middle 2020s. Higher penetration is hard to predict, and the study stops short of suggesting it. Why? One reason is the high cost of ownership. BCG points out that the decrease in fuel use comes at a corresponding increase in vehicle cost. Advanced internal combustion engines can achieve about a 20 percent increase in fuel efficiency at a cost of about $2,100 per vehicle, about the same cost increase associated with the mild hybrid. Right now a full hybrid carries an additional $7,000 cost burden compared to a conventional engine. BCG estimates the battery cost for a fully electric vehicle at $14,000. Those cost differentials would pay for a lot of gasoline over the life of a conventional vehicle.

When the average salary in the country is less than $50,000 and the mean salary is in the high $30,000s, electric cars for mass adoption need to cost less than $20,000. I don't see or hear anyone predicting price levels like that for plug-ins or electric vehicles. With the Tesla electric car priced at $100,000 now and projected to perhaps one day achieve a $40,000 price tag when it reaches mass production, and with plug-in hybrids expected to be priced in the high $20,000s to $30,000s, these are not the cars that average Americans, or people in other countries, are going to be buying anytime soon. And beyond the initial costs, there is the additional issue of lifetime cost of ownership, especially with battery electric cars. Using lithium ion battery technology, the more the battery is expended, the shorter its life. Therefore, the more you drive, the more you pay, especially when replacing the batteries costs several thousand dollars each time. Just the opposite occurs with an internal combustion engine, which is designed for long life.

The range issue is another unresolved challenge. Although many individuals drive 35 miles or less per day—less than one battery charge—most individuals need vehicles that can handle longer-range activities, such as visiting relatives, weekend get-aways, or a trek to the outlet mall. Those who can afford more than one vehicle will enjoy the choices available. People limited to one vehicle may not be able to partake. Moreover, recharging batteries is easy if you have an all-weather garage or carport, less so if you park on a street or rely on public parking facilities. It's hard to imagine local communities strung with extension cords across lawns so that remotely parked cars can get recharged at night, or apartment dwellers fighting over available plugs in nearby parking lots.

The environmental benefits of battery vehicles are unclear. The source of electricity is one issue; decommissioning of used batteries is another. If batteries are recharged using electricity generated from coal, the carbon dioxide problem is not solved, just shifted. Disposal of depleted batteries is also troublesome. If tens of millions of old batteries end up as so much electronic trash does, in landfills in developing counties where environmental rules and practices are haphazard at best, the world will be recycling such wastes in our waterways for centuries.

None of this means we will not see more hybrids and electric cars in our future. But we are unlikely to see the demise of the internal combustion engine based on these products. We therefore will continue to rely on vast amounts of fossil fuels to run these engines, unless something else is available.

Hydrogen Fuel Cell Vehicle

There is something else available. We can develop an alternative personal mobility power system, the hydrogen fuel cell vehicle, as the successor to the long-range internal combustion engine and put to rest forever much of the demand for liquid fossil fuels. As a member of the U.S. Department of Energy's "Freedom Car" Task Force (in my role as Shell's president), I was able to sit behind the wheel of a hydrogen fuel cell car on a test track in Dearborn, Michigan, in late 2007. The experience was as memorable as my first experience behind the wheel of that Allis-Chalmers tractor. This all-electric, non–battery-powered vehicle offered acceleration, power, durability, distance, and speed that equaled, but mostly *exceeded*, today's vehicles powered by internal combustion engines. The additional beauty of the hydrogen car was the potential—not yet fully developed, but possible—to use hydrogen, the most abundant element on Earth, as a 100 percent carbon-free energy option, by producing it from water (H_2O: hydrogen and oxygen) with water vapor as its only exhaust.

I admit a bias toward this technology. I remain a member of the Department of Energy's Hydrogen Technology Advisory Committee because I believe the research and early on-road vehicles offer extraordinary promise to revolutionize personal mobility. Critics suggest that the cost of the fuel cell will never be commercial. Others say that the infrastructure to deliver hydrogen to retail outlets will never be built. Some argue that fossil fuels will be the source of hydrogen (second to water, natural gas [chemically CH_4], is the most common source of hydrogen), so why bother? With incremental change, such as biofuels, hybrids, and plug-ins, they say, there is safety in moving forward. With revolutionary change—battery electric for short runs and hydrogen fuel cells for distance—they contend, there are greater risks and more complexities.

I say that knowing what we know about the century-old inefficiency of internal combustion engines and their reliance on liquid, mostly fossil, fuels, let's move on. Although we don't know everything about the future, we know enough to take the risks associated with both batteries and hydrogen fuel cells. Let's get the public policy support in place to make it happen and stop dodging the inevitable uncertainty of our continued reliance on dirty liquid fuels.

Are we ready for hydrogen fuel cell vehicles? Speaking personally, and not for the Hydrogen Technology Advisory Committee on which I serve, I have to say, not yet, unfortunately. Like so many energy initiatives, it's been politicized. The Bush administration pushed it; the Obama administration, eight weeks into its first term, proposed to cancel funding for hydrogen fuel cell research for personal mobility. The new secretary of energy, Stephen Chu, without consulting the Hydrogen Technology Advisory Committee, informed his department and later Congress that he would zero out the budget for 2010 because there was insufficient immediate promise of success versus other prospects, such as biofuels and batteries. Congress, fortunately, mandated continuation of the program in the 2010 budget. And yes, there are infrastructure and cost challenges. But such challenges exist for batteries and biofuels as well.

The ultimate question we must answer is whether the United States will choose to be a global player in the future of the automobile industry. While the nation dithers and politicizes key questions on the future of personal mobility, the rest of the world is moving ahead. Major programs exist in Germany, China, Korea, and Japan to advance both battery vehicles and hydrogen fuel cell vehicles. They do not seek an either/or solution; they seek a both/and solution in order to lead the way forward. It's crazy to have Republican or Democratic Party solutions to the future of mobility. We need *American* solutions if we're going to compete.

Natural Gas

One additional option: should we develop a natural gas infrastructure for personal transportation? We discussed the pluses and minuses of natural gas as a source for electricity, but it is also possible to burn natural gas in the internal combustion engine, replacing gasoline or diesel. I'm not a fan of the idea because natural gas is a fossil fuel that has multiple other uses, such as electricity production. Extensive use of natural gas for transportation will have a price impact on natural gas fuel supplies. In view of the electric and hydrogen fuel cell options for new power trains in vehicles, it is probably not worth building out a new national infrastructure of retail natural gas pumps and storage. Fleet conversion for local transportation needs, such as the U.S. Postal Service and UPS or FedEx deliveries, with centralized refueling, might be useful applications. Beyond that, I'm not sure it's worth it.

This discussion raises the question of how many refueling infrastructures the nation can realistically afford. For maximum economic benefit, retail fuel needs to be ubiquitous (everywhere) and homogeneous (the same) for all vehicles. Multiple infrastructures drive higher prices, limited availability, and driver insecurity. We've had one infrastructure, oil products, for decades. Building out multiple infrastructures for biofuels, electric batteries, natural gas, and hydrogen compromises ubiquity and homogeneity. It is simply impractical. When 60 or 70 million customers per day show up for fuel at the nation's 150,000 gas stations, you don't want to disappoint them. Take it from me, they are an impatient group. The impracticality of multiple infrastructures is why we need to answer these questions: Where are we going? And how are we going to get there?

■ ■ ■ ■ ■

The abundance of Earth's energy resources, from fossil fuels to noncarbon fuels, renewable and manufactured, is unquestionably greater than we commonly know. Unfortunately, politics has a way of rationing energy such that we needlessly overpay for it and live with massive uncertainty about our energy future. Every administration since Nixon and every Congress since the 1970s has in one way or another dealt with the politics of energy rather than the substance of it.

The bitter experiences of the 2005-to-2008 years of pain at the pump and the whiplash of price volatility and hurricane-induced insecurity of supply are still fresh in people's memories.

We should not forget the experiences of those years because they are certain to return. Economic and personal mobility growth, globally and nationally, will stress our supplies of fossil fuel, our only near-term source for significant new quantities of liquid fuels. Alternatives are years, or decades, in the making.

We need to look at radical shifts away from our dependence on the internal combustion engine and pulverized coal-fired electricity plants. Hydrogen fuel cells and niche battery applications work for transportation. Nuclear energy and gasified coal with carbon capture and sequestration work for electricity, along with wind and future solar, augmented by natural gas. But we need to transition to these options without chasing down a lot of additional trails sponsored by narrowly focused, bloviating politicians and greedy venture capitalists. When their corn ethanol and other creative solutions fail, they are nowhere to be seen. Investors and taxpayers are stuck paying for their passions.

We can promise ourselves many things and aspire to invent what isn't. But what is real is day-to-day short- and long-distance mobility, wrapped with ubiquity and homogeneity, in vehicles we can afford, fueled by product we can afford while sustaining our environment. What is real is reliable, affordable electricity that lights our darkness and powers our smart economy while sustaining our environment. The combination of the two provides national and economic security and a lifestyle unrivaled elsewhere on Earth.

We will never lack for energy in the future because of scarcity of resources. We will, however, face serious shortages of energy in the future unless we start making better, often harder, choices about what will supply our future needs. Such supplies will also need to work in an environmentally challenged world.

INCONVENIENT OR NOT, THE TRUTH IS THAT CLIMATE CHANGE IS NOT THE ISSUE

Let's quit debating global warming and manage gaseous wastes as we do other trash.

On a hot, muggy August afternoon during the summer of 1996, I was hard at work in a conference room of the Ministry of Aviation Industries of China (AVIC) in Beijing, discussing human resources for a potential joint venture between AlliedSignal, the company for which I was then international human resources vice president, and AVIC. When the meeting ended, one of my hosts from the ministry graciously accompanied me outside. As we waited for the car, he noticed that I was looking up and down the street and then skyward. Visibility was only about a hundred yards in any direction. I was shocked. The executive looked at me and said, "My children do not know the sky is blue."

He said he had discovered this when he had taken his family on an outing to the Great Wall of China, some 45 miles north of Beijing. When the children got out of the car, they shrieked and began crying: they thought something was terribly wrong because the sky was a brilliant blue. He said it took him considerable time to calm them and to explain the difference between the polluted Beijing air and the blue sky.

A decade earlier, my wife had visited Beijing in winter. She recalls it as "like being inside a vacuum cleaner bag while vacuuming in a freezer." A decade later, when I visited in 2006, my lungs were so affected by the atmospheres in several China cities, I could not return to work for a week after the trip.

The air quality problem is not restricted to China. During the (illegal) forest burning season in Indonesia, the air in Singapore or Malaysia is horrific. People wear masks, children are told to remain inside, at times even aircraft are diverted.

The problem is not even restricted to Asia, however. How many times I recall recently flying into Los Angeles, Seattle, Denver, Phoenix, Chicago, Washington, Atlanta, New York, Philadelphia, Dallas, Houston, and so many other U.S. cities, only to see the sickening, sultry brownish layer of smog, from vehicle and building, factory and utility exhaust, accumulated in the sky several thousand feet aboveground.

Greenhouse gases and airborne particulates from exhaust are humanity's trash in the atmosphere. There is no plainer way to say it: air pollution is garbage in the sky. By what we do, we make a mess. We've been making a mess for a pretty good while. Each year, at least since the beginning of the industrial age, we have made more of a mess. As the world employs massive quantities of hydrocarbons, industrializes production, uses electricity, we throw ever more garbage at the sky. Some argue that one of the gases, carbon dioxide, is a natural gas needed in the balance of the atmosphere and that although it is created by the destruction of carbon molecules, it is also absorbed by the growth of new carbon molecules in biomass and other living matter. The ultimate issue regarding carbon dioxide is whether man-made molecule destruction is putting too much of it into the atmosphere for nature to absorb. In my view, it is.

In Beijing and elsewhere, the level of particulates in the atmosphere is so great that visibility is reduced. In other places, the waste molecules are essentially invisible but still present. Chimneys, exhaust pipes, and tall industrial emission stacks all are designed to move the exhaust as far away from us as reasonably possible, yet we continue to breathe it in. Our lungs capture molecules of substances that were never intended for human consumption.

We're intelligent beings and mostly rational. To remain so we must continue to breathe. As rational beings, we have choices about what to do when we make a mess. We can ignore it, pretend it doesn't exist, acknowledge it, talk about it, debate over it, blame someone for it. We can also emit less of it and even clean it up.

So what are we doing?

In the face of ever-increasing amounts—measured in the thousands and even millions of tons—of garbage in the air, we are having a monumental, never-ending, fundamentally dysfunctional national and international debate over global warming and the possibilities of climate change. This debate over whether the climate is changing has been going on in earnest for at least two decades. The United Nations Intergovernmental Panel on Climate Change publishes periodic warnings of how much worse global warming is getting, only to be refuted by other bodies of scientists who challenge its assumptions and conclusions. Charges and countercharges of manipulating data to prove a point raise questions about the legitimacy of the science. Some politicians run for office on the platform of protecting their electorate from global warming; others run on the platform of protecting their electorate from the ravages of expensive public policies put forward by global warming scaremongers.

In every discussion I've been a part of regarding climate change, someone has challenged someone else on the reality of such claims. Scientific amateurs, including current and former elected officials, set out to prove their points for or against global warming. When someone cites warmer temperatures, someone else cites lower temperatures. Some argue that Earth has never been warmer; others argue that Earth is in the fourth or fifth year of a cooling period. Late in 2008, the Prince of Wales warned that Earth has less than a hundred months left to address climate change. His argument was that if dramatic steps were not taken forthwith, Earth would enter an irreversible and catastrophic era of unstoppable global warming.[1] Seven months later, at the Group of Eight meeting in Italy, no western nation other than the United States was willing to discuss interim targets on global warming, preferring to commit to a reduction in greenhouse gases some 40 years hence. Meanwhile, China and India not only scoffed at the notion of interim targets but also refused to set any targets for any time in the future.

By August 2009, in advance of the Copenhagen climate conference later that year, developing countries were preparing their claims for economic adjustments to be paid for by developed nations. The African Union's claim was for $67 billion per year to enable member states to adjust to the consequences of climate change. How hot has Africa been throughout history? How much hotter could it get? Ultimately Copenhagen achieved little, other than an informal understanding among a few attending countries that has no legal impact on participants or signatories. Friends of mine who attended came away encouraged by the depth and breadth of the dialogue, believing that the conference was in the end a necessary step along a pathway. Undoubtedly there will be more debate and discussion, functional and dysfunctional, along that pathway in the coming years, as long as the frame of reference is global warming and/or climate change.

The point here is that debating climate change is a fantastic waste of time and human energy. There is no agreement on what it is or isn't. There is no set of measures accurate enough to be credible to present a clear and present danger. There is no rebuttal for the argument that we have always had cycles of global warming and global cooling, and Earth has adjusted accordingly.

During a May 2009 visit to Washington, DC, I met with the staff of Congressman Joe Barton (R-TX), former chairman and now ranking Republican on the House Energy and Commerce Committee. My goal was to introduce them to Citizens for Affordable Energy, the nonprofit organization I was starting to educate grassroots Americans about energy and the environment. The congressman happened to see me and said, "You're an oil man, or at least you were, so I want to know, how did all the oil get to be off the coast of Alaska? How come it's there and not somewhere else?" He explained that he had just asked the secretary of energy the same question and wanted to compare our answers. He was bemused by the secretary's answer, which he explained was based on tectonic movement and the south-to-north drift of Earth's plates resulting in oil moving with the plates and now being located well into the northern hemisphere. I pointed out that I was not a geologist, but the congressman pressed me for my answer. I said I expected that oil came to be off the coast of Alaska in much the same way it was off the coasts of Louisiana, Texas, Nigeria, Siberia, Brazil, and Angola: biomass sediment carried by rivers into oceans over hundreds of millions of years, causing a buildup of such materials and converting it, under pressure and heat, from one type of carbon to another.

He said he thought the same, but for the secretary to agree, he would have had to acknowledge that at some time in the past, Alaska must have had a warmer climate, to produce the biomass that would have flowed into the oceans. He couldn't do that, because it would destroy his case for global warming. With that comment the Congressman helped himself to a piece of strawberry shortcake and munched off into his inner office.

■   ■   ■   ■   ■

As the debate rages on, we're throwing ton after ton of gaseous effluent into the atmosphere and doing little or nothing about it. That's wrong. It's wrong for today, tomorrow, and forever. We breathe what we put into the air. It is time to come to grips with gaseous waste in much the same manner that we have tackled other waste problems. If we did not deal with physical waste in the modern age, we'd be suffocated by our own trash. If we did not deal with liquid waste in the modern age, we'd be poisoned by our own filthy water. The fact that we are not dealing adequately with gaseous waste is wrong, wrong, wrong. How strongly can I say it?

When is the last time you asked how much it cost to deal with your physical trash? When is the last time you worried about it? Perhaps when your local garbage collectors last went on strike. While not perfect, physical waste management in America is a system that works. Companies like Waste Management, Inc. are so good at what they do that they actually report on their commitment to sustainability and are publicly recognized for their efforts.

Physical waste management is now a multibillion-dollar industry employing tens of thousands of people in jobs that pay a decent wage. Historically municipalities have provided the service as a last resort. But the industry has professionalized, developed its own science and methodology, and most cities now outsource the service to companies that compete for the contracts. We pay our fees, many of us not even knowing what they are.

We see continuing advances in trash management. If you watch trash collection in New York City, where more than 36,000 tons of solid waste is generated every day by the city's 8,300,000 residents and millions of workers and visitors,[2] you can see dedicated trucks that haul only certain types of trash. At trash-receiving sites, there are processes in place for treating it responsibly—whether it is buried, recycled, burned, or even reprocessed to generate biofuel.

Companies take physical waste so seriously that many make policy choices to eliminate certain types of waste. During a recent visit to the headquarters of Bank of America in Charlotte, North Carolina, I learned that a policy to prohibit the use of disposable foam cups was under deployment. All staff members were given reusable cups for use at their work stations. They were everywhere. To facilitate use of the cups, dishwashers were installed in coffee break rooms. Americans take physical waste management seriously, and our society and environment is better for it.

When is the last time you asked how much it cost to deal with your liquid waste? When is the last time you worried about it? Perhaps when your sewer line was last clogged. While not perfect, liquid waste management in America is a system that works. Liquid waste management, like trash management, has become a multibillion-dollar industry employing tens of thousands of people, utilizing specialized science and methodology. Local, state, and federal rules and regulations require that no home, building, factory, processing plant, or utility can dispense specified untreated liquids into the public sewer or waste disposal system; rather, each must have its own treatment system or eradicate or capture and treat harmful materials before they enter the system. If you think your home does not fall under these regulations, check your local rules for disposing of oil paint, turpentine, or other hazardous liquid waste. As a consequence of such regulation, we live in far greater safety, and our surroundings are much cleaner than before.

There are still liquid waste issues. Runoff from rainstorms continues to carry pollutants from the surfaces of roads, highways, parking lots, playgrounds, yards, and fields into our water systems. But overall, the nation's rivers, ponds, and lakes are cleaner than they were a generation ago when factories, processing plants, and utilities, as well as homes and offices, emitted wastes directly into waterways. I have been to refineries that pull water from rivers and emit water back into the river that is cleaner than what they removed.

The amazing thing is that I never hear anyone bellyaching over the costs of water treatment. They know better. They know that if they did not do the right thing for their company and society, if they dumped foul wastes into public waterways, it would only come back to haunt them. They know that water is finite and we need to have clean water to drink. In the past 25 years, in all the plants that I have been a part of, from manufacturing electric motors or jet engines or telecom switches to processing oil and chemical products, I do not recall one lament over the costs of water treatment. It was simply a part of doing business responsibly. Costs of investments were capitalized, preventive maintenance was built into the operating plan, staffs were trained to do their jobs. As long as the plant was up and running, water treatment was part of its operations, no ifs, ands, or buts.

So why are we debating climate change instead of managing gaseous waste the way we manage physical and liquid waste? Is it because we can't see it or taste it; is it because often it simply blows away, out of sight and out of mind? I suspect the answer is just that simple. We can't know what we can't see. We can't understand what we can't taste. Yet aren't we smarter than that? I think so.

■ ■ ■ ■ ■

I believe we're mired in a dysfunctional debate on climate change because it's a classic way for politicians to exhibit their self-professed profundity. What I object to are self-declared experts who, lacking any scientific knowledge or credentials, basically repeat what they've read, have no certainty other than their opinion, and believe themselves omniscient on the subject. They can present themselves as the saviors of humankind, the protectors of the biosphere, the heroes of modernity, the avowed enemies of the unclean. Those on the opposing side can profess their anti–climate change counterarguments in much the same way, directed at defusing the ramblings of the self-anointed saviors. In other words, politicians have taken on the climate change debate for their own purposes and skewed their dialogue for political outcomes. Those on both sides of the issue become unbalanced, unrealistic, and ideological, which fundamentally doesn't solve the problem of needing to manage gaseous wastes as we do physical and liquid wastes.

It's not that I dislike politicians. I actually enjoy and respect them immensely. They have tough jobs in a difficult profession. But let's get real. There is a craft to their trade, and they are skilled craftsmen and women. What they are good at—and I give them every credit for it—is the use of language that captures and captivates, expressions that impact thinking and belief, the turn of phrase that creates fear or confidence. So it's no wonder that politicians prefer to talk about climate change, global warming, and its certainty or improbability. It beats a simpler, more mundane conversation about managing gaseous wastes. There is little political mileage in arguing for a sanitation department for the atmosphere. It is not dramatic enough. However, we would solve our problem of too much gaseous waste emitted across the land and into the sky if we dealt with the rules and regulations for gaseous waste the way we have for garbage and sewage.

But wouldn't it make more sense and couldn't we get a lot more done if we brought the conversation down to where it belongs, to the multiple types of such waste we're pushing into our atmosphere and how much the remediation is going to cost? I do not doubt that either Congressman Henry Waxman (D-CA), chairman of the House Energy and Commerce Committee, or conservative talk show host Rush Limbaugh, both of whom have strongly held views on the subject of climate change and global warming, would decline the offer to stick his head over a utility's smokestack or stand behind a city bus, breathing diesel exhaust fumes, for any period of time. At a practical level, every person has a stake in the outcome of reducing gaseous waste.

We actively try to avoid breathing gaseous emissions—whether it's in our own garage, a municipal parking garage, the city street, the shopping center parking lot; why don't we also try to figure out how to manage these wastes as quickly as we can? Many people deliberately choose to live upwind, not downwind, from a factory, a utility, a refinery, a processing plant, a highway, or any other gas-emitting facility or place; why don't we also figure out how to manage these wastes as effectively as we can?

Why is it that coal and gas electricity plants are located as far from established civilization as economically feasible? Is it so that people do not see the smokestacks or smell the emissions? Of course it is. Why do we not mind solar panels on our rooftops or in our backyards? Is it because there are no emissions? Of course. I can't tell you the number of people who have said to me, "I wish I could install a wind turbine in my backyard. I wouldn't mind it at all." Is it because there are no emissions? Of course.

Can we agree that we don't like emissions? Is it because we don't think they are safe to breathe? Is it because we don't understand what they will do to us? Is it because we want to protect our children and their young lungs? Is it because we have seen or experienced respiratory ailments and we know how painful and life-threatening they are? Is it because we've been in stinky, cough-producing, sickening atmospheres at some point in our lives and knew it was bad for us? Yes, yes, yes, yes, yes, and yes!

Let's recognize gaseous waste as the trash it is and get on with treating and managing it. Let's create a new multibillion-dollar industry called gaseous waste management that produces tens of thousands of jobs utilizing science and process knowledge to systematically manage, clean, and in some cases capture and sequester our gaseous waste.

As we have with physical waste and liquid waste, let's turn a social and environmental problem into value-creating enterprises that improve society and the sustainability of the planet. Forget about arguing for or against global warming or climate change—that's not the point. Forget the images of ice falling off a glacier into the ocean—which, by the way, it's been doing since Earth cooled—and clucking our tongues over the melting of the Arctic. Forget the extortion by developing countries for climate change remediation payments. Instead, let's help them with the technology of gaseous waste management at the same time we're working on it ourselves.

■   ■   ■   ■   ■

Gaseous waste is nasty stuff. It can sicken and/or kill you. Why do we tolerate its release into the atmosphere if there are alternatives to managing, capturing, and treating it? What does such management cost? Does it matter? How much is life worth? Earth's atmosphere is large; thank God for that. But no one has ever argued that the atmosphere is infinite because we know it is not. There are limits to how much waste the atmosphere can absorb and disperse. At some point, we harm ourselves.

I can't for a moment believe that the people of China are not harmed by the significant atmospheric pollution they experience. The lack of controls and the violations of regulations are so severe that I shudder to think of how many times I visited China. Chinese citizens breathe the air there every day. The consequences are unimaginable.

There is a little-understood link between gaseous emissions in China and the record oil prices in 2008. Many people blamed the high cost of crude oil in the spring and summer of 2008 on oil-trading speculators. What a waste of time and verbiage. When I testified before a congressional committee in May 2008 that the crude oil price should be in a range of $35 to $65 per barrel, at a time when it was above $130, I knew that gasoline demand was shrinking. There was too much already in the market. But crude oil prices were not falling because the demand for diesel and aviation fuel was still growing. The world was short of what are technically referred to as middle distillates: diesel, aviation fuel, and heating oil. The only way to get more of these distillates (which make up a fraction of the end products of refining) was to produce more crude oil. Production was maxed out at 85 million barrels per day. So the price of crude kept going up as purchasers continued to buy the diesel they thought they needed.

Where was this demand coming from? Airlines, for one: they were still going strong in the first half of 2008 and coming off a frightening winter period where their chief concern was the short supply of aviation fuel, not its price. But the major demand for more diesel was coming from China. Why? What was going on in China in the summer of 2008? The Olympic Games.

The threat of significant air pollution was a major risk for the Olympic Games. The fear that athletes might refuse to train or perform because of atmospheric pollution was top of mind for Olympic planners. China's plan to deal with air quality had two parts: (1) Put plants and factories on an extended holiday so they didn't burn their soft coal, which emits significant particulate waste, along with other pollution; and (2) buy up as much diesel for distributed electrical generation as might be needed for critical facilities, like hospitals, in the event that coal-fired electricity plants had to be shut down to keep the air clean enough that it would not impact the games and athletes. It wasn't oil speculators who drove the price of crude to record highs; it was demand for middle distillates to keep people flying and to substitute for coal in China to generate electricity, if needed. Did you notice that as the Olympic Games proceeded and the air quality was acceptable to athletes, the price of diesel collapsed?

■　■　■　■　■

How do we move forward to reduce and manage gaseous waste? As one of the early members of the U.S. Climate Action

Partnership (a voluntary coalition of companies and nongovernmental organizations that came together in late 2006 and early 2007 to promote legislative solutions to climate change), I acknowledge that I'm partial to a cap-and-trade mechanism to put a lid on gaseous waste entering the atmosphere (the "cap") and then incentivize companies to find creative ways to reduce their pollution. This is done by offering credits for reduction below the permitted cap that companies can sell for real value (the "trade") to companies that can't meet the cap.

I believe that a system of credit trading using a classic carrot-and-stick method is the most effective means of creating a new multibillion-dollar value-creating industry to control and manage, and in some cases capture and sequester, gaseous emissions. I believe there is an opportunity to do for gaseous trash and poison what we've done with physical and liquid trash and poison.

We can't go on the way we have. The world's population is growing; its demand for industrial production and electricity and transportation increases every year. The most useful energy source we have for now and the near future is hydrocarbons. The world's use of oil and gas and coal is going to intensify over the next 20 to 50 years or longer. We can't afford the risk of significantly more man-made pollution entering and fouling our lungs day in and day out for decades to come. Young, old, or in between, life is precious to everyone. And life is short enough. We don't need to shorten it further by refusing to manage man-made gaseous waste.

How much will this management cost? Seriously, no one really knows. Estimates are all over the map. My own view is that the costs will be offset by other factors, including the value creation of a new industry, cleaner air, and more efficient ways of managing energy. Do we have the technology to cap, manage, capture, and possibly sequester gaseous waste? Yes, we do. Why aren't we doing it already? In large measure, because we don't have to. Any company or country brave enough to unilaterally reduce its gaseous waste, when its competitors don't do so, will face cost pressures that makes it noncompetitive. This is why we need legislation or regulation to make reduction imperative, to keep the competitive playing field level. It is also why we need international leadership and cooperation as we proceed, so that the whole world buys into gaseous waste management, not just a part of the world.

Experts can probably make a wild guess at the costs based upon certain assumptions, but ultimately those costs depend on how we go about the process. If we rush too fast, it could cost too much. If we legislate in a way that companies and polluters have time to manage their investment future to reduce emissions and do not overly penalize emissions from the start but do so progressively over time, the costs will be less, the resistance will be lower, and the speed of lowering emissions will be that much faster. The costs will inevitably vary based on the gases to be managed, the method of management, the choice to sequester or not, and the economies of scale to be established in the methodologies, technology, equipment, and systems deployed. There are three ways to assist companies that must endure mandated costs: one is the use of free credits for a time, which the government basically subsidizes; the second is the use of tax incentives, such as accelerated depreciation, which are also a form of government subsidy. Yes, taxpayers get into the mix as industry moves to clean the air and manage the wastes that taxpayers are currently inhaling into their lungs. The third is to use a staggered approach over time. I offered Congressman Ed Markey (D-MA) in November 2009 a suggestion for a hypothetical "plan B" for the Waxman-Markey climate bill, which had passed in the House in mid-2009, and appeared unlikely to be supported by the Senate. My proposal was to give, instead of free credits to some, a few or none to others, five years of no-cost transition time to polluters, followed by an implementation plan that held polluters accountable for an additional 20 percent of their emissions in each five-year period following. This would provide 30 years to implement the law, which should be sufficient time for companies to figure out how to implement and pay for reducing, eliminating, or capturing and treating emissions.

I'm not arguing that gaseous waste management or carbon capture and sequestration is free. It's not. But the creation of jobs, the economic value in new construction, and the value creation by a new cap-and-trade industry put gaseous waste management into the same category as the challenge the United States once faced with physical and liquid waste management. We feared the cost increases of managing wastes would make us noncompetitive compared to other countries. It turned out that physical solid and liquid waste management produced as many benefits or more than it cost and stimulated technological advances in chemical and biochemical treatment technologies as well as safe storage of inert liquids and solids.

When we know we can do something, why don't we do it, when it is in our own best interests? That is where we are now with managing gaseous waste. There are some unknowns; there are costs. At the same time, we cannot go on as we have, particularly when we see what lies ahead. Therefore, let's move forward, utilize technology, create jobs, create value, choose credits or tax incentives, or use time to our advantage to make a new industry come to life, and enjoy cleaner air for the rest of our lives.

Considering the global warming and climate change debate and the polarization that we've seen on the issue, there is a wider implication that affects the future of our energy and environmental system and energy and economic security. It is the significant right and left division in the United States and the fact that its rhetoric has changed the political conversation and fueled extraordinary partisanship. We should look at the impact of partisanship on the future of energy.

BEWARE THE RECKLESS RIGHT AND LUDICROUS LEFT

Put in charge of energy, the right wing will destroy the earth; the left wing will destroy our society.

One of the images from the 2008 presidential campaign that sticks in my mind is vice presidential candidate Sarah Palin enthusiastically leading a campaign rally in the chant "Drill, baby, drill!" Who would have thought that this catch-phrase would come to symbolize the Republican campaign? It brought to my mind scenes from the movie *Giant*, where the glamorous homestead of the super-rich was contrasted with the proliferation of oil wells around it—with fences and landscaping around the house blocking the view of the wanton destruction.

Yet the chant resonates because of the truth behind it. There is within the nation's right wing a determined element enam-ored with the idea of achieving energy independence by intensely exploiting domestic oil, gas, and coal. It is a way of telling the oil-exporting nations to "Go to hell" and also telling the left wing of the nation "To hell with your airy-fairy idea of 'no more hydrocarbons.'" This mind-set says: "We have the technology, the people, and the money to produce our own resources. After all, oil, gas, and coal are well understood and have served the nation for most of the last century or longer. They have carried the nation to its economic peak, enabled our comfortable life-styles, and fueled our global leadership."

Such ideas were captured in the No More Excuses Energy Act, introduced in 2007 and cosponsored by 88 Republicans (although it never came out of committee). It had as its stated goal "to secure unrestricted reliable energy for American consumption and transmission."[1] The bill would have removed all offshore and nearly all onshore drilling restrictions and required the federal government to designate 10 sites on federal land for private refinery construction. Never mind that we don't and probably won't need 10 new refineries; never mind that refineries on federal land would be sited without regard to where crude oil was produced or where the markets for refined products are; just "Drill, baby, drill." As a nod to clean energy, the bill also extended tax credits for wind energy production.

These conservatives, including former Speaker of the House Newt Gingrich, whose American Solutions organization promotes the "Drill, baby, drill" mantra, don't reject alternative energy and they embrace nuclear power. They accept renewable and alternative forms of energy, provided they are unsubsidized, convenient, and usable...and as long as the price is no greater than energy from traditional sources. As Houston congressman John Culberson (R-TX), a proponent of the No More Excuses Energy Act, put it in his 2008 campaign: "While it is important to explore alternative energy resources such as wind and solar power, the production of these resources should be driven by the free market, not mandated by the federal government."[2] In other words, go ahead, but it's your dime.

That is a sure way of guaranteeing that alternative energy won't move forward, since the costs of the required massive infrastructure investments are beyond the scope of private enterprise at this stage.

This traditionalist group also rejects carbon and other greenhouse gases constraints and trashes the idea of global warming as an environmental hoax foisted by what columnist George Will calls "eco-pessimists"[3] on otherwise intelligent and prosperous people.

The right-wing solutions of unconstrained drilling and coal development are simply too destructive to be considered sustainable. The notion that the right wing, left to its own devices, will destroy Earth may seem like hyperbole. Unfortunately, I've witnessed excesses and abuses of land, water, and air—shoddy construction, inadequate retaining walls, water erosion due to poor land management, and excess flaring of natural gas—by irresponsible, hurry-up, get-it-done-and-move-on drillers who embarrass responsible operators. It is no wonder that in parts of Wyoming, Colorado, and Alaska, for example, local opponents to drilling become so enraged at what happens when self-interested operators get the leases. I do not mean to imply that all "Drill, baby, drill!" conservatives endorse irresponsible acts. But when mob enthusiasm runs amok, caution often disappears. Oil and gas excavation is risky business, not to be taken lightly. The consequences of loosely managed operations can be devastating in terms of land erosion, gas leaks, oil spills, even explosions. Regulations and restrictions exist for good reasons. The notion that they can be lifted and we can trust everyone to do the right thing is naive at best.

Yet I can point to best practices and technology for drilling and mining that provide for sustainable energy development. As I have discussed, the world will need more hydrocarbons for decades to come. They should be developed responsibly. The technology and operational best practices to do so exist and have for years.

From my own experience in the energy industry, I can also say that there are sensitive areas of our world where no one should drill. For example, we should leave the Arctic National Wildlife Refuge alone. The amount of oil to be obtained from it is not worth the environmental and social cost. There are far more oil and gas resources on the Alaska outer continental shelf that can be developed without disruption compared with on-land arctic surface drilling.

∎　∎　∎　∎　∎

Contrast Vice President wannabe Palin with Vice President used-to-be Al Gore, the icon for the left wing demanding the elimination of most carbon-based energy within ten years. Using dramatic images of natural disasters or serene, picturesque wind and solar farms, real and simulated, to make their points, the Alliance for Climate Protection, founded and chaired by Gore, and similar groups, such as Repower America and the Center for American Progress, advocate a rapid transformative process to deliver U.S. energy independence. Their prescription: green energy sources, battery-powered and plug-in hybrid vehicles, no coal (except "clean coal"), limited or no more drilling, limited or no more nuclear, but the maximum use of biofuel, wind, and solar sources—in as short a time period as possible. The Web site for Repower America, as this book is being written, for example, in its plan A, drastically calls for no more coal in just ten years; its plan B, an accommodation to clean coal advocates, says 2 percent of our energy from "clean coal with carbon capture and sequestration"[4] within ten years is OK. The rest of our nearly 50 percent of electricity from coal, however, must be shut down in favor of renewables. The rejection of oil, gas, and coal is intended to protect this and future generations from the devastation of land, water, and atmospheric abuse of Earth and to sustain our collective future.

The implication of what is proposed, apart from being preposterous, is potentially the outright destruction of the society in which we live. By eliminating hydrocarbons and restricting nuclear power, the left-wing solution will cripple the sources that now account for 93 percent of our current energy system, without a realistic plan to replace them. The ideas presented in the name of clean energy are so outrageous and the timelines so aggressive that America and its hundreds of millions of people would face unprecedented high energy costs, shortages, interruptions, and ensuing chaos. The powerful ideological and emotional public messages, combined with the aggressive legal and activist tactics to prohibit and prevent domestic hydrocarbon projects from moving forward, add up to an incredibly expensive and socially irresponsible effort that will impoverish America. The energy system in this country is so vast and energy projects take so long to execute that proposing radical change in a short time frame is destructive of the system we have and disenfranchises every American, but in particular those on low, fixed, and moderate incomes. It represents an ideology of imposed righteousness from the left that discounts the lives and futures of individuals and their families who live in thousands of communities and work in as many legitimate businesses that produce or use hydrocarbons.

If its ideas become public policy, Repower America would single-handedly cripple the U.S. economy and challenge the nation's foundations of social and civil harmony. Its plan to close 600 operating coal plants in 10 years means we'd need to shut down 60 plants a year, starting right now. Coal-powered electricity provides most of the power for the East Coast and upper Midwest. Imagine life in the nation's most urbanized region without coal-fired electricity. Thanks to the ideologues promoting this concept, life where our nation began would be miserable. Apart from the millions of newly unemployed Americans this proposal creates, there is no way to replace the dramatic loss of coal-fired electricity to supply the ongoing needs of society and the economy. The organization's proposals also include no domestic expansion of drilling for oil to feed the 250 million cars and trucks in America today, about 80 percent of which will still be on the roads throughout the next decade and beyond. The feasibility of Repower America's plan is zero.

When people can't afford gasoline for their cars or electricity for their homes or businesses; when supplies are cut off for nonpayment of bills; when shortages of liquid fuels lead to gas lines; when brownouts and blackouts turn off the lights, eliminate heating and cooling, and shut down the electronic equipment that keeps our economy going—we'll realize we've gone too far too fast.

∎ ∎ ∎ ∎

The right and the left. Whose vision is the correct one? Neither.

The right's unconstrained exploitation of hydrocarbons will in time destroy Earth's environmental balance, making the planet ever less habitable. Unrelenting production of hydrocarbons is very difficult to achieve in sustainable ways. There are natural and risk-based limits that must be enforced for the protection of society. At the same time, the left's ideologically set timetable to transition the country to unproven, untested, not-yet-built new sources of energy to power the entire national economy and hundreds of millions of vehicles, while shutting down the existing infrastructure in just a decade, is both destabilizing and physically impossible. If attempted, it will price energy out of reach for tens of millions of Americans, and companies that rely on affordable energy will become economically uncompetitive, eliminating tens of millions of jobs as a consequence. The actions of the left will fundamentally destroy our pluralistic society and its economy.

Clearly, the solution lies between the extremes. My worry is that the nation's energy and environmental debate is taking place in a U-shaped model instead of our historic reliance on a bell-shaped curve. Most people claim to be centrists or moderates and believe that they are part and parcel of a social and political system that looks like the shape of a bell, where most individuals' opinions occupy the center of the bell shape, shifting over time slightly to the right or left of center, while a few extremists hold forth on the far right or left. Too often, in the face of so many years of fierce partisan acrimony and paralysis in Washington, the bell curve has been inverted. The interests of the people sit unrepresented at the bottom of the U and the outcries of right and left at the upper extremes of the U reverberate across radio, television, and print media.

In Houston, radio station KTRH offers a typical menu of right-wing perspectives, broadcasting Glen Beck, Rush Limbaugh, Sean Hannity, local conservative Michael Berry, and Mark Levin, one after the other, for about 12 hours every day. The rants from these outraged celebrity info-tainers draw an audience that hangs on every word. Listeners call to offer paeans to the radio hosts. Challengers sometimes get through, but their comments are twisted and they are churned into virtual mincemeat before they are cut off the air. In a similar manner, MSNBC serves as a medium for the left's organized rebuttal, whether for proposing and supporting left-wing policies or for positioning, or demeaning, key personalities in or out of favor. *Countdown* with Keith Olbermann followed by *The Rachel Maddow Show* provide viewers with their daily fix on far-left-of-center priorities, policies, and people.

The fuming and bloviating and demeaning and cynicism would be seen as entertainment, sophisticated wit in Britain or France, and maybe even in some parts of American society. Too often, however, people actually take these right or left media messages seriously, to the detriment of our rational, pragmatic future. In the past decade, energy and climate bills have been driven by left- or right-wing polarities, as determined by the dominant party in power at the time.

On July 17, 2008, for example, then-senator Barack Obama said, "I strongly agree with Vice President Gore that we cannot drill our way to energy independence, but must fast-track investments in renewable sources of energy like solar power, wind power and advanced biofuels, and those are the investments I will make as President."[5]

Obama's remarks came three days after President Bush said: "Today, I've taken every step within my power to allow offshore exploration. This means the only thing standing between the American people and these vast oil resources is action from the U.S. Congress."[6] Is it any wonder the American people have sunk to the bottom of the U when they are presented such polarizing opposite leadership directions? Both men sit on the top of the U-shaped curve promoting opposing approaches, leaving Americans to choose one or the other. That is hardly a centrist approach for a bell-curve society to come to grips with.

The country does not need right-wing or left-wing extremists beating their drums for radical, ideological energy and environmental systems changes. Neither extreme understands the implications of what it promotes. Nor does either offer solutions that meet the complex combinations of energy supply sources, environmental protections, and energy demand solutions that are warranted in our nation's and the world's future.

You might think that the oil companies are the fomenters of the rabble-rousing right-wing political movement. While the oil companies certainly favor additional access to domestic resources—as do I—they tend to be more tempered in their approach, recognizing that there are places that are both too risky and too sensitive to drill.

Energy companies' hands are not completely clean, however. The money ExxonMobil has put behind anti–climate change research is frequently cited, and a coal industry coalition was outed in August 2009 for hiring a public relations firm that forged letters to legislators opposing the carbon cap-and-trade bill.[7] Such faux grassroots efforts (often referred to as "astroturfing") are yet another reason the energy companies have such a black eye. Even the American Petroleum Institute is being called to task by media for its behind-the-scenes role in promoting 2009 "Energy Citizens" rallies aimed at defeating the cap-and-trade bill. At least Valero Energy, a San Antonio, Texas–based oil refiner and marketer that opposes proposed climate change legislation, has been up front about its position, posting its anti–cap-and-trade message right on its gasoline pumps. ExxonMobil has also spoken publicly about its preference for carbon tax instead of a cap-and-trade system, if any public policy is moved forward.

■ ■ ■ ■ ■

Beyond the polemics and the extremes, what are the real-world implications of polarized policy making? Is a balanced, centrist approach to energy and environment solutions possible?

One way to examine this issue in depth is to take a close look at two recent examples where the ideological extremes played out to the detriment of the economy, jobs, America's energy security, and affordability. These are events of which I have firsthand knowledge. While the examples are real, the outcomes are surreal. They are indicative of the dilemma this nation has created for itself and why this book is being written. Both examples demonstrate that our nation's energy future must be predicated on the hard work, determined efforts, and sound business and environmental plans of energy providers, technology innovators, and responsible consumers. Extremists from either side only hold us back from achieving energy, economic, and environmental security.

The events took place while I was president of Shell Oil Company and while prices of both oil and natural gas were spiking. Although both involved Shell investments, I think I can be somewhat dispassionate in looking at what happened because they were intended as long-range projects that would develop long after I had retired, and I'm no longer tied to either one.

The first involves Alaska—not the onshore Alaskan National Wildlife Refuge, where congressional opposition to development is clear and sustained, but offshore Alaska in the Beaufort and Chukchi seas.

Alaska is a treasure trove of oil and gas resources, both onshore and off. That is a fact. It also has significant social and environmental risk issues to be addressed, from fragile ecosystems to native peoples who use the waters for subsistence living, to a tourist economy that depends on preserving its unspoiled beauty.

Alaskans also pay some of the highest energy prices in the nation, and on the North Slope, a vast region of the state bordering the Beaufort and Chukchi seas, they pay about double the national average price for gasoline. The state is dependent on supplies of finished products from the lower 48 states because little refining takes place in Alaska due to its relatively small consumer market. The harsh climate on the North Slope means that all oil and gas must be barged in during the short summer months. Basically Alaska is an oil and gas upstream play, where the natural resources abound but local consumers hardly benefit from them, apart from the state's annual payout to all residents of a residual amount of the royalties from oil and gas production. This payout can be in the hundreds or thousands of dollars, depending on the crude oil price and the state's royalty levels.

There is no agriculture in the Arctic Circle. For the local Inupiat people, the sea is their garden. It provides the marine life—marine mammals as well as fish and shellfish—on which they live. But beyond this, the sea is a cultural and historical symbol of a people proud of their long heritage in North America. The traditional whale hunts are not only a source of food, fabric, and bone put to practical use, but also a coming-of-age ceremony for young men and women.

Through personal interactions with Alaska governors, legislators, appointed officials, and local regional authorities, including elders of the native Inupiat tribes, as well as federally elected senators and its congressman, I became convinced during my time as Shell Oil's president, especially during 2006 to 2008, that the State of Alaska is determined to develop its natural resources for the benefit of its citizens and its economy while balancing that development with environmental, social, and cultural risks.

There are difficult trade-offs to be made. I've had Inupiat elders tell me that the state ignores their points of view and works against their subsistence lifestyle. At the same time, I've had conversations with officials in Anchorage and elsewhere that describe how critically important it is to preserve the subsistence lifestyle of the people of the North Slope. There's just disagreement on how to go about it. Others have told me that decisions in Juneau, the state capital, are made with the best interests of all stakeholders in mind; dissidents have said the good-ol'-boys'-club rules applied for too long (which is why the voters chose Sarah Palin to set new rules). Governor Palin told me point blank in a private meeting in February 2008 that the oil companies do not run the state; she said that the state would determine where and when the oil companies would operate, provided they were cooperative and followed the rules. The point is there is a wide diversity of strongly held opinions. The small population does not make governing any easier.

Beginning in the early 2000s, Shell Oil Company began looking into the opportunities for reentry into Alaska to develop oil and gas resources off its coasts. Company experts looked at the range of issues: the technical challenges of arctic operations; environmental risks and mitigation; production potential; commercial feasibility, and state, regional, and local community impact issues. Feeling confident in its studies and capabilities, Shell participated in multiple federal lease auctions that were part of the Bush administration's efforts to increase national energy security in the post-9/11 world. Members of Congress from Alaska were instrumental in building support in both houses for major efforts to develop these resources.

Shell succeeded in acquiring rights to explore in the Beaufort Sea and, later, more Beaufort rights, as well as significant rights in the Chukchi Sea. But the company's exploration plans were brought to a halt by the same federal government that had awarded the rights. Because of a lawsuit brought by plaintiff attorneys, who attracted clients in local North Slope villages, the United States Court of Appeals for the Ninth Circuit effectively stopped Shell's plans by blocking the government's environmental permit that enabled Shell to operate. Today, almost ten years into Shell's reentry efforts, billions spent on leases, hundreds of millions expended on local development efforts, and tens of millions in community outreach and grants have yet to bear fruit or are on hold, while the nation has become ever more dependent on foreign imports of crude oil. New Alaskan offshore efforts are essentially at a standstill.

What went wrong?

In a general sense, there is governmental dysfunction (more on this in a later chapter) where the priorities of one branch of government are stymied by another branch. In addition, there is a decades-long history of suspicion surrounding oil company operations in Alaska because of environmental damage and rumored backroom deal making and political payoffs. In this specific case, Shell's own actions, or failures to act, may have also contributed to the setback.

The first of Shell's problems was speed—too much. Although the company engaged heavily with local communities to build understanding about its plans, the efforts, in retrospect, were inadequate. The urgency of the opportunity, the pressure felt within the company to address the country's energy security, and the messages from state and federal executive and legislative officials to move forward were received as signals to *go now*. Then-governor Frank Murkowski, Senator Ted Stephens, and Congressman Don Young (Alaska's sole representative in the House) were all supportive of Shell's plans to develop in the Beaufort and Chukchi seas. They were also aware of the sustained decline in oil and gas production from existing North Slope operations and the corresponding decline in state revenue, and recognized the need for new Alaska crude oil production to generate needed royalty income.

Senator Lisa Murkowski, also supportive, gave me one prophetic insight in a private meeting: "If you do not have the

[Inupiat] whaling captains with you, your chances of success are severely limited." In retrospect, Shell should have taken more time to ensure that the community views and issues were factored into the deliberation process as enablers, not disablers, of its development plans. Governmental organizations, including the North Slope Borough and individuals in the villages, needed to know that their views mattered and their subsistence way of life would be protected. They needed to know that they had had direct input into the plan *outcomes*. Because that did not happen at a level sufficient to thwart dissent, some villagers were left feeling vulnerable. That gap between assurance and vulnerability was an important lesson learned for me and the rest of the Shell organization.

I think ultimately Shell could have worked through that issue, however, had not the second factor intervened: plaintiffs' attorneys. These lawyers, from law firms (not just in Alaska but in the lower 48 states as well) with histories of using the left-wing mantra of "environmental justice" to scout out new revenue by attempting to legally block energy projects, quickly connected with vulnerable villagers. The promise that becoming a party to a lawsuit would potentially slow or stop the development—or, better yet, pay enormous sums for the right to development— became a means to an end to strengthen the voice of the Inupiat people.

Spurred by the attorneys, an Inupiat village, joined by various environmental groups, raised legal objections, suggesting that the government's environmental permits were flawed, and filed suit to stop Shell's exploration project. Since Shell was acting fully within the laws and regulations of both federal and state governments, the lawsuits were filed against the Minerals Management Service (MMS), an agency within the U.S. Department of the Interior that is the ultimate licensing authority. The suit challenged in part the scope of the environmental impact statements prepared by the MMS and enjoined companies from certain operations on the leases while the case was being heard. The MMS would be defended by government lawyers arguing on behalf of the nation's energy security. Shell was an interested party named in the filing but not the primary party sued. This is not an atypical approach. Plaintiff firms would rather fight the government than companies directly. Their track record seems to be better against the government than it is against companies, and they know that the government's timetable to fight cases is longer and more drawn out than that of companies, leading to potentially larger fees for legal services. Experience leads me to the not-so-surprising belief that these cases are more about the money, for lawyers and plaintiffs, than they are about environmental justice for the aggrieved.

The lawsuits found their way to federal court in San Francisco, where there is a decades-long history of judges finding fault with natural resource extraction for any variety of reasons, including what many people infer is a fundamental ideological opposition to environmental risk. While an executive branch may make energy security a national priority, and a legislative branch might fully support such a priority, the judiciary is free to take a completely independent view of what is in the interest of law, whether it is compatible with executive or legislative branch governmental interests or not.

After three years of injunctions, appeals, and counterappeals, the court ruled that the Minerals Management Services' 2005 Environmental Impact Statement—the basis of all leasing since that time—was inadequate and must be redone.

Despite the federally approved lease sales and the support of state government, the project was halted in its tracks by the judiciary. Plaintiff attorneys are awaiting handsome fees, Alaska's oil and gas revenues continue to decline, the nation's energy security is handicapped, Inupiat peoples are missing out on job opportunities. Shell has moved on to work on other projects around the world while it waited for clarification on the Alaska situation. Meanwhile, high energy prices helped push the nation into recession.

Some clarification has more recently occurred, but not nearly enough. In late 2009 Shell Oil was granted a license and permits for test drilling for the summer season of 2010 by the Interior Department and Environmental Protection Agency. In January 2010 plaintiff lawyers, villagers, and environmental groups filed suit all over again to stop Shell's plans.

Russia, China, and other interested nations, partnering with international oil companies, are moving forward to develop the natural resources around the Arctic Circle. They do not face lawsuits by left-wing plaintiff law firms because they are not operating in U.S. waters. Arctic oil and gas will be developed elsewhere. No body exists that can stop its development. But the United States is literally and figuratively out in the cold with nothing to show for its vast Arctic resources except a handful of happy, well-paid plaintiffs' attorneys, temporarily satisfied environmental activists, and hundreds of unfortunately jobless Inupiat people.

■   ■   ■   ■   ■

Moving from the sparsely populated, resource-rich extreme northwestern edge of the continent to the densely populated, natural-resource–poor New York metropolitan area, let's look at a second energy initiative where similar polarization of the right and the left has stymied improvement in energy security.

A horseshoe-shaped region encompassing southern Connecticut, the New York northern suburbs, New York City, and Long Island is the most energy-constrained market in the nation. Despite a large and growing population and a huge demand base for electricity and fuel, this region has not built new sources of energy supplies in more than 20 years. No material amounts of new electricity power generation, no new pipelines, no new supply and distribution facilities. This area also pays the highest electricity rates in the country, the highest heating oil prices, and the highest natural gas prices, and generally suffers the greatest price volatility, both in summer and winter, of any region in the country. With high demand and constrained supply, it is a market ripe for a project to bring new, more affordable and reliable energy supplies to the millions of people in the region. So you might think.

It was in that context that in 2004 Shell Oil Company joined in a venture to increase the supply of natural gas (the cleanest-burning fossil fuel) to the region. Supported by the federal government's energy policy promoting increased imports of natural gas, the Broadwater venture (in which Shell partnered with TransCanada, a Canadian pipeline company that has infrastructure already in the area) was designed to import lique-fied natural gas by ship and regasify it at a terminal tied into the region's infrastructure. It would bring a billion cubic feet per day of natural gas, enough to power 4 million homes, into a region currently paying double the average electricity cost of the nation (with peaks even higher).

In recognition of both the natural beauty of the coastal area and the dense population, the project partners decided to site the project offshore.

The choice of location had to take meteorological issues into account as well. Anyone who has read *A Perfect Storm* knows the violence of winter storms in the north Atlantic. The respon-sible choice was to build the regasification terminal within the calmer waters of Long Island Sound. A site was identified that would not interfere with the thousands of commercial vessels that traverse the sound each year; it would be 11 miles from Connecticut and 9 miles offshore New York, hardly visible from either shoreline (equivalent in the field of vision to an eraser tip of a pencil held at arm's length, and that only on a clear day). It seemed to be a perfect site, and not in anyone's "backyard."

As an added benefit, the project brought with it steady new jobs in an area of Long Island that had seen little new job cre-ation in decades.

The venture was approved by the partners' boards. As in Alaska, experts assembled a commercial, technical, and stake-holder plan and approached the stakeholders of New York City, Long Island, New York State, and Connecticut.

It was anticipated that memories of the Shoreham nuclear power plant on Long Island Sound—completed but never oper-ated and ultimately dismantled after the incidents at Three Mile Island and Chernobyl raised local concerns—would not have faded. But liquefied natural gas is very different from nuclear power, and the offshore location was technically and visually unthreatening. In fact, the facility would look like and function as a stationary vessel. The proposed site was so far removed that a 25-mile pipeline would have to be built under the Long

Island Sound to bring the gas into the existing Iroquois pipeline infrastructure.

Given the size and diversity of the region's population, including two (politically very different) states; multiple municipalities, counties, and other governmental units; and business interests ranging from Fortune 500 operations to lobster fishing; with countless cross-relationships and points of connection, it was difficult to determine how to approach which stakeholders and when. Shell and TransCanada laid out a multiyear, multifaceted community-based stakeholder approach that included early engagement with both potential supporters and potential opponents of new infrastructure. An office was opened in a Long Island community, and staff members were carefully chosen for their ability to relate openly and transparently to members of the community. Plans were also laid for company executives to communicate directly with governmental, business, and other community leaders over a sustained period of time.

The technical and commercial aspects of the plan presented few difficulties. Regasification of liquefied natural gas (LNG) and its environmental and security issues are well known around the world and in parts of the United States. It is the cleanest hydrocarbon fuel; there has never been an explosion of an operating LNG facility; there is less environmental risk both on land and in water than with other hydrocarbons. Public acceptance also seemed feasible. Communications about the prospects of new energy were well received by many stakeholders: commercial interests, ratepayers, low-income and fixed-income residents, and many elected officials at state and local levels. Polls showed that the general public supported access to more energy.

But slices of the environmental community raised vocal opposition, as did wealthy landowners along the east coast of the sound. New York State elected officials, where the approval decision remained since the site was in state waters, reserved judgment on the project until all the facts were known. Connecticut's governor, opposed to the project from the outset, refused even to meet with company representatives. The state's long-standing attorney general, Richard Blumenthal, although lambasting the project, did meet with me. He listened respectfully to the project's rationale but remained adamantly opposed, suggesting that it was the wrong project, at the wrong time, in the wrong place. While agreeing that the region needed more energy, he suggested that Broadwater should be built off Rhode Island or Massachusetts, or Maine even, but not in the Long Island Sound, directly adjacent to the Connecticut coast. He stridently demanded cessation and withdrawal of the project, leaning forward to emphasize his message and then offering an apology that media cameras might be awaiting my exit from his office, feigning surprise that information about our private meeting had leaked to the press.

Meanwhile, Mayor Michael Bloomberg of New York City, who wanted to know all of the operational details as well as the effects on the supply chain and benefits to ratepayers, decided immediately that people across the region would benefit from the project, even if some individuals might not like it. Some major environmental groups, including the Natural Resources Defense Council, quietly endorsed the project by indicating their lack of opposition. Labor unions, including the Teamsters and Building Trades Council, not only endorsed the project but engaged with local stakeholders and elected officials on behalf of the project. Local congressional representatives on Long Island and coastal Connecticut and the senators from both states opposed the project to varying degrees, even though all agreed the region needed new energy sources.

With this mixed bag of responses, the companies continued years of engagement and moved toward the permitting stage. Then on March 17, 2008, just 30 days before the final New York State go/no go decision was due, Eliot Spitzer resigned and David Paterson became the new governor of New York State. Given Paterson's request to become more familiar with the decision process (although he had been continuously briefed and had met with company executives as lieutenant governor), all parties agreed to extend the decision for an additional 30 days. After five years of sustained community engagement, another month was not material to the project.

But at the end of the agreed two months, the governor ignored the polls, the labor unions, most of the business community, the mayor of New York City, the needs of low- and fixed-income residents, and the many hospitals, schools, community associations, and interested parties who had prepared endorsement letters for the project. He said no.

Why? Vocal objections from eastern shore landowners along with a thin slice of local environmental groups, increasingly heated threats from Connecticut officials, and lackluster or negative support from local power generators (many of whom saw Broadwater as either a competitor or a source of potentially lower margins) persuaded the new governor to rule against the project. The state Department of Environmental Resources had also advised Paterson to reject the project, issuing a factually flawed opinion that served the narrow interests of the landowners rather than the wider interests of the region. Even though stakeholders on this issue were coming from multiple directions and self-interests, the left/right polarity was clear. Democratic leaders of Connecticut, New York, and Long Island were united in opposition. Republican leaders, including the now Independent but former Republican mayor Bloomberg, were generally for it.

The two companies appealed Paterson's decision to the U.S. secretary of commerce, which is the appropriate recourse for such infrastructure projects. In the final nine months of the Bush administration, the commerce secretary never made a decision. The new secretary in the Obama administration ruled against the project within his first few weeks in office.

Down the drain went five years of planning, millions of dollars of investment, and thousands of hours of stakeholder engagements. Clear evidence from the larger public that new energy was needed and wanted in a region that is energy short, where costs are already beyond affordability for many, was ignored in deference to the special interests of a few louder and wealthier voices. Because of the left/right divide and inability to reach a middle ground, residents of the region will continue to live with high prices and their economic ripple effect on the business community, taxes (to pay for energy for public facilities, including schools, jails, and municipal and state offices). There is no new energy infrastructure on the horizon.

■   ■   ■   ■   ■

Alaska and New York—the lessons to be learned are the same.

First, the demands of both right and left are inconsistent with the expressed needs of the broader public for balancing both more energy and more environmental protection. However, a dearth of public education, due in part to decades of noncommunication by energy companies about what's at stake in our energy future and in part to government indifference toward informing the public on the realities of our energy options, makes it easier for a small vocal minority on either side to derail plans that can benefit the wider public. In the Alaska case, Shell underestimated, as did many public officials, just how much public engagement and interaction was needed. Our future economy, well-being, and security are increasingly at risk by the day, month, and year that we fail to educate the people about all aspects of energy and the environment.

Second, the energy industry must take seriously the emotional and cultural sensitivities reflected in public concerns. It is not enough to use technical and commercial arguments to make the case for new initiatives. Companies that want to provide new energy must fully appreciate and take responsibility for engaging with all stakeholders, regardless of who they are, what they believe, and what they know or don't know, in order to improve outcomes.

Third, it is important for elected officials to recognize and not be swayed by the one-trick ponies of public policy debate, whether companies or environmentalists. Public officials must stand for the good of society rather than rely on the money and influence of a small sector of society. In the Broadwater instance, the polls showing consumer-based public support should have been given at least as much attention as the shrill outcry of a few narrow dissenters. The willingness of the companies to discuss differences, modify plans, and provide full transparency on the project was rebuffed in favor of well-to-do proponents of the status quo.

Given all the frustrations in trying to serve the New York and Connecticut markets, there are those in the energy industry who mutter, "Let them freeze in the dark." This argument, of course, is as untenable as that of an elected official who says, "We need more energy, but take your project somewhere else."

Fourth, the nation cannot rely on a random few infrastructure initiatives to meet its energy security and affordability needs. While perhaps not every project proposed will be approved, there must be a comprehensive short-, medium-, and long-term plan to meet the needs of the country from all sources of energy, to improve efficiency, and to protect the environment.

Without a comprehensive plan, balance will never be achieved. The nation will continue to ride the pendulum swings from the right to the left and back, all the way to inevitable economic and social decline. But if the government cannot provide clear direction, can the free market do a better job?

6

FORGET THE FREE MARKET

Let's quit pretending. Energy access, production, storage, distribution, and sales have been regulated for decades.

During my years on the board of the National Association of Manufacturing (NAM), a membership organization of small, medium, and large U.S. manufacturing companies that promotes sound public policy to support competitiveness, I had the pleasure of meeting some of America's finest business leaders and entrepreneurs. Over many years, the NAM has watched out for manufacturing interests and has wrestled with every imaginable challenge that anyone could throw at industry.

There were moments at board meetings when frustrations with government policy boiled over on issues such as immigration, taxes, and government subsidies. Of course, companies that benefited from subsidies and other policy proposals were generally in favor of them; companies that competed against subsidies or other government support were generally opposed. The conflict in the room was sometimes irreconcilable.

At such moments, there was always a rearguard response, one that has echoed across the country repeatedly over the years, proud and patriotic: "Let the free market decide." Let the market decide what products, services, technology should be available to consumers. Let the free market determine prices, availability, and quality. The market is the ultimate arbiter of what works, what sells, what happens. Isn't that American free market capitalism?

If only it were so. Around the boardroom, some of us felt that confidence in the free market was overstated. These were my counterparts in oil refining and chemical processing companies as well as coal companies and electric utility and transmission companies. We had seen market "freedom" in our industries shrink and disappear over many decades, to the regret of our customers, shareholders, and suppliers.

Market freedom was eaten away for many reasons, some due to legitimate government protections, such as land and natural resource management, health, and safety; others were punitive measures applied to all companies in response to abuses by a few individuals, such as anticompetitive behavior, environmental degradation, supply constraints, or excessive risk taking. Some loss of freedom came from legal judgments; some came from progressive legislation, such as rural electrification and offshore exploration, or regressive legislation, such as production prohibitions and multiple, unnecessary categories of gasoline.

I am not arguing for or against the past actions of either the industry or the government, nor do I intend to provide a history of legislation and regulation affecting energy. The point is that energy, which once was developed, bought, and sold in a free market, is now constricted and constrained in ways that the government determines and in ways that exceed the limits on most other industries. Although energy companies remain involved in discussions of legislation and regulations, when the debates are over, the government makes the rules and the energy companies comply or forfeit their licenses to operate.

The reason government energy policy becomes so important in terms of national security, economic competitiveness, and American lifestyles is that the government sets the market for supplies: where companies can explore for natural resources or produce power. The government also tries to determine demand both by limiting supply and by restricting products that consume energy. It is no overstatement to say that the government has progressively, to use an old analogy, moved from the camel's nose in the tent to the whole camel in the tent. When something goes wrong, as when prices skyrocket, the government first blames industry. Yet later analysis often shows the root cause is traceable to government policy, as in high prices caused by prohibiting access to natural resources.

So when I hear media, consumers, politicians, and various interest groups attack energy companies over supply shortages, price increases, and infrastructure breakdowns, and accuse them of mismanaging America's energy supply as if the companies were free market operators, all I can say is, "I wish."

The following exchange illuminates what energy companies faced in the recent debate over prices and supplies. It took place when I interacted with Congresswoman Maxine Waters (D-CA) in a hearing of the Committee on the Judiciary Anti-Trust Task Force and Competition Policy on May 22, 2008.

At the time gas prices were nearly at their 2008 peak: in California, prices were approaching $5 per gallon, while the rest of the nation was experiencing prices well over $4 per gallon, levels unprecedented in the U.S. retail gasoline marketplace. Diesel prices were even higher. Pain-at-the-pump stories were everywhere in the press. Both houses of Congress were holding hearings with market analysts, oil companies, and consumer groups to explore the connection between the high prices and what were seen as excessive profits, with a view toward doing something about the problem. Oil companies were being threatened by members of Congress with punitive legislation on virtually a daily basis. With that backdrop, my dialogue with Congresswoman Waters represented the direct opposite of free market prospects for companies that produce and sell gasoline in the wider energy marketplace.

WATERS: There's nothing that you can tell us here...about how you could guarantee a reduction of the price at the pump if you were given the ability to go and drill where you say there is oil deposits.

ME: On the contrary, I can guarantee to the American people, because of the inaction of the United States Congress, ever-increasing prices, unless the demand comes down, and the $5 [in California] will look like a very low price in the years to come if we are prohibited from finding new reserves, new opportunities to increase supplies.

WATERS: And guess what this liberal [meaning herself] would
    be all about? This liberal would be all about socializing—
    would be about basically taking over and the government
    running all of your companies, and that, I tell you, is an
    extreme position.
ME: Venezuela...has been nationalized and we see what is
    happening under the government's leadership in Venezuela.
WATERS: I don't want to hear about Venezuela...So don't talk
    about what they're doing. What I'm telling you is you don't
    want to see that happen in the United States. You guys have
    got to get off of this [high prices]. You cannot keep coming in
    here with all of these profits and tell us you can't give us any
    guarantees [on lowering prices], even if the liberals are con-
    vinced that you should go into some of the protected areas.[1]

The exchange continued with the congresswoman continuing to
insist on reductions in gas pump prices, regardless of the supply/
demand balance in the marketplace. It was clear that Waters, like
many other politicians, had no concept that government energy
market supply constraints cause higher prices in the face of continued demand by consumers. The only logical way to address
demand in the face of constrained supply would be gas rationing.
Of course, elected officials are not about to restrict consumers,
who vote for them, even while they work hard to restrict companies, which don't vote. With such convoluted thinking about
how the market works, it's no wonder that the nation's energy
policy has been in tatters for decades.

■   ■   ■   ■   ■

Added to the domestic constraints on oil and gas supply and
their impact on prices is the enormous complication called the
Organization of Petroleum Exporting Countries (OPEC). This
cartel exists for one reason and one reason only: the self-interest
of its oil-producing members. Sovereign members with oil reserves
available for export collectively determine a production quota
and a price target for the crude oil that they sell on the global
market.

OPEC members, including countries in the Middle East,
Africa, and South America, control approximately two-thirds of

the world's oil reserves and meet approximately one-third of the world's daily oil demand. OPEC produces twice as much oil per day as the combined global output of all the major international oil companies, including ExxonMobil, Royal Dutch Shell, BP, Chevron, ConocoPhillips, and Total. OPEC is the antithesis of the free market. The volumes of oil it controls dominate setting the crude oil price. It withholds oil from the market when prices move below its consensus-driven price objective; it may choose to produce more oil when prices move so high that its members fear the price impact could drive customers to alternative energy sources or cause demand to decline. If the international oil companies did in the United States what OPEC does internationally, their executives would be locked up for price fixing.

Recently international dialogue has been growing among sovereign nations that are natural gas producers. They propose to create an international cartel for natural gas similar to OPEC to protect their interests. From 2007 to 2009 there were a series of meetings among gas-producing countries to consider the prospects. The discussions are particularly worrisome to European countries, because of their dependence on natural gas imports from Russia, North Africa, and the Middle East. For now, the U.S. market is relatively unconcerned, given the geographic abundance of natural gas reserves in the United States and North America generally. But ultimately, international cartels inevitably destroy market forces.

■　■　■　■　■

Pain at the American pump prompts the predictable knee-jerk reaction by Congress to call U.S. oil executives on the carpet and drag them through a hearing or two in the Senate or the House. On the surface, this gives the impression that Congress is doing something about the "pain." If Congress really wanted to do something, though, it would direct the administration to provide leasing rights to American oil companies for additional offshore or onshore production of more natural resources. Such action by Congress would both serve consumers' interests and deliver a double whammy to OPEC. For one thing, it would increase global energy supplies, putting downward pressure on the world-wide crude price. OPEC could do nothing, other than restrict its own production, thereby reducing its take of the oil market and reducing the inflow of money to its national treasuries. It would also give Americans the benefit of lower-cost domestically produced crude oil, which would improve affordability and reduce the pain at the pump. It would do for oil what T. Boone Pickens is arguing should be done for U.S. natural gas.

But Congress has chosen not to do what is in the people's interests. Instead, it has preferred to undertake the sham exercise of harassing American oil executives rather than tackle the actual problem of too little petroleum in the market while distracting attention from the sustained nature of the problem over the next decades by promoting so-called clean energy proposals. The eventual snap-back of gasoline prices promises to be excruciatingly painful. No doubt we will once again see sham hearings to blame the oil companies, accelerated taxpayer subsidies for higher-priced biofuels, and continued avoidance of the fundamental issues. The U.S. government is inflating the price of liquid fuels by virtue of its anti–free market policies while pointing fingers and blame at the companies whose prices are reflected on street corner sign posts. At the same time, the sustained difficult relationships between oil companies and government set the stage for a contest that neither the government nor the companies win. And consumers, stuck with the higher prices, lose as well.

Legislators have searched far and wide for a rationale on which to base their accusation that oil companies are withholding production. During 2007 some smart staffer in the House or Senate who may never have set foot on an oil rig or visited a drilling site "discovered" the idea that oil companies were sitting on thousands of leases that they could otherwise be producing, deliberately forcing the price of oil higher. Over and over I have been asked how many leases Shell Oil was sitting on that were not producing oil or gas. Over and over I have explained that if Shell had a lease on which it was not producing, it was for one of two reasons: either there was no commercial deposit of hydrocarbons to produce, or the lease was in a queue to be developed as soon as the financial capital, engineering, production, and other infrastructure plans were complete.

New oil and gas wells are not turned on with a switch. It takes time, money, and people to bring a new well on line once it is shown that there is oil or gas to produce. In a period of high prices, no oil executive could look shareholders in the eye and say, "We're withholding production," and survive. More production means more income, more return on investment. What is in shareholders' interest is also in consumers' interest. The sitting-on-leases argument is a quite pitiful display of government ignorance playing out as arrogance.

Posturing and pontificating by elected officials will not produce an additional barrel of oil. Having stripped the free market mechanisms away from energy suppliers, the officials themselves are the source of any and all new production prospects. Without new access provided by the U.S. government, there is no response to OPEC other than to be held hostage to its price cartel while we send hard-earned American dollars to countries that generally could not care less about the American consumer.

Aha, you say, but what about biofuels? Don't they release us from the power of the cartel? Aren't they a free market solution? In fact, biofuels are one of the beneficiaries of high gas prices caused by lack of access. High prices are the only reason we are making a play for biofuels production. But the manufacture of biofuels is a government policy, not a free market response. There is a story circulating that early in the Obama administration, Secretary of Energy Stephen Chu, in a meeting with oil executives, asked what it would take to keep the crude oil price in the range of $75 to $95 (at the time it was bouncing between $50 and $60), because such a crude price would on one hand make biofuels competitive with gasoline and on the other hand keep pump prices from going out of sight, as they had when crude oil prices exceeded $100 per barrel. It was an unanswerable question, in part because oil company executives are competitors. They cannot act like a cartel and cannot collectively discuss the future price of crude oil together, even if invited to do so by a government official, without perpetrating a collusive, illegal act. But the take-away from the meeting was that biofuels meant more to the administration than the affordability of fuel for consumers. So let's just say our government's policy, as expressed by the energy secretary, is to actively promote higher fuel prices by constraining supplies and diverting attention to other high-priced alternatives.

■   ■   ■   ■   ■

In conversations that I have had with executives at American Electric Power, Duke Energy, Florida Power and Light, and Exelon, four of the largest electric utilities in the country, they describe their own world of operating a business outside a free market. Discussions of future electric supplies turn on a common phrase: "We can't get price." Over and over executives have described how public utility commissions will not grant the price relief needed to fund the technology and capital investments they could make to bring in new clean energy technology to make more efficient use of traditional energy. This is a serious problem for America.

For Exelon, one of the nation's premier nuclear generators, the issue is even more complex. Not only can't it get the price that would be needed to fund development of new nuclear electricity production; siting and other permit requirements, together with the national debacle over nuclear waste management, also hold back development of new nuclear-sourced electricity.

In a free market, price pays for everything. From research and development, to product design, to manufacturing, distribution, and retailing, price is the mechanism that enables commercial products to get to customers. Customers may not like the prices charged, but if they want the product, they will pay the price. Think about the introductions of the iPhone, Viagra, the Nintendo Wii, or the Toyota Prius. Later, when volumes increase and competition enters the market, prices trend downward. But by then the original investments that were needed to bring new products to market have been paid off. If that is not the case, new products never reach the market or companies go bankrupt.

This is not what happens with electricity. In regulated states, public utility commissions are the final authority on the prices that electricity producers can charge. In deregulated states, public utility commissions are the final authority on the *range* of prices that producers and/or distributors or resellers can charge. Public utility commission charters, as set by state legislatures, contain a general provision that the commission operates in the consumers' interests by establishing rate structures that essentially insist on lowest-cost sources of electricity. This was a logical response nearly 70 years ago when the electrification of America was well under way and being extended to rural areas. But all these years later, in the face of continuing demand growth and the critical need for gaseous waste management, with the technology evolution that has occurred, is occurring, and will occur, isn't it time to rethink this ancient principle?

There is obvious democratic logic in such provisions: the state is looking out for the financial well-being of its citizens. That's hard to argue with. But many of those charters have their origins in the days when electricity was a new market phenomenon. Lowest-cost sourcing was seen as protection from monopolistic providers and a way by which essentially all Americans could benefit from the comforts and security that electricity provided. At the advent of the new electricity marketplace, environmental impact was not a high priority. Little enough was known. It was wise legislation—at the time.

But things change, don't they? Public utility commission authorizations have not been adequately updated to reflect new technology and environmental sustainability needs in today's society. If utility companies and power generators cannot charge the prices needed to pay for investments in either or both, they're not going to spend shareholders' money to pay for such investments. Why aren't they? They'd lose their shareholders.

Yet public utility commissioners chartered to do what is in the consumers' best cost interests cannot go against their charters without being tarred and feathered and run off the commission on a rail. The lack of free-market dynamics in electricity supply costs and demand pricing is just as problematic as governmental prohibitions on new gas and oil exploration and production. The government is essentially restricting the future supply of cleaner, more efficiently produced electricity in the name of protecting consumer prices. As the nation moves toward a more restrictive carbon management regime, it will ever more frequently come face-to-face with this dilemma, and the outcome is uncertain.

One consequence of tighter carbon management rules could be higher prices to pay for the construction and commissioning of clean coal electricity generation. Another consequence could be the elimination of the source of carbon emissions by simply shutting down pulverized coal plants that do not have carbon mitigation technologies, thereby reducing supplies of electricity to the market and causing prices to rise anyway.

■　■　■　■　■

What do we do about carbon management and the use of clean coal technology? It's not that difficult a problem if we're open to some constructive, depoliticized conflict and debate, long-term investment and appropriate pricing, and a change of mind-set (and official charters) within public utility commissions and state legislatures. Since the government now has ownership over the market and has eliminated the basic free-market functioning of utility companies, it has a responsibility to make the required hard decisions so that citizens continue to have affordable energy and a cleaner atmosphere. If we clean the atmosphere by shutting down pulverized coal plants, which produce 50 percent of the nation's supply of electricity, we have no way to replace that amount of power, given the course we are on today. There is no way, under any intelligent analysis of future electricity demand/supply requirements, to grow wind and solar and natural gas to replace half our electricity supply overnight, if ever. In the best of circumstances it would take many decades to even come close. And significant additional new, clean coal plants with carbon capture and sequestration and expanded nuclear power would be needed as part of the mix because of the advanced ages of the existing coal and nuclear fleets of power plants, which are not currently in the cards we're playing. A new public utility commission price formula that enables price increases to pay for new capital investments from the beginning, rather than upon commissioning of the new facility, could take us to clean coal utilization and new nuclear plants as a major part of the solution to future clean energy needs.

Coal gasification technology, which uses coal much more efficiently than traditional pulverized coal, has a higher up-front cost, perhaps as much as 20 percent, but can essentially pay for itself over the life cycle of an electric power plant. Attaching carbon reduction or elimination technology onto coal gasification technology is both feasible and doable. It also adds cost, perhaps another 20 percent, and cleans the air, reducing other social costs, such as health care, that are borne by all of society.

Nuclear electricity production is carbon-free. It is expensive, however, because of the safety and security precautions, siting challenges, custom designs, and long construction cycles that seem to prevent cost efficiencies from materializing among equipment suppliers and engineering, procurement, and construction suppliers. But over the life of a nuclear generating plant, the high up-front costs are essentially more than paid for by the efficiencies and reliability of the technology. As a result, the per-kilowatt-hour cost of electricity from a depreciated operating nuclear plant is arguably one of the cheapest available. The burden of the capital cost of construction, however, makes it one of the most expensive.

Faced with the dilemma of making future electricity affordable, sustainable, and plentiful, public utility commissions and state legislatures would be well advised to suspend the current prohibitions on front-end ratepayer funding of capital investments in order to pay for both new technology and environmental sustainability. Current practice generally prohibits rate changes by utilities until new plants are operating; utilities must borrow from shareholders the capital needed to build new facilities, which depresses the rate of return to shareholders and makes new investment decisions very difficult for utility management and boards. It simply makes common sense for the future of energy security to change the charter wording from lowest-cost sources to something like "sources that deliver responsible investments in future availability, sustainability, and best technology." In addition, it makes sense to allow for innovative utility financing and accounting treatments that lead to rate leveling over extended periods.

By enabling rate changes from the beginning of projects, such new direction and regulatory logic would unleash additional supplies of clean, efficiently produced electricity to meet future market needs. As the economics of front-end funding for such capital investments become better understood and realized, it will also become obvious that consumers will ultimately be the beneficiaries of the combination of cleaner air, more efficiently produced electricity, and a long-term future of potential price reductions as depreciation costs are written off and the efficiencies pass through the production system, assuming supplies of fuel are not constrained by public policy.

With regard to nuclear plant construction, standardization of designs, siting, waste management, and safety and security plans, along with liability reform, could lead to dramatic improvement in new construction and operating costs. Government policy has made it so difficult to build new nuclear operating capacity that no one dares take the risk. The government, through its anti-nuclear representatives and leaders, has also tolerated, even participated in, the demonizing of nuclear energy, adding to the costs of taking the risks. Americans deserve better than politicization of energy to achieve selfish local or regional electoral outcomes. They need to be informed of the facts in order to make their own analysis of preferred outcomes. The government and industry share collective blame for the general absence of the facts in communities across the nation.

Such logic applied across the entire system of electricity supply, even taking into account the future cost implications of carbon management restrictions, should deliver a supply of energy that is cleaner, more efficient, and continuously affordable by virtue of the judicious balancing of investment costs and efficiency rate relief applied over decades, not years.

■   ■   ■   ■   ■

The headway the United States is making in pursuit of renewable electricity, especially wind and solar, is happening only because energy is not a free market. I pointed out earlier the extraordinary level (more than $20 per megawatt-hour) of subsidy that is being provided by Congress, which I support as a part of the energy system transition, but not forever. In addition, many state legislatures are providing renewable energy incentives (equivalent to taxpayer subsidies) to promote construction and deployment of wind and solar initiatives that would not otherwise be built. The subsidies are hidden in the general tax fund. If they showed up on consumers' monthly electric bills, it would provide useful education and could impact the artificial comfort many draw from expansions of these forms of costly renewable energy. It might prompt them to ask whether they wouldn't actually be better off, from the standpoint of both affordability and sustainability, to promote more clean coal and expanded nuclear and natural gas electricity production.

An unanswered question is whether renewable energy will ever be competitively commercial, relative to more traditional forms of electricity generation, even with carbon management costs factored into the equation. I doubt it can be, at least in my lifetime. That doesn't mean that we shouldn't build more wind and solar. It means that we should be honest with ourselves about their real impact on affordability and availability. We should not pull wool over consumers' eyes and pretend that renewable energy is the nation's salvation. If the government is going to own the market, we citizens must demand honest broker accountability and truth from the government.

A second unanswered question in this government-mandated market is how utilities will manage the twin challenges of distributed power (consumers incentivized by state or federal programs to install private solar or wind power units that provide partial power to the consumer for parts of the day and potential off-take power to the grid at other times) and electric cars (a huge potential draw on the system and also a potential source of distributed power to the grid). While in theory such systems create new supply, at what point does the primary power provider build ratepayer costs into the grid and power supply system to adjust for the alternating demand/supply imbalances created by such push-and-pull forces? Individual decisions by millions of consumers to impact the flow of electricity onto or off the grid could be enormous. Someone has to manage that inflow or outflow and make sure it doesn't lead to surges or drops in supply that prompt the shutdown of the grid to protect itself. Proponents suggest that grid intelligence will provide the necessary protections. At the conclusion of the construction and implementation of smart grid technology 25 or more years from now, they may well be right. It's how we get there from here that will be critical to the affordability and reliability of electricity supplies.

The social and economic costs of distributed power and the requirements for sufficient backup power to reliably sustain the grid should be shouldered by all ratepayers, including those who think they should have the right to opt off the grid. No one can really opt off entirely. Even if consumers self-generate residential power, they still are the beneficiaries of schools, community buildings, shopping centers, traffic lights, streetlights, and numerous other public uses of electricity. No one should be excluded from paying for the advantages of twenty-first-century energy.

■   ■   ■   ■   ■

The absence of a free market for energy, and the likelihood that the nation will never again enjoy free-market availability and pricing based on true supply and demand, come down to two unchanging realities.

1. Electricity and all other forms of energy are for everyone individually and for society collectively.
2. There is simply insufficient trust to go around.

So let's quit pretending there's a free market and manage the future more constructively. This means that government, the energy industry and consumers all have to change, as hard as that may be, or we will end up without enough energy, with too much dirty energy, or with prices higher than they need to be—or all three.

We have the choice to create a future where everyone wins or everyone loses. It all comes down to how we develop and use public policy, regulation, and supply/demand balance to impact pricing.

For the electricity market, our current course means a future where power from primary sources will be tight and erratic and more than likely insufficient to meet future demand. We're simply not building enough new core electricity production to meet future demand growth. We will pay a price later for shelving more than a hundred coal plant projects in the past five years. Likewise we will pay a price for not building more nuclear plants when we could have. We are not allowing utilities to pay for the building of cleaner, more efficient primary source supplies through start-of-project rate structures, yet we're planning a carbon-restricted future as if we were. All this will lead to significantly higher costs for utilities and distributors to provide or purchase both the electricity and the credits needed to continue to supply dirty power, or more likely it will result in the elimination of such power sources, further diminishing supplies and dramatically increasing costs to ratepayers as shortages grow.

This situation will lead in turn to more distributed generation—consumers investing in their own electricity production, which further suboptimizes the benefits of the larger grid. The efforts to make up for the diminishing supplies of dirty power by constructing significantly more wind and solar power add more costs to energy supplies because of the subsidies needed to build them. When they are built, they will not deliver sufficient new power to make up for the retirement of old, or lack of new building of, traditional power sources. Current-course proponents claim they will make up for the differences by improving energy use efficiency. No doubt efficiency will make a difference. But American electricity consumption history is not on the side of the argument, especially when increased population is factored into the balance.

For transportation fuels, the lack of a free market and the continuing reluctance or refusal by Congress and the current administration to seriously address the responsible development of domestic supplies will only lead to higher costs and tighter availability. Biofuels may add marginally to liquid fuel supplies in coming years, but no one I know can explain how biofuels compete without both public subsidies and higher-cost crude. Current U.S. policy is to inflate the cost of liquid fuels to pay for biofuels in the name of less dependence on foreign oil. If as citizens we demanded truth from our elected officials, they would have to acknowledge that they prefer inflated prices over the development of new domestic resources. This is not new with the Obama administration. It's been going on since the Nixon administration. The problem is that we Americans have not demanded and therefore have not been told the truth by the people we elect. They've gotten away with it to the point that most of us believe we're short on crude and high prices are inevitable. Nothing could be further from the truth, if truth be known. What a pity for each and all of us.

Here's the trust problem in its clearest, most visible, most frightening climax. With no free market, if our government refuses to support access to more domestic oil supplies; if the government will not allow the electricity industry the price relief it needs to produce cleaner, more efficient electricity in a carbon constrained future; if the government decides that the only new supplies of energy we can produce are both noncommercial and taxpayer subsidized, what are we doing to ourselves as a society? We are setting ourselves up for less energy availability, higher costs, loss of competitiveness compared to other nations, and a poorer quality of life. Promoting green jobs, wind, solar, and biofuels as a new energy system for America is fodder for unthinking herds. It is not a new energy system for the future; it's a symbolic tack-on to a huge existing infrastructure in dire need of reinvestment. We need more supplies from every source of energy, produced more cleanly, and distributed universally.

And since we're now nearly 40 years past the time when we should have been addressing these issues, investing in more domestic supplies, and reinvigorating the traditional infrastructure in cleaner ways, where will the political leadership, the past Congresses, and administrations that led us into this debacle be when these effects become seriously evident as shortages grow over the next decade? We all know they will be as far removed from accountability as possible. When have our political leaders ever taken responsibility for the problems they create? But now we know that since there is no free market, they can't blame the industry for the problems they created. We're screwed. They screwed us. Shame on us for allowing them to do it to us.

It's not too late to correct the mess they have made. But as a society, we need to make a lot of difficult decisions quickly and implement a lot of practical solutions faster than ever. We are facing simultaneously a future energy abyss and price inflation unprecedented in our history. We can't wait until the lights go out and gas tanks run dry to fix the problems that have been passed down the line and are even now being passed along to the next round of political-time operators.

Are we ready and willing to trust the oil companies and utilities to play a larger free-market role in determining our energy future? So far, Americans have not found them to be very trustworthy.

7

THE INDUSTRY IS PAROCHIAL. SURPRISED?

The energy industry cannot solve our energy crisis.
I should know.

As I entered the hearing room of the Subcommittee on Energy and Resources of the House Oversight and Government Reform Committee, I felt a touch on my shoulder. I was one of several energy executives called to testify before the subcommittee on the thorny topic of royalties that had been waived for Gulf of Mexico leases during the Clinton administration. It was June 2006, and rising oil profits had brought into question why price caps were not written into the waivers.

Turning around, I saw the hard-jawed face of an official from the Washington government relations office of ExxonMobil. He was there in support of his colleague who would also be testifying. With his arm around my shoulder, he leaned close to my ear and said, just above a whisper, "John, I read your opening statement. If you happen to see a live grenade on the floor of the hearing room, do us a favor, jump on it. We'd all appreciate it." He then removed his arm, grimaced, and proceeded to take his seat.

Anyone who knows the energy industry from the inside knows that there are sharp, defining differences among its players. When I have told this story to others in the industry, they just smile and shake their heads. It is no surprise to them that ExxonMobil would disagree with Shell Oil or that a wise-crack would be offered with an air of intimidation disguised by false collegiality.

Since the person making the remark knew I was not about to be intimidated, I took it as a stab from the "we're right, you're wrong" singsong collection in the ExxonMobil versus Shell "Book of Barbs" that has been around for over a century.

ExxonMobil's testimony that day stated its position on the sanctity of contracts and its unwillingness to amend them. Shell's testimony explained its open mind on the controversy and its recent decision to fix the problem with the Department of the Interior by renegotiating pertinent contracts.

This sharp divergence on the issue before the subcommittee that day is a prime illustration of how substantively differenti-ated the supposedly monolithic "Big Oil" really is.

■　■　■　■　■

During the middle and late 1990s, when oil prices were lower and actually hit just below $10 a barrel in 1998, new investment in oil drilling in the Gulf of Mexico was dramatically slowing. Rigs were idled, layoffs were widespread, and companies were girding themselves for a long period of low-priced oil. The cover of *The Economist* magazine on March 6, 1999, showed several oil workers hovering under a shower of crude oil trying to con-tain an oil well blowout. The headline: "Drowning in Oil?"

The Clinton administration and Congress feared that a sus-tained drilling drought would result in ever-increasing depen-dence on oil imports and cost the United States thousands of high-paying jobs on a permanent basis. In response, the adminis-tration considered incentives that would entice and reward those companies willing to maintain capital investments and keep their drilling programs and jobs going. The device it chose was a suspension of royalty payments for a specific round of leases that would be auctioned off in the coming months. Allowing the oil companies that participated in the upcoming lease auction to forgo the federal government's royalty (basically the suspension of a tax equal to about 16 percent of the value of the oil produced) meant that the companies could generate a higher return when they later produced oil from the lease.

At the time of the policy incentive and in the initial drafting of the leases, there were at best ambiguous discussions about whether the leases would be capped at some hypothetical crude oil price. Frankly, at the time no one saw oil prices rising above the current low levels or even returning to their average levels for years to come, so neither the government nor the oil companies considered a price cap germane to the discussions. However, there was precedent in other federal leases that included price caps. (In retrospect, the government's position should have been that price caps belong on all incentivized leases.)

The Clinton administration handed over the process of finalizing the leases to the Bush administration. This was not unusual; it is normally a multiyear process from the time leases are auctioned to the time that contracts are drafted, reviewed, negotiated, and ultimately signed by the government and the companies. The contracts that were signed contained no price caps.

The price of crude oil rose from 2003 through 2006, given higher global demand and industry's inability to increase production rapidly after years of low oil prices and correspondingly low investments in new production. The price of a gallon of gas rose correspondingly, and in 2005 Congress began a series of its periodic gas price inquests, taking aim at alleged Big Oil collusion, pain at the pump, and oil companies' rising profits. The first hearing followed the gasoline price spikes after Hurricanes Katrina and Rita. The next spring, reports regarding the 1999 leases and the so-called sudden discovery of the absence of price caps surfaced and attracted considerable attention. Allegations that the Bush administration and its Interior Department "colluded" with Big Oil were juicy, testy, attention-grabbing revelations, especially in a midterm election year, when the Democrats stood to gain seats from the Republicans.

To the credit of Representative Darrell Issa (R-CA), as chairman of the Subcommittee described previously, he led a thorough investigation without prejudging the parties. In the end, he discovered that regulatory language dating back as early as 1995 was unclear and not adequately corrected by the Department of the Interior. His subcommittee did not find collusion or illegality. The issue of the uncapped leases went unresolved and remains to this day a matter of dispute between the government and some oil companies.

Why were the positions of ExxonMobil and Shell so diametrically opposed? ExxonMobil argued that a contract is a contract; Shell voluntarily agreed to renegotiate the contracts with the Department of the Interior and to include a price cap. Besides Shell, two other companies, BP and ConocoPhillips, had also come to the same renegotiation conclusion. Other companies took the same position as ExxonMobil.

Essentially the divergence reflected the extraordinary differences that abound in the industry. Shell believed that a mistake should be correctible, considering its own imperfect track record. The public was already upset about oil company profits; the image of the industry extracting the last possible cent from the government played to the anti-profits crowd and those who were clamoring for a "windfall profits" tax. Shell felt there was more to gain than to lose by being flexible. On a long-term basis, Shell believed that the better position was to acknowledge and correct mistakes by mutual agreement, with the idea that future potential corrections could be reciprocal.

ExxonMobil was not the only oil company that day to claim the contract-is-a-contract argument. Another one, Kerr McGee, argued the same point with as much passion as if the future of the capitalist economy and viability of the industry were at risk. Each company's perspective reflected its own worldview—and its own self-interest.

■   ■   ■   ■   ■

The point of all this: Don't count on the oil and gas industry to take common positions on solutions to the nation's energy security, volunteer to work together on what benefits the common good, or consistently agree on what policy choices the government should make on energy and the environment.

By extension, don't expect the whole energy industry to speak with one voice. Within the electric power generation industry, companies that produce electricity from coal, nuclear power, hydropower, or natural gas are as different from one another as their sources of supply. Likewise, the alternative and renewable energy industry, including wind, solar, and biofuels companies, hydropower, and geothermal, have no basis to work together on the nation's common good. On the contrary, each energy company has every imaginable reason to work in its own selective best interest, even in opposition to one another.

This parochialism is not new. It started when coal displaced wood and oil first competed with coal. It is framed in anti-competition law; demanded by historic adjudication; promoted in modern times by local, state, and federal policies; rewarded by investors and venture capitalists. And it's all paid for by consumers. How about that?

Admittedly there are some superficial linkages that seem to tie energy companies together. Electrical power plants all (or nearly all) feed into a common electrical grid. Crude oil, liquid fuels, and natural gas are fed into common carrier pipelines. Oil field drilling rigs move from job to job working for competitors. The intense capital requirements of today's difficult exploration projects have led to what is known as co-opetition: joint ventures or co-investments by competitors. But such ventures are managed with extreme care to avoid any crossing of competitive lines. You have only to try to enter any oil company office in Houston to see how intensely the companies guard their secrets from each other.

What we have across the United States is an industry that is our largest by revenue and employment, most capital intensive, highly sophisticated, yet utterly, irrevocably parochial and fragmented.

Considering the lack of a true free market and the commodity nature of the ultimate products (both electrons and liquid fuels), and in the face of urgent national needs for energy security and quality of life, why does this industry remain so parochial?

There are two reasons. Both reinforce the status quo, which means nothing's going to change anytime soon.

ANTITRUST

The first reason is U.S. antitrust law. On May 15, 1911, the U.S. Supreme Court decided to uphold the findings of a lower court that Standard Oil of New Jersey was an "unreasonable" monopoly under the Sherman Antitrust Act and to break it into 34 independent companies with their own boards of directors. A few years earlier, in 1904, Standard Oil had produced 91 percent of the nation's refined products and had 85 percent of retail sales. (By the time of the Court's decision, this figure had declined to 64 percent of retail market share.) The oil industry as a whole has yet to live down this decision. It may never.

Nearly a century later, the entire industry is far larger in total; the nation is essentially dependent on liquid fuels for transportation, and oil is still the primary natural resource for those fuels. ExxonMobil, considered to be the descendant of Standard Oil, has achieved the role of largest publicly held oil company by market capitalization and other rating factors. Royal Dutch Shell and BP are generally second and third, followed closely in size and scope by Chevron, a former Standard Oil company in later historic iterations, and then ConocoPhillips. From the consumer's perspective, they are all generally lumped together as one faceless insensitive monolith.

The integrated oil companies are among the largest publicly held companies in the world, dwarfed in size only by the much larger state-owned oil companies around the world, including Saudi Aramco (Saudi Arabia), Kuwait Oil (Kuwait), Petronas (Malaysia), and Petrobras (Brazil). Yet, as we know, size matters in the oil and power generation industries. The capital investment, technology, staffing, and financing requirements necessary to succeed in this high-risk, long-payback, competitive international industry are extraordinary. If an integrated company cannot achieve size, it has a limited future.

The U.S. government believes it best manages that size and behavior by enforcing long-standing antitrust policy and threatening to pass industry-handicapping legislation.

Let me point out that antitrust legislation matters to corporate executives. Every year for 35 years of corporate life I verbally or in writing signed off on a briefing on antitrust rules and regulations. I will never forget what I was told at General Electric's 1974 annual review of anti-competition rules, when I worked in Lynchburg, Virginia. The company lawyer conducting the session said, "Remember this: Your company lawyer is at your service and may even be your friend. If you are accused of antitrust behaviors, your lawyer will stick with you through thick and thin. He or she will work with you and represent you faithfully to the best of his or her ability for however long it takes. He or she will sit with you, talk to your family, support you in every way possible and do whatever is needed to protect you. He or she will argue your defense and do everything legally permissible to ensure that justice is done. There is, however, one difference. Your lawyer will always go home at night (meaning: while you return to your cell)." Thirty-five years later I still remember that lesson. I've never known anyone who was found guilty or even charged with antitrust violations. I hope to preserve that record. So does everyone else I know in the energy industry.

Here is an example of how antitrust works in real life. The American Petroleum Institute (API) is a third-party organization that is funded by oil and gas producers to represent legally permissible common interests of the member companies, such as technical standard setting; health, safety, and environmental protection best practices; public policy positions; and industry reputation. It's not unlike similar associations in other industries. It is governed by a board of directors, which meets periodically to review the business of the institute and to agree to specific matters. Every meeting includes a reminder of antitrust obligations, and an antitrust lawyer is always present to make sure that no improper activity, behavior, or conversation takes place while conducting API business.

The special guest at an API dinner in the fall of 2006, with the antitrust lawyer present, was Al Hubbard, President Bush's chief economic advisor, a person who joined the administration in its second term to work on, among other things, energy alternatives such as biofuels. Most attendees were looking forward to hearing from someone so well positioned at the White House in the run-up to the November elections.

As Hubbard stepped to the podium, he remarked that he would prefer a conversation to a one-way speech. He then asked the audience a question. He wondered whether anyone thought the rise in the crude oil price was likely to continue and what levels it might reach in the coming months. He was met with dead silence. He looked around the room, unable to make eye contact with anyone, and reframed the question, saying he couldn't imagine anyone not having a point of view. Again silence, but also some squirming in seats. After a pause, he reddened slightly and asked what was wrong.

Red Cavaney, president of API at the time, rose to explain that everyone in the room was a competitor and no one was able to respond to the pricing question, since it would be an antitrust violation to do so. He said individuals could discuss the matter privately with him but not collectively. Even if President Bush himself were to demand a reply, no one would risk a jail sentence to answer. Hubbard blushed deeply, cleared his throat, and apologized.

No one fools around with antitrust.

COMPETITION

The second reason the industry remains parochial is competition—the kind that raises blood pressure and stimulates fierce loyalties, just as in sports. Why are the Olympic Games so eagerly anticipated? Why is the World Cup the most important event in the world every four years? Why do the World Series, Super Bowl, and Final Four matter in the United States? Why do political junkies like me stay up all night to watch election returns of races clear across the country? People love competition. It's important to us. It's a life force. It's also fun, exciting, keeping us on the edges of our seats. It brings out the best in us and rewards those who win. There are intrinsic and extrinsic satisfactions to being or choosing a winner.

So it is in the business world of energy. Coal wants to win against gas and nuclear. Oil independents want to beat the major companies to access and leases. Major brands fight over the best corners for retail stations. Electricity resellers want to take market share from big utilities. Biofuels proponents want to win against oil products. Wind wants to beat solar. Everyone in the energy space wants top talent, top dollar, top market share with lowest costs. Brand matters, so advertising and public positioning never stops.

Go to an industry meeting and watch the tribal behaviors, hooting, and chest-pounding when a brand gets recognized. Announce your intentions to go to work for a competitor and you earn the persona non grata frog-march out of the building.

To see how competition drives fragmentation, watch how the energy industry plays its cards in the public policy world of Washington, DC.

Coal companies work hard to de-position nuclear or natural gas companies in competition over favorable public policies in electricity generation. Coal executives emphasize their economic contribution and job creation across mining, transportation, and utilities. They bring along the United Mine Workers and their fraternity of other unions. They leverage their geographic spread across the country. They define "clean coal" to their own advantage. They describe the potential economic impacts of job losses on remote rural communities in coal states. They are deeply involved, and have been for years, in supporting many long-serving elected officials, helping to preserve the advantages of member seniority for their causes. For whatever tarnished history they may have, they are and will continue to be not just survivors but fighters for what they believe is their privileged role in affordable energy production in the United States.

A near-50 percent market share of electricity production is a good base of strength. A 200-plus-year reserves base of future energy production is a strong platform to invest in America's future. An improving health, safety, and environment record, regardless of what coal's critics say, creates a credible position on coal's ability to continue to take corrective actions. Verbal posturing against nuclear energy ("We can't manage the waste," "A nuclear plant is a national security time bomb," "A nuclear meltdown is one bad valve away from occurring") helps their cause. Their arguments against natural gas ("We're running out, let's conserve what we have for the future," "Tight gas fracturing pollutes our water and creates subsidence") prop up coal.

Meanwhile, the nuclear industry, looking out for itself, has plenty to say about coal. It argues that mountaintop removal is an environmental travesty. It adds that coal is the dirtiest and least efficient hydrocarbon fuel on earth, especially in comparison to carbon-free, incredibly efficient nuclear power by a factor of 2 million to 1.

Natural gas weighs in with claims it is 50 percent less polluting than coal and has a long-life reserve base well in excess of what others acknowledge. Clean Skies internet television, operated by a nonprofit founded in large part by Oklahoma-based Chesapeake Corporation, broadcasts the news about and advantages of natural gas from its studio in Washington, DC.

And on, and on, and on.

The industry segments all make legitimate points about themselves and don't mind shooting sound-bite bullets at their foes. The same public policy battles take place through the associations that form to promote their products and policy recommendations across Washington and the states, funded by the companies in their industries.

Does so much competition harm us? Absolutely! Or, not at all! It depends entirely on your perspective.

Advocates point to the advantages of a specific source of energy; contrarians point to the consequences of the sources. Presidents and members of Congress and their appointees and advisors come to Washington with their individual policy perspectives on display. These views are formed based on what they know about the various sources of energy and from whom they learn it.

George W. Bush's interest in biofuels had a direct connection with Al Hubbard from Indiana, where the corn grows high, and the unrelenting sales pitch of venture capitalists who, in frequent White House meetings, described the domestic economic value creation of this potentially vast new source of energy in the post-9/11 energy security era.

The Obama administration's rhetoric on green jobs created through investing in new forms of clean energy satisfies its environmentalist supporters. The otherwise complete silence on the potential loss of oil and gas "brown jobs" reflects the team's ongoing disconnect with the hydrocarbon industry and its customer industries.

What should we do about it? What *can* we do about it? Associations have the legal right to exist, and they're good at complying with the laws and regulations that define their limits.

But anyone who wants to have the complete picture of how competition works across the industry has to learn the facts, the implications, and the consequences of each source of energy. Each source is powerful, practical, and affordable under the right enabling public policies. Each can do harm in a wide range of technical, environmental, operational, and community settings—yes, even wind and solar, as regards land abuse, water erosion, and loss of aviary wildlife on wind farms, and land abuse and consumption of scarce water by solar farms. None is risk free or entirely nonpolluting. None is free.

Frankly, our security and economic competitiveness are better ensured through diversity of supply. Public policy, hand in glove with competition, joined to the hip with knowledge, information, and education are natural allies for a safe, secure, and affordable energy future. But such a future comes with the baggage of never-ending competitive positioning by every source of energy. Unless the government were to waive anti-trust laws, which won't happen, the fragmented companies across the expanse of energy sources are not about to work in what might be considered the nation's interests when those goals don't align with their individual parochial priorities.

Bottom line: We have a lot of sources of energy. They all work. They all compete with one another in both the political arena and the consumer marketplace. The fragmentation of energy is historic and unlikely to change. The various elements of the industry all see their job as to make and distribute energy in a competitive economy. There is no industry monolith looking out for the general interest of society. So don't expect industry to solve our energy future. Instead—no surprise—parochialism reigns.

Besides making it difficult to develop a cohesive, multisource energy strategy, this self-interested behavior also feeds the public's negative perception of the energy industry as a whole. Collectively we tend to see all members as part of a down-and-dirty lot.

8

OIL AND GAS: UNLOVABLE AND UNAVOIDABLE. UTILITIES: DITTO!

The oil and gas industry, locked in its paradigm, is unlovable but essential. So quit complaining and get used to it.

On a brilliant, blue-sky Saturday morning in August 2006, I found myself in Erie, Pennsylvania, on a side trip during my Shell Oil outreach tour. My weekend itinerary included stopping by local Shell stations, unannounced, to chat with store managers and customers. Erie is a friendly, family city. Its industrial past is being transformed by postindustrial efforts from entrepreneurial services and information management companies. I was familiar with the area, having lived there for several years early in my career. The summers are fantastic; people get out and enjoy their weekends. I wanted to talk with them.

My first store visit could not have gone better. The manager was not present but the cashier, a young lady with less than a year of experience, greeted me with a friendly hello and smile as I entered. She was cleaning an already shining checkout counter, and her broom and dust pan were right behind her. The store was bright, cheery, with plenty of Shell promotional materials highlighting our popular NASCAR sponsorship. The shelves were stocked, neat, the freezers full, the beverage refrigerators well arrayed. You could smell the morning coffee, and that's where I went first.

Over a fresh cup of black coffee we talked about her time at the Shell station. She said her customers were mostly local, friendly, and regular. They weren't too happy about the rising gas prices, but she said no one had so far blamed her, so that was good. She asked who I was. I explained that I worked for Shell out of Houston and, when I was on the road, liked to drop into local Shell stations to get a sense of how things were going. I didn't play the president card; that's a good way to close down an otherwise open conversation. She said she didn't know much about Shell, since her station was operated by a jobber, a third-party intermediary, a person who leases and runs but does not own the station. But she thought the tanker delivery people were really nice, always prompt, regardless of the weather or time of day.

Strolling outside I found a few customers filling up. In response to my questions, people seemed friendly and open. Interestingly, no one asked me who I was. One person told me he stopped here and always bought Shell whenever he needed gas because of his Shell MasterCard and the discount he got. Another person said he and his family lived a few blocks away, and he believed in doing business in the neighborhood. He also said he liked the people who worked at the station and confirmed that it was always clean as a whistle, not like some other stations around town. Another person said he bought gas there because he believed in supporting American companies first, either Shell or Exxon.

A stop to see the bathroom, which was as clean as the store, and I was off to the next station on my itinerary, after telling the cashier what a great job she was doing and how pleased I knew her manager must be. I assured her that people in Houston would be happy to hear about my visit and to have Shell's name on her store.

My next stop was a Shell store near the interstate. What a disaster! There was so much gravel and dirt covering the forecourt cement that it must not have been cleaned in many months.

The store manager was inside, behind the counter, surrounded by trash, piles of old newspapers, and store records, as a radio played loud music. The shelves of merchandise were haphazard; the coffee counter filthy, the coffeepots empty. Aisles were blocked by stacked merchandise waiting to be shelved. A departing customer said to his buddy, "Forget the restroom, it don't flush; you don't need to see how bad it is. Let's get out of here."

As I approached the manager, he turned his back and went into the office, leaving me standing at the register. When he came back I asked how business was. He ignored the question. I asked a second time. He said, "None of your business, that's how."

If nothing else, I'm persistent. "No, seriously," I said, "how's it going, what with the prices and all?" He shook his head at me and asked if I was buying anything. I could have just left and reported the condition of the station to the regional manager. But no, I decided to play the president card—literally—and handed it to him, explaining why I was there. He looked from my card to me in silence, then suddenly erupted.

"Do you know you are putting me and my family in the poorhouse? Who do you think you are? I saw Shell's profit report two weeks ago. You disgust me. You make billions and I squeeze nickels to keep up with my bills. My take-home pay is less every month. Your profits are larger every time I hear about them." He then called back over his shoulder to the office, asking a colleague to come see me. "Look at him. He's the reason we're poorer while he's richer. He's Shell's president, the man who could care less about real people like us."

I asked if he was a jobber and if he leased his store. He said he leased it and that his manager and the wholesaler who supplied him were bad people. I asked about volumes. He said they were down because of the high prices, "so you can make more profits." I asked if he had been visited lately by anyone from Shell. He said I was the first Shell visitor he ever knew. I asked how long he had been in his store and what motivated him to get into the business. He said it was presented to him as a moneymaking proposition by his manager and wholesaler and that he had signed a lease about 18 months earlier.

Despite the unpleasant circumstances, I decided not to give up yet. I talked candidly about high prices and high profits, global supply/demand pressure on prices, failed energy policies in the United States, dependence on expensive imports, prohibitions on domestic production, challenges for retailers, all the themes I was talking about across the 50 cities I was visiting. I also brought up Shell's standards for swept forecourts, tidy stores, and clean restrooms and the critical importance of the store owner as Shell's face to the customer. We went head to head for a while. He wasn't buying it; I was still selling it. My final advice to him was to visit other stations, Shell's as well as competitors in the area, and talk to other store owners. We didn't part friends, but we did talk in respectful tones. He did say he was surprised that I would take this much time to talk with him. When the person wearing your logo sees your company as the problem, you know you are in trouble.

■   ■   ■   ■   ■

The United States is a big retail gasoline market. There are more than 150,000 retail stations across the country, mostly locally owned and operated by jobbers or wholesalers. Every day tens of millions of Americans stop at a retail gasoline station. For many, especially with the run-up in prices, it is their most negative experience of the day, unless they have to have a tooth pulled or, even worse, talk to their electricity provider. Whether it is cold, hot, rainy, or windy, a retail customer has to stop, get out of the car, figure out the pump, feel like a suspected criminal for having to pay in advance or enter a zip code to confirm ownership of a credit card, pump the gas, trying not to acquire the smell of benzene on one's hands, maybe clean the windows with the dingy water available, decide whether to chance the restrooms (probably locked with a key attached to a giant tag, a double sign of distrust).

For this delightful experience consumers pay a price that they don't understand or believe, to a huge company of which they have at best a faint knowledge. Need mechanical help or directions? Good luck. Whatever happened to "You can trust your car to the man who wears the star" or even the "Shell Answer Man"?

On an annual favorability rating poll by Gallup covering the 24 largest industries in the United States, the oil and gas industry as a whole has for the past seven years been rated twenty-fourth out of 24.[1]

When the major oil companies run their retail businesses in such a consumer-unfriendly manner, why are they surprised when they are not welcomed with open arms by both local and national government officials? (As a side note, the federal government is included in the above poll and ranked twenty-second in the most recent rating, up from twenty-third the year before, displaced by real estate. The bottom-ranked industries seem likely to remain so for some time to come.) Even the product is unappealing. From the time it is extracted from the ground—a dirty, backbreaking process—to the time it enters a vehicle's tank, oil companies go to extreme lengths to make sure their product is not seen, smelled, or touched—much less tasted. "Loss of containment" of crude oil or refined gasoline is not only an unpleasant experience for those around it, but dangerous. The products are flammable, and some elements within them are known carcinogens.

Nearly every American adult has seen images of the devastation wrought by the oil spill in 1989 when the tanker *Exxon Valdez* ran aground with a full load of crude oil. More than 10 million gallons of oil fouled the waters, beaches, and wildlife off the pristine Alaska coast, causing extraordinary environmental and economic damages. Exxon was faulted over its handling of the aftermath and for the next 20 years was embroiled in legal battles over the event.

When Hurricane Katrina hit the Gulf coast in 2005, the water surge burst open crude oil and natural gas pipelines and lifted 40,000-gallon storage tanks of crude oil off their foundations. Oil ended up on the roofs of homes, in living rooms, kitchens, and bathrooms, thousands of yards from where it had been contained, adding to the challenge of the poststorm cleanup.

Fortunately, such catastrophic events are rare, and the industry precautions and the skills of its workers mean that few people are exposed to the product unless they mishandle the gasoline pump. For many years, even that possibility was minimized by having attendants pump the gas. (Self-service is still not legal in New Jersey and Oregon, with safety cited as the primary issue.)

There are other products we use every day that we wouldn't want to be exposed to in their raw form. Computer chips and circuit boards are made using a toxic mix of chemicals (hence they are disposed of as hazardous waste). But companies like Apple Inc. are able to build a loyal following of customers who are passionate about their products.

The basic difference: Apple sees itself as a consumer products company and works hard to educate customers and build relationships with them. In contrast, although their brand signs may be on every street corner, oil companies see themselves as wholesale producers of high volume products.

■   ■   ■   ■   ■

From mid-2006 to early 2008 I interacted with tens of thousands of Americans, visiting with them where they lived in 50 U.S. cities. I was probably out in front of the public more than any of my peers on the American Petroleum Institute (API) executive committee during those years. But as a share of my time, it was roughly 6 percent—not all that much. And that outreach was focused more on shaping public opinion on energy issues than on building customer relationships. Although the outreach did seem to have a positive effect on our market share, it was a secondary goal.

At the top level of an oil company, minimal time is spent considering the retail customer's experience. In eight years of executive meetings in my global role at Shell headquarters in The Hague, I can recall very few discussions about the retail end of the business, unless it had to do with selling off stations from company ownership to wholesalers. Retailing fuels is basically an off-take exercise from the oil company's point of view, a way to get rid of the product it has spent so much time and money producing. The oil company makes virtually all its money from discovery, to production, to trading and shipment of crude, to refining, to shipping to wholesalers. Retailing is the end of the oil company's business process, a part of the business value chain that makes virtually no money for the company relative to the total. (Although the gross margin on a clothing or similar retail store is typically 35 to 45 percent, gross margins on gas stations—even with convenience stores—have been as low as 12 to 13 percent in the last few years, according to public data from the Retail Owners Institute, a U.S. association of retail store owners.) This makes retailing the least valuable part of the business, more often a nuisance than a value creator, and worst of all the source of much public scrutiny and enmity.

With such low profit potential, ownership of the retail end of the business has shifted from oil companies to local business owners, who purchase supply and branding rights for products. Legally, the oil company is separated from the customer, although the oil company is still responsible for the quality of its products. As a result, top-level oil executives spend virtually no time on the retail end of the business. They delegate responsibility to those farther down the management hierarchy—in some of the major oil companies, you have to dig three or four layers down from the top to find someone dedicated to the retail stations.

There are more reasons than value chain to explain why, from the major oil company's perspective, the retail end of the business is better off being owned by others. One is the concept of disintermediation. Oil companies that own the retail network have historically faced innumerable antitrust charges, especially over pricing and availability of supplies. After hurricanes or other supply disruptions, I could always count on attack letters from state attorneys general who accused the company of conspiring to raise prices or withhold supplies, or both, and threatened antitrust charges and other legal action. Retail outlets have also been a source of fines and permit violations, when local staff cut corners or fail to pay attention to operating requirements. There's nothing like local officials going after the deep pockets of a big oil company over a single gas station violation of a local ordinance. Creating a legal separation reduces the oil company's liability for local infringements.

Given that retailing gasoline is at best a low-margin business for large, national companies, it simply makes sense to disaggregate the business by selling off the real estate and local operations to people who want to manage a high-volume, large–cash flow, real estate–intensive business.

Basically the oil majors have helped to create a distributed business of local owners and operators who become the face of the major oil company. Some do it very, very well, like the first retail station I visited in Erie. Some don't. Some may even damage the major's brand to make a more profitable business for themselves. But through this system, many oil executives absolve themselves of direct responsibility for consumer relations.

Of course, from the consumers' perspective, they are buying the product of a major oil company and they don't know or care about disintermediation. They place responsibility and accountability for the product they buy and the experience they have on the shoulders of the brand that they purchase.

In the middle of the controversy over rising oil prices in late 2005, one oil company executive is rumored among members of the American Petroleum Institute to have told then–Speaker of the House Dennis Hastert that if the American people didn't want his gasoline that was fine with him, there were plenty of people around the world who did. (Of course, this remark was not made in a public hearing.)

And oil companies wonder why they are hated.

■　■　■　■　■

When oil executives do speak publicly, they focus on what they believe is the best thing they can be doing to benefit the consumer: finding more oil and gas supplies for the future. The oil that will be in gas pumps and cars and planes and ships for the next eight to ten years has already been found. Oil executives are looking beyond that time frame to the resources that are still to be discovered or tapped. Within the industry, "positioning" means planning the future. The future is now for every oil company. The clock never stops ticking on the need to identify and access future supplies, or reserves. It is a compelling, ongoing obsession for top leaders.

Not only must each oil company build and sustain relationships (with governments, other companies, and mineral rights owners) to develop access opportunities, but it also must invest in talented people, the most advanced geology and drilling and production technology, logistics management and refining equipment, not to mention safety and environmental management, to stay in the game. Competitors are strong, unrelenting, and working on the very same time-focused activities.

Time is the most critical resource. How much can be done in what period of time? What risks and opportunities will present themselves in what time frame to enable or disable future endeavors? Shell is famous in the industry for its hundred-year forecasts and even more so for its longitudinal scenario planning. Both are time-based analyses that attempt to describe the future of resource supply and depletion while anticipating global, regional, or local events in society, culture, economy, and politics that may or may not impact supplies with higher or lower degrees of expectancy. This work informs executive thinking, but it is far removed from the retail station where the product is purchased. By the time a tanker's load of gasoline is delivered to the retail station, the oil executive has moved on to think about the gasoline that will be delivered 10 to 25 years in the future.

This difference in time perspective further distances the oil executive from the consumer. Imagine the dumbfounded oil executive who is jerked back to today's market reality by public opinion issues. The executive is further perplexed when public officials inevitably side with consumers. If I heard it once, I heard it a thousand times over the years: "How could these elected officials be so dumb, so detached, so distant, and so unrelenting in their opposition to what it takes to meet future demand for gasoline? Don't they know everyone needs gas?"

What do oil and gas executives do in response? Rather than engaging and informing government officials across the board, they tend instead to seek out their friends in the political arena, looking for help, solace, and understanding, pledging their support to their friends and like-minded officials while complaining about those who don't understand them. They then ignore or disparage their contrarians. They essentially compound their problems, especially if their friends are in the political minority, which happens regularly over long cycles. Nonfriends of the oil industry delight in confronting and publicly humiliating oil and gas executives when their misfortunes and travails prompt a public outcry. It is seen as fair payback for otherwise being ignored by industry executives. "Feeding frenzy" is not too strong a phrase to describe the predicament. "Bunker mentality" describes many oil company responses to public outcries.

■   ■   ■   ■   ■

There is one area where oil executives are focused firmly on the present: profit. Investors, financial media, executives, bonus-eligible staff, and many other stakeholders care a lot about a company's profitability. If you doubt that, watch what happens when a company misses expectations. It's not good. The share price, reputation, and credibility of executives are all negatively impacted. So top executives spend considerable time asking questions, reviewing results, looking at problems, examining near-term opportunities, and frankly watching revenues and costs, to assure themselves that operations are proceeding according to plans and profit objectives are being met.

Constant effort is expended on cost management. It was amazing to me how hard it was to manage costs. The temptations to spend, to address issues with more money, are ever-present. And all budget planning has to take into account the volatility of oil prices. Huge capital expenditures, investments in growth and new facilities, staffing levels, positioning plays, and day-to-day operations must carry on despite unpredictable and extreme fluctuations in the oil price. It may seem from the outside as if higher oil prices were a win-win for oil companies, but those higher prices also drive up competition and costs for new oil leases, drilling equipment, and oil field services. When prices later fall, especially as dramatically as they plunged in 2008, recouping those costs becomes difficult.

Yet financial performance is measured quarter by quarter, and while the raw profit numbers for oil companies are huge, earnings, measured in net income as a percent of sales, are actually fairly modest, in the range of 6 to 8 percent. Even at the peak of crude oil prices in mid-2008, oil company margins were just 6.8 percent. In mid-2009, they had fallen to 5 percent. These numbers are fairly typical for manufacturing companies and (as the API frequently points out) well below the earnings of pharmaceutical, telecommunication, and beverage companies.

■   ■   ■   ■   ■

Granted, I may have been extreme in describing oil executives' lack of concern for retail customers. Giving credit where credit is due, in Shell's case, for example, during the period when prices were rising, the company took on a number of customer initiatives beyond the outreach tour that I mentioned. Its investment in NASCAR sponsorship, the most popular fan sport in the United States, as measured by fan attendance, was one method for building stronger customer loyalty. In addition, there were significant efforts to attract consumers to the Shell MasterCard via exceptional discounts on gas purchases. Fuel improvements were made and advertised with additional additives configured into Shell gasoline to keep engines cleaner by burning hotter, which also helped to improve mileage. Driving tips for gas conservation were made available at all 14,000 Shell gas stations. However, top executives were not necessarily directly connected to the exercise of a local retail market initiative. They were time-obsessed by the demands of pursuing future oil and gas resources.

The disconnect between oil industry top management and consumers comes to a head when things go wrong—when prices rise or supplies are interrupted. Political leaders looking out for their constituents immediately tie top executives to the plight of the consumer. They want desperately to demonstrate that they are doing something, anything, to or against the "nasty" oil executives so they look like they are on top of the price rise or fuel shortage. Whether that means dragging the executives into public hearings for verbal thrashing or lambasting them in absentia, such behavior feeds consumer disdain and confirms the overall disconnect between oil executives and consumers.

■   ■   ■   ■   ■

Are we stuck with this paradigm forever, unlovable and unavoidable? Is there nothing that can be done to patch up the relationships between the oil companies and the consumers, or the oil companies and the politicians? From where I sit now, and based on my years in the chair where I sat then, I see little hope that things will change for the better. As a realist, I think it more than likely will get worse over time. Why? I see two areas where the industry has failed and is unlikely to change course: poor politics and poor public relations.

The industry is stuck in its own political purgatory. The best recent hope for the industry's future was extinguished early in the first administration of President George W. Bush, when so-called secret meetings took place between industry representatives and the White House. The lack of transparency hurt whatever best intentions were in play. But ever since muckraker Ida Tarbell took on Standard Oil in 1904, the industry has lived with a victim mentality, especially when the Democratic Party is in power. Over a number of years, this investigative reporter publicly lambasted what she determined were Standard Oil's anti-competitive, anti-consumer behaviors, using research that included direct interviews with Standard Oil's chairman, John D. Rockefeller (who reportedly participated in the interviews against the advice of his advisors). Her reporting called public attention to the company and the industry, and some argue that the negative public reaction played into the dramatic anti-trust case that ultimately led to the Supreme Court's breakup of Standard Oil in 1911. Since the Democratic Party has long been associated with consumerism and anti-monopolistic regulation, members of the oil and gas industry are perceived as friends to Republicans, not Democrats. Personally, I believed in walking down the center of the aisle politically as Shell's president. It was, however, a lonely walk relative to the rest of the industry.

But much of its poor image is self-inflicted by an industry that has allowed itself to appear to not care about customers and political stakeholders, an unforgivable transgression in a consumer society and political democracy. The industry has been shortsighted and one-sided in its political relations. When its friends are in the majority, there are efforts to use public policy to enable the business. When its enemies are in the majority, the industry hides in its bunker to wait out the cycle.

Today's green initiative is seen by some as the industry's comeuppance. Politicians have seized on the opportunity to displace a century of investment in the hydrocarbon (oil, gas, and coal) infrastructure with a rush to invest in whatever magical, especially green, formulas can rewrite the future history of energy and make new fortunes for its adherents. They see themselves as saviors of the economy and the environment without regard to the fact that they are effectively disregarding about 75 percent of the nation's energy supplies. Add disregard of nuclear, and it totals 93 percent. The Democratic Party gives the impression that it is out to save our new energy future from the oil and gas industry dinosaurs and the mad nuclear scientists. As a new breed of populist politicians promote what's new, industry reminders that we will be dependent on fossil fuels for the next 50 or more years, even if true, sound like automakers' empty protests from the 1950s that seat belts were an unwarranted expense, and the computer mainframe manufacturers' denunciations in the 1980s that personal computers would never catch on.

Even those in the industry who are making serious efforts to diversify the future fuels mix gain little credit for their efforts as long as they continue to drill for more oil and gas, lobby for access to new hydrocarbon resources, and build more infrastructure—all necessary to enable affordable energy during the transition to a new energy age but denied credence by new-energy-age aspirants because of the basic distrust of the industry.

The industry's poor political skills have been neatly complemented by even more abysmal public relations, the other area where industry has failed. Transparency and open communications have never been a strong suit for the oil companies. Yes, they comply with public reporting requirements. But from the earliest days of the industry through the boom periods of the middle of the twentieth century, to the secret deliberations of the Organization of Petroleum Exporting Countries, to the price volatility of recent years, the industry and the companies have resisted the candor and forthcoming style of communications that other industries call best practice.

When the industry makes operational mistakes, they can be spectacular: refinery explosions, well blowouts, shipwrecks, and oil spills. Equally spectacular is the industry's poor handling of such incidents, to the point that they live on as case studies of what *not* to do in a crisis.

The oil industry is not the only high-risk industry in America, but it seems not to learn from its mistakes. The airline industry makes tragic mistakes and has an incredible track record for recovering quickly. But the entire oil industry carries the burden of the aftermath of the *Exxon Valdez* spill, pitting a hugely successful company against hardscrabble fishermen, low-income Native Americans, and photogenic oil-soaked animals. When criminal gangs in Nigeria poke holes in gasoline pipelines to steal gas—leading to conflagrations that consume hundreds of people wanting to take advantage of the "free gas"—the gangs seem to carry more credibility than the oil companies they attack.

Over the decades, the industry has done many good things that it has failed to capitalize on. It has carried the United States to victory in two world wars by supplying its allies with ample supplies of U.S. oil, and to this day oil supplies are a part of our national defense strategy. The industry supplied the fuels that helped power the nation's industrialization through the twentieth century; it enabled the freest people in the world to enjoy virtually unlimited and (usually) affordable personal mobility.

Oil companies have also provided hundreds of millions of dollars in philanthropic support to organizations and communities. One firsthand example: after Hurricane Katrina, Shell provided tens of millions of dollars in financial support for rescue, education, and rebuilding, including underwriting the cultural classic of the New Orleans community, JazzFest. The company also provided significant in-kind contributions of fuel and other supplies to first responders. Including the wages and benefits of jobs that remain in the community, Shell and its partner Motiva (a joint venture between Shell and Saudi Aramco that owns several former Shell Oil Company U.S. refineries) contributed hundreds of millions of dollars to New Orleans and surrounding Louisiana parishes in the first year of recovery. The company's monetary and manpower support, which continue to this day, have been a mainstay of the rebuilding of New Orleans.

Best practice doesn't just mean taking credit for the positive steps the industry has taken; it also requires public exposure by top executives, a human face on a complex organization, consumer empathy and engagement, obvious and intentional. Twenty-first-century engagement demands a commitment to transparency. That concept, which was behind the outreach tour I undertook at Shell, was not an easy initial sell to the Royal Dutch Shell board, although its members quickly saw how it paid off in reputation improvement and ended up encouraging similar initiatives in other areas of the world.

More recent decisions by the oil companies to fund the API with education outreach funds are useful but too little and too late. Until the individual companies move their public relations models from least amount of information necessary to most amount of information possible, the oil industry will continue to hold twenty-fourth place out of 24 industries and be the recipients of harsh public policies and sustained criticism as a result.

Will the companies still make money? You bet they will. And if that is all individual companies care about, it will be a profitable and perpetually disliked industry that's seen as the problem rather than the solution. Best practice companies also make money. But the way the oil companies do it, hiding in their bunkers, will continue to be a major part of the reason why we hate the oil companies.

■ ■ ■ ■ ■

I've focused on the oil industry, which is the arena I know best, but the dichotomy of customer dependence and customer avoidance is just as pronounced in the electric utility industry. While many of the reasons for this dichotomy are similar, the role of state public utility commissions (PUCs) and similar intermediaries adds a unique barrier between utility companies and customers. Compared with gasoline purchasing, which is a straightforward consumer choice at a preferred corner gas station, electricity purchasing is arguably simpler but ever so much more complex for the consumer.

This regulatory complexity generally feeds the levels of distrust that exist between electricity providers and the average consumer, to whom the work of the state PUC is basically a mystery. Ostensibly its operations take place in the public domain, but unless you are keenly interested in following arcane filings reported in the back pages of local newspapers, or you track down the PUC's website, and are able to translate the language and terminology used by utilities and regulators, it's hard to know what is actually happening.

Even if you find the information, you may not believe what you are seeing. For example, in August 2009, the Texas PUC approved a $115 million rate hike for Oncor, the transmission and distribution company serving much of the northern portion of the state, even though the PUC's own staff reportedly recommended a rate reduction of $101.9 million. The $115 million rate hike was estimated to increase customers' monthly charges by $2.50 to $3.00. Why did Oncor need a rate increase in the middle of a recession and falling energy prices? In part, it was because Oncor had ordered 898,000 "smart" remote control electric meters without waiting for the PUC to issue its standards for the meters. You guessed it: the meters fell short of the standard. Now customers in Oncor's service area are being forced to reimburse Oncor for the noncompliant meters—on top of a $2.21 monthly charge previously assessed (over an 11-year period) to buy meters to replace the noncompliant meters.

Alas, the mystery of electricity rates continues to befuddle the average person. Like gasoline buyers, electricity consumers want to spend the least possible amount of time thinking about electricity supply or reliability or price, unless bad things happen and they are forced to confront their electricity reality. Whether it is an outage or an unexplained spike in billing, it is almost always a bad experience. As a consequence, the electricity company is unlovable and unavoidable, just like the oil company.

And in 27 states, electricity is still regulated, giving consumers virtually no choice (assuming they draw electricity from the grid). In deregulated markets, there are limited choices.

I recall a conversation in 1994 with a Southern California Edison executive at a social function in Hollywood. He told me that he was retiring from the company so that he would not be part of—and therefore not bear responsibility for—the pending upheaval and ultimate catastrophe that deregulation would mean to customers in the years ahead.

He said, in essence, that California consumers did not know how good they had it in their regulated markets and that it was a shame that they would have to experience deregulation to learn how good it once was. He predicted that deregulation would lead initially to lower consumer prices but ultimately would take the market to unprecedented high wholesale prices and then lead to shortages of power because of the illogical legislation that capped internal wholesale prices to "protect" retail prices.

Turns out he was pretty much right on all counts. Power trading abuses in a deregulated California market in the late 1990s—which came about due to capped wholesale prices, leading to shortages in the state's internal supply system upset by high costs, compensated for by hugely expensive uncapped supplies from outside the system—not only inconvenienced people but led to a number of tragic deaths from heat stroke and traffic accidents caused by nonfunctioning lights. Like the Standard Oil abuses in the oil industry 90 years earlier, the experience has tarnished the power industry and poisoned the well of deregulation for a long time to come.

Some states have slowed or stopped the deregulation process, while some deregulated states have considered re-regulating.

When oil and utility companies are seen as the problem, it is easy to avoid looking at some of the deeper social and political issues that need to be addressed.

9

CONSERVATION STARTS WITH LAND USE MANAGEMENT

If we are unwilling as a nation to address urban and rural planning in more significant ways, let's quit pretending we're serious about energy efficiency.

In July 2009, *Texas Monthly* magazine subtly mentioned my name as a potential "white knight" candidate for the upcoming Houston mayoral election. In fact, there had been some conversations along these lines among members of the business community. I had name recognition both from my Shell tenure and from my community involvement; I was viewed as politically engaged after speaking out locally and nationally on energy issues; and as a recent corporate retiree it was assumed I had time on my hands.

However, not only did I have different plans—to continue grassroots engagement on a national energy agenda—I was also in the middle of pulling my thoughts together for this particular chapter. I knew my ideas on this subject would not be popular in some quarters of Houston, where unrestrained development and lack of zoning regulations are considered birthrights of a city founded by two land speculators with a highly creative approach to marketing bayou swampland.

When 5 percent of the world's population uses 25 percent of the world's energy, questions about sustainability need to be asked. I believe such questions must start with the rules we apply to land use. Conservation doesn't start by easing up on the gas pedal or jiggling thermostats. Real conservation starts with the basics: the manner in which we develop and use land, water, and air resources in the world around us. There is a direct relationship between such utilization and energy consumption.

To be blunt, the unconstrained geographic growth of communities that became a way of life in twentieth-century America has got to change in the name of sustainable growth and energy management in the twenty-first century. Other countries have recognized the problems of unconstrained growth, especially in Europe and Asia. The Houston area is one of many U.S. communities that will have to come to grips with this outdated, utterly wasteful form of so-called economic development. As we look ahead, the long-term costs of sprawl far outweigh the short-term benefits. James Kunstler, a New Englander who has studied this issue over many years, says in his book, *The Long Emergency*, that it is already too late. He adds that as energy becomes fully priced to reflect the cost of carbon management (which is as necessary as it is inevitable), travel distances, size of buildings, and consumption of energy will take on new significance to individuals as well as communities as both price and availability of energy reach a crisis stage.

I'm less pessimistic than Kunstler. While he thinks we're past the tipping point, I believe there are far more energy resources than he does and that we will eventually develop them. But energy may be more costly for some decades—because we have avoided new supplies—before we have sufficient surplus energy to drive prices back to appropriate affordability.

Fortunately, some of the unmitigated spread is already being reversed in certain communities, including Houston. Civic leaders and developers, with and without regulation, are discovering economic advantages to reusing idled urban land and finding that many citizens want lifestyles that depend on vibrant urban cores. Builders are touting new building construction methods and technology to promote energy-efficient yet comfortable new multi- and single-family homes in regentrified urban neighborhoods. They are also converting and upgrading old buildings to new uses and improving energy efficiency at the same time. Retailers are betting on the success of such ventures, placing grocery, drug, clothing, convenience, entertainment, and food service establishments within the new inner-city growth areas. Government is cooperating by ensuring that green spaces, security, and transportation needs are factored into the plans. Schools, churches, and community centers will ultimately follow and participate in the new growth areas of renewed urban America.

New jobs are critical enablers of successful development of historic downtown living centers. Fortunately, technology and entrepreneurial start-ups, services, and the professions, such as finance, law, and medicine, find urban locations as compatible to success as suburban. The Houston Technology Center, a venture capital and new technology incubator, located in the central business district of Houston, adjacent to new condominiums and regentrified warehouse flats, is such an example. And all such new job creation brings with it a certain number of service and support jobs for those with lesser skills. So market forces are bringing out some voluntary densification and rejuvenation of America's urban areas. But it is not enough, nor is it happening quickly enough, to make the difference we need in the next several decades. Why is that?

"Manifest destiny," a uniquely American sense of national entitlement heralded during the growth of nineteenth-century America, helped develop the country from coast to coast. It was predicated on the theory that God brought America's settlers to its shores and that their descendants were preordained to establish a nation that would develop its many strengths from nature's bounty to firmly establish twentieth-century growth and economic leadership of the world. That growth was fueled by the cheap and plentiful hydrocarbon energy supply—wood, oil, gas and coal—all of which, supplemented by nuclear power later in the twentieth century, supported seemingly endless transport and infinite electricity supply. And energy in the United States has been oh-so-cheap for so long, its affordability has been ingrained in Americans for generations.

Immigration and population growth fed economic expansion throughout most of the twentieth century. Urban centers gave way to suburban growth. Suburban growth gave way to ex-ur-ban growth, including the rise of satellite commercial centers and remote expansive developments, positioning major commercial campuses and large homes on enormous lots. Close-in farmland transitioned from supplying beef and potatoes for McDonald's to supporting exclusive McMansions. Utilities saw market growth as they strung lines longer distances; fuel retailers saw the same.

But as my former boss and frequent teacher Jack Welch, former chairman and chief executive of General Electric, used to say: "Trees do not grow to the sky." Sometimes we need to prune as well as plant more trees. The nation's growth cannot be predicated on manifest destiny forever.

Land use is about more than suburban sprawl, housing and shopping developments, highways and parking lots. It is really about people, nature, energy, society, and sustainable accommodations of one to the other. Land use management does not mean we stop growth or economic development. But it does mean we need to find the ways to harness both growth and economic development to achieve the balance that ensures future generations will benefit, rather than suffer, from the effects of prior generations. In reality, this takes more than enlightened individuals or voluntary efforts. It takes thoughtful, well-debated planning choices, regulations, and enforcement. It requires that the balance shift to the greater good of the community and away from the historic practice of rewarding especially and primarily the entrepreneurs, first movers, and sometimes exploiters. Those who emphasize growth for its own sake and those who promote preservation at the expense of growth should be equally unhappy with the outcomes of planned and balanced growth.

■   ■   ■   ■   ■

It was the early 1980s before I had my first opportunity to visit California and, in particular, to experience the San Francisco Bay area. Later I had the pleasure of living in Los Angeles for nearly five years, and since then I have been in and out of California repeatedly. My time there has given me a feel for the California mind-set. During my Shell years, I also met hundreds of Shell staff members in California and heard their firsthand experiences with their businesses, their life choices, and political life in the state. A lot of the conversations bordered on the impractical, if not impossible, propensity of state leaders to oppose everything hydrocarbon. The efforts to prohibit drilling of oil and gas resources and refining are markedly greater than virtually any other state in the nation, except perhaps Florida. Considering the role hydrocarbons play in Los Angeles, the mobility, and oftentimes immobility, capital of the nation, or the San Francisco Bay Area, and the manner by which the state's population has spread itself across the state without benefit of mass transportation, it looked to them, and to me, like a wag-the-dog kind of public policy: a limited number of political activists and their leaders making decisions that impact the whole population. The net effect would only be to make business and life in California more difficult, with little if anything to show for it among the special interests who were promoting such anti-hydrocarbon policies. My own objective as Shell's president was to promote pragmatism among policy makers. An example was to bring Shell's voice into the State Assembly and regulatory drafting rooms, in legitimate ways, in both the framing and subsequent regulation writing of AB32, a bill to manage greenhouse gases, so that California residents could continue to purchase the fuels they needed at prices they could afford.

When it comes to land use issues, I think back to my first visit to the Bay Area. Northern California was going through one of its periodic wet periods. The rains seemed endless. It was March, the grass and hills were green as Ireland, and downtown San Francisco was saturated; some streets were streams, some intersections ponds. The nightly news was keeping citizens up to speed with highway closures, landslides, and, most agonizingly, house slides. I recall at breakfast saying to my colleague, an older, more traveled and weathered labor management professional, what a pity it must be to lose your home to a landslide. His response was immediate: "What are you talking about? How crazy do you have to be to build your house on stilts on a steep hillside in earthquake country? California has always had land movement. Don't pity the homeowner, he bought the risk. How much is a view worth? Pity the stupidity of the developer who put the house there and the government official who gave the permit."

Fair enough. This man hailed from upper New York State, where hillsides and mountaintops are more protected and month after month of ice and snow are reasons enough to avoid hillside home construction.

California now possibly leads the nation in land management planning regulations and restrictions. It learned the hard way. It may even be going too far, in fact. There are growing frustrations among many businesspeople and ordinary citizens with the state's lack of economic growth, inability to create necessary infrastructure to support the current population—let alone future populations—and the stifling bureaucracy and regulatory impediments to commonsense quality-of-life improvements. Narrow special interests that define the art and practice of politics in California are positioning themselves to obtain their near-term priorities—more restrictions and fewer freedoms to develop land and businesses—at the expense of larger numbers of citizens. Industrial and infrastructure development, manufacturing, energy, agriculture, and a wide range of other commercial activities and their associated jobs are at risk under increasing regulatory constraints.

Out-migration of jobs and people and the thinning of the tax base can be a consequence of too much regulation and associated higher costs. Immigration without a robust economy adds stress to a tax-challenged social system of education and health and welfare benefits. There is a case to be made that too much land use regulation, coupled with other rules and regulations, stymies economic development to the disadvantage and unsustainable shrinkage of the communities, infrastructure, and energy systems needed to sustain and grow large complex societies. Sustainable growth is one of the most challenging issues California faces.

■   ■   ■   ■   ■

If some argue that Texas is a state with too few constraints and California a state with too many, as the July 9, 2009, edition of

The Economist magazine so neatly suggested, what is the right balance? What is the formula for sustainable growth? Let me try to answer by first offering a working definition of sustainability that characterizes my view of land use management, energy, the environment, society, and the future.

In providing this definition, I reject an either/or dichotomy that frustrates and politicizes outcomes to the detriment of community harmony; I recognize that extremists on either side of the issues, growth and the environment, will probably not be happy with it. But my experience is that the extremes on either side of the issues in our pluralistic society are generally unhappy most of the time anyway, which is perhaps why they remain on the extremes. They get wrapped up in a one-size-fits-all solution and lack the ability or willingness to accommodate the legitimate interests of others. They see the world as black or white, on or off, right or wrong. They see growth as good or bad; environmental protections, the same.

Fortunately, there is a history of the great bell-curve middle in America and other democracies. I still believe that when the majority of people are adequately informed, educated, and engaged, they can overwhelm the extremes and their often vocal and noisy objections from the end tails of the curve, right or left, and establish through their elected representatives the appropriate ways forward within a community and a nation at large.

I define *sustainability* as the outcome of practices, customs, beliefs, rules, regulations, and decisions that, over time, enable one generation to leave to the next generation a legacy of land, water, air, infrastructure, energy systems, health systems, education, social and civic relationships, and economic well-being that is better than what it received.

This definition emerges from my experience with Native American history and my reflections on it as a modern industrialist and concerned citizen. Manifest destiny had its pluses; it got us to where we are. It also had its minuses; it was carried too far and lasted too long. As the population grew and expanded across America, many people laid waste to what they encountered, including the social and physical genocide of people they did not know or understand. America in the nineteenth century was not the only "civilized" society impressing its peculiar form of "civilization" on otherwise "uncivilized" aboriginal people. The world looks back in horror at what was done in the name of "civilization" on other continents, as well. Sustainability is about weeding the last vestiges, implicit or explicit, of such unsustainable expansionism out of twenty-first-century social and economic growth and, in the United States, consigning manifest destiny, especially in the sense that it was actually God's will, to the annals of history.

A small Native American museum on the Warm Springs Reservation in central Oregon contains artistic expressions of this idea of sustainability, derived from the Native American experience. There are paintings and other examples of normal life scenes of hunting, fishing, food preparation, other domestic chores, home building, children's education, love and marriage, birth, coming of age and death, preparations for seasonal change, play and celebration, neighborly relations with visitors, and preparations for defense. I also recall a bronze image of an elderly Native American couple looking into the distance of unending time and a simple expression that went something like: "We do what we do for our grandchildren's grandchildren."

Sustainability is the outcome that makes life better for future generations, not worse, utilizing everything we can know and learn in the process of life. Can anyone disagree with such an objective in principle? Can't we focus on a nationwide land use management framework that meets this definition of sustainability? I believe it is not only possible, it is essential to our future economic and energy security; indeed, it is necessary to protect life itself.

Why start with land management, not atmosphere or water management? The reason is because land determines so much of the human ecosystem, and it is also the resource most vulnerable to abuse. It is ultimately the most precious of our natural resources. When we waste land, we waste life. When we destroy land, it is gone forever. Land feeds, clothes, and secures us. It makes life possible. The oceans, lakes, rivers, and the atmosphere reinforce and reinvigorate each other through seasonal change and weather systems. But they are so immense relative to the land on Earth, let's start by protecting what we can see, walk on, and depend on every day. It's a practical place to establish sustainability, and sustainable land use simultaneously benefits water and air resources, too.

■   ■   ■   ■   ■

Development, by its common definition, takes land from one use and turns it to another. People pay for the privilege and benefits of the new use. Land use and development in our country's history originally came from the monarchical privileges and grants of kings. (So for sure we got off to a bad start!) Explorers identified territories and claimed them in the names of their monarchs. Divinity was invoked somehow in arbitrarily determining that current occupants had no property rights in the sense of actual ownership.

Certain amounts of remuneration, or wampum, were given to ensure the release of any right to ownership, which was not an active concept among natives anyway. Yet there were negotiations around retaining certain uses of land and which lands would remain available for use. Inevitably skirmishes, wars, and annihilations took place in the aftermath of the nation's first system of land use management. What else would you expect? In the finest American tradition of subsequent individualism and inalienable rights, land use practices were handed down from sixteenth-, seventeenth-, and eighteenth-century European monarchs and their barons whose absolute authority and divine wisdom determined what was best for society. As America grew out from its early pioneer settlements, its first cities—Boston, Philadelphia, New York, Baltimore, Williamsburg, Albany, Hartford, and Charlestown, to name a few—became land use pioneers. Today they remain epicenters of the ongoing land use alternatives that we employ. The American Revolution was in part an effort to remove the shackles of monarchical rights over land and to transfer ownership to individuals, governed by a representative democracy that serves the interests of the majority. Land is now owned by individuals, corporations, and various levels of government, including the federal government. Use of that land is variously circumscribed or authorized by the authority of the state.

For most landowners in America, their land is their private property, available to them 24/7 to do with what they choose: hold, develop, sell, or pass on to heirs, subject only to subdivision deed restrictions or local bylaws. As long as claims of the state, county, or municipality on property tax and use is satisfied, and no liens or other officially sanctioned encumbrances are present, in America, your land is your own. Eminent domain is an exception that is exercised ever more rarely. The ramifications of a government declaring eminent domain and taking over a landowner's property are serious and of concern to not just the individual but also the larger community. What happens to one could happen to all, so there is a community of interest protecting individuals from government eminent domain.

The point: we cherish our real property rights. We don't want others to tell us how to manage our own property, yet we have an implicit responsibility as landowners to sustain our property for future generations. We're not growing more land.

■   ■   ■   ■   ■

Why is land use so critical to sustainability and energy? Everything about the land gives or takes from the balance of energy and nature. Land left in its natural state generally gives more than it takes. It supports life as nature has established it. When we make use of land, we remove it from its natural state and transform it to another. Developed land uses energy and, depending on the amount of development, may give little or nothing back.

Imagine Manhattan's progression from a fully forested island, to a mixture of farms and trees, and now cemented and paved to support a mountain range of buildings aboveground and mined and excavated to support an infrastructure of water, sewer, transportation, electrical transmission and communications, parking, storage, and countless other uses belowground. Would anyone dispute that Manhattan is forever transformed? An island that perennially gave back more than it consumed is now the consummate consumer of energy, water, and air, where millions of residents and visitors occupy the most densely occupied land in the country, giving essentially nothing back but taking, taking, taking day after day.

Or take a car or train from Boston to Washington, DC. Imagine the original state and condition of the land you are traversing and how it has been transformed. Any argument anyone chooses applies to the stretch of land between these end points: it's been used, abused, valued, diminished, irretrievably destroyed, grandly upgraded. You name it, all of the above apply. What also matters is the amounts of energy, water, and air that are consumed, dirtied, exhausted, and released to forever contaminate the land, waterways, and atmosphere surrounding these areas. In some respects, the Northeast Corridor is an embarrassing junkyard of American history. The generations that have come and gone have not left behind a better legacy to their heirs.

In fact, I would submit that a ride on the Acela Express, a high-speed train from Washington, DC, to Boston, Massachusetts, or a trip up or down I-95 between the same two cities, is nothing short of an embarrassment to any citizen with a sense of decency about his or her country. How does one explain the conditions along the highways and train tracks, especially the train tracks, to the new or next generation? What an appalling disgrace. In recent months as I have made the trip more often, I can only reflect on the missed opportunity to restore this corridor with funds from the 2009 stimulus bill. Imagine how many jobs could have been created and how much sustainable cleanup and restoration of America's backyard could have taken place with some of the billions of dollars in the act. Whole swaths of former commercial and industrial as well as all-but-abandoned residential tracts in Baltimore, Wilmington, Philadelphia, Trenton, Elizabeth, Newark, New York, Bridgeport, New Haven, Providence, and Boston could have been cleaned and fixed up rather than left to rot and represent the worst of America's past abuse of land, water, and air.

My intent is not to pick on the Northeast. Travel anywhere across America and many other parts of the world: Land use is a frequent disgrace with admirable pockets. Make no mistake: there are many beautiful developments, well designed and maintained, old and new, across the country. And many citizens, voluntary associations, government officials, developers, businesses, and institutions are determined to work together to make communities responsible and accountable for the sustainable use of land, water, and air. They are determined to leave a legacy that is better than what they received. But not every citizen, government official, developer, business, and institution is equally involved and committed. That is the root of the problem. Too much wasteland, too much abuse, and too much unregulated, unmanaged, irresponsible development continue to occur. We must attend to this issue as a matter of both national and local priority. Our energy future depends upon it.

■   ■   ■   ■   ■

Unsustainable population density also wastes energy and fouls water and air more than we can tolerate in the future. *Cadillac Desert,* by Marc Reisner, a classic work by an environmental activist who attracted much controversy regarding ill-advised efforts to develop the vast desert tracts in America's West from the 1970s, describes the unsustainable development of the near-waterless West. The principles Reisner espoused—leaving to nature what nature designed and avoiding man-made "corrections," such as artificial water resources—were never taken seriously. The situation west of the Rockies is a good example of developers and officials ignoring common sense, let alone principles of sustainable land use. The unmanaged growth of cities in Arizona, Nevada, Utah, and California, and the extraordinary consumption of energy, building materials, food, and everything else in water-deprived geographies, will have to be resolved in the twenty-first century. Humans have to work with, not against, nature to deliver sustainable outcomes. Current development of the West is anything but sustainable, consuming too much of everything.

We can't do much about the extraordinary growth of cities and populations that has occurred since Reisner's views were published in 1986, short of arbitrarily dislocating millions of people and dispersing them to more habitable parts of the nation. We overthrew the divine right of kings to do just that a long time ago. So now we have a much more intractable set of issues to overcome in democratic fashion. It may be messy to deal with the problems, but continuous migration of more and more people to these states is not sustainable. Local and state officials will have to come to grips with public policy prohibitions on expansionism to avoid economic and human catastrophe at some undetermined time in the future. Not only do trees not grow to the sky in these thickly inhabited desert cities, trees do not grow at all—at least not naturally. Yet developers and land-owners pretended that they did, establishing water-dependent land use practices that led to lots of luscious greenbacks in bank accounts at the expense of future generations who will have to deal with the consequences.

In midwestern and southern cities, suburban and ex-urban sprawl cannot continue forever. There is a cynical joke in Texas that, left to their own devices, developers from Houston will pave the whole of East Texas. The example cynics point to is the I-10 expansion west of the central business district, from the I-610 beltway west to the ex-urban community of Katy. State and federal officials, working together, obtained more than $2 billion to create Los Angeles–style five-lane-wide roadways, topped up with an additional two-lane (each way) high-occupancy vehicle drive path. For miles on miles, drivers are intimidated by 14 lanes of traffic. Beneath the thick concrete lies buried forever a set of railroad tracks that some imaginative local people thought could have served as the foundation of a light rail system. No way. Land use management, at least in this part of Texas, means concrete pads for passenger cars, inestimable water runoff when tropical deluges hit (a regular occurrence), loss of terrain used by migratory birds, and massive car exhaust contributing to the region's inability to meet Environmental Protection Agency emission standards for at least the next decade.

I remember talking about this in 2005 with then-Congressman Tom DeLay (R-TX), one of the local legislators responsible in large measure for the major federal appropriations that paid for the "pave-over." DeLay's district included major suburban areas of Houston. At the time, I was incoming vice chairman of the Greater Houston Partnership (GHP), an organization that combines economic development and normal chamber of commerce activities into one large set of efforts for the ten-county region that includes Houston. The GHP was strongly advocating expansion of light rail and working closely with the bus and rail transportation agency for Houston and the congressional delegation on a major federal appropriation. The request was for $4 billion for light rail expansion, which could ultimately benefit millions of residents of Houston and the surrounding region—especially low-income commuters. For months, the $4 billion was written into the draft language of the appropriations bill. When it was finalized, however, the amount was cut in half. Representing the GHP, I visited with DeLay, who was in a key House leadership role, to ask that the $4 billion funding be restored. His response was succinct and direct. He made certain I understood that we should be satisfied with the $2 billion; that it could have been zero; that not all Houstonians were interested in rail; and that especially in his own suburban district, people preferred to drive cars.

To complete the story, a year or so later, as the clock turned toward the 2006 elections, DeLay visited me to discuss his upcoming reelection campaign. He noted that he was likely not only to face local opposition but also to come up against funding from the Democratic National Campaign Committee because he had acquired something of a "reputation" among Democrats. He had provoked too many too often, and he thought they would be out supporting his opponent in every way possible. He asked me to commit to raising $100,000 for his campaign, in view of all that he had done for the community and the energy industry. I thanked him for his visit and all he had done for the energy industry, then reminded him of our difference of opinion on the critical matter of mass transit and told him that it would be unlikely that I could raise money for his campaign. On the following Monday, having probably heard similar responses from other people he had visited, DeLay announced that he had decided not to run for reelection. But Houston has its oversized

$2 billion 14-lane freeway and has broken ground for its much-too-limited $2 billion expansion of light rail.

■ ■ ■ ■ ■

Land use management affects how much energy we use, what happens to water and water runoff, and how air is fouled. In addition, land use management can be the basis for governing the use of technology and construction for building and energy efficiency. Our highways, parking lots, housing and commercial developments, industrial and light industrial plots, schools, churches, shopping centers, parks, green spaces, recreation centers, and every other manner of land use have energy and environmental consequences. Population density or sprawl determines the infrastructure needed to connect people to the electric grid and to transport them to work, school, and recreation. The more we spread out, the more energy we consume per capita—as we live our lives at more distance from offices, friends, and power plants than do those who live in other parts of the world.

Americans now consume 10,000 gallons of oil per second, or 20 million barrels per day, due in large measure to how far spread out we are. How much longer do we continue to grab up land for low-density uses and consume more energy in so doing? How much longer do we contribute to water runoff at rates such that many areas are prone to flooding because they are paved and unable to manage excess water? How much longer do we add to man-made pollutants in the air we breathe locally?

We have choices. I advocate community, regional, state, and national planning in ways we have not welcomed heretofore. It's time. Manifest destiny is dead—or should be. Let's behave that way. We know we've spoiled too much land, spread out too much, lost sight of the economic, social, community, and environmental benefits of living more densely, and created a socioeconomic imbalance with the keeping-up-with-the-Joneses style of material abundance promoted in suburban or ex-urban subdivisions.

I do not advocate Politburo central planning. I do, however, advocate 50-, 25-, 10-, and 5-year planning for land use management by every level of government that dispenses land use permits. I also advocate that such plans be amalgamated, rationalized, and enforced by citizen councils at county, county-regional, state, multistate regional, and national levels. Democracy, economic and energy security, and land-use planning, including water and air management, must come together to support sustainable land use management. We don't need and cannot afford more shameful Northeast corridors and unlimited expansion on waterless deserts. Mindless expansion for the sake of lining a few developers' purses is but a lingering hangover of manifest destiny. Our future and that of our grandchildren's grandchildren depends on democratic planning where responsible commitment to sustainability is the outcome.

This may not be the platform that gets one elected as mayor of Houston in the near term, but it should be the platform of every elected representative at every level in America. Don't we want to leave to our next generations a better future than what was bestowed to us? Doesn't that beat the unsustainable mess that we've been left with in large parts of the country? Real energy conservation must start by addressing the root cause of excess energy use: too much expansionism.

10

ENERGY AND POLITICS: OIL AND WATER

There is a basic conflict between "energy time," which is defined by decades, and "political time," which is defined by two- and four-year cycles.

*I*t's All in the Timing is the name of an off-Broadway play that my wife and I saw more than a decade ago. The stage is a monkey cage in which four or five actors and actresses behave like monkeys. Their life's work is to produce the world's greatest novel. Upon its completion, they will be given their freedom. They create the novel by conversing on the history and state of the world, society, literature, philosophy, and economics, and by taking turns, when so inspired, to hit a typewriter key on a manual machine at stage center. Most hits are one letter at a time. Occasionally an extraordinary inspiration will result in two hits. There is no deadline for completing the novel so that time will ensure it becomes the world's greatest. Time, therefore, is everything: moments in time, as letters are typed, and the whole of time, as the novel is completed. In other words, eventually enough of the right letters will be typed to create the greatest novel of all time. As the play unfolds, it becomes obvious, however, that there is no relationship between moments in time and the whole of time.

In politics "it's all in the timing" means election cycles. I once asked a political consultant who used to work for several members

of Congress how long a member has after an election before planning starts for the next election. Her reply was, "In a contested
district, about 30 days." Presidents and governors, arguably, never
stop campaigning until they reach their term limits. Their visibility
is enormous, their stakeholder population huge, their supporters
and opponents seldom separated by more than a few percentage
points. Politics is dynamic and unpredictable. Events, personalities, issues, headlines, stories, opposition candidates, special interests, families, and personal strengths and weaknesses never stop
playing out both in the private and public lives of elected officials. And because the costs of running for or retaining office are
extraordinary, there is never a moment between elections in the
American system that a candidate or incumbent doesn't consider
where the next contribution is coming from.

So it is hardly an overstatement to say that election cycles
never end. Instead, they have an ebb and flow that never stops.
This means that public officials are always, always on guard
regarding what they say or do about every issue or event that
occurs. They must consider their position and response as part
of the calculation that impacts the next election. Accountability
for elected officials comes down to one day every two or four
years: election day. What they did or said, or didn't do or say,
can and will benefit or hurt them on accountability day. Timing
is everything. Get out of sync with your electorate on issues or
timing, and the opposition is all over it. There is no relief for
an elected official. The elected official or candidate has to be
always in position to hit the typewriter key at exactly the right
moment.

■   ■   ■   ■   ■

For an energy executive, it's the opposite. A moment is nothing.
Timing exists on a near-endless spectrum. Just as energy supply knows no beginning, energy demand knows no end. Supply
has always been there; demand will always be there. The energy
executive's job is to figure out the best way to convert supply to
meet demand. Rush the process and you're likely to spend too
much money, suboptimize the conversion, upset relationships, or

overstress the infrastructure, each of which has ramifications for future supply conversion. Take too long and you risk competition taking away some of the future demand. Capital investments are the most important decisions an oil company executive makes. How much, which countries, what type of resources, where in the value chain, and when to invest—the decision process can take a few months, even up to 20 years.

So timing does matter, but only in relative terms, compared to the immediate timing that an elected official confronts every day. One of the complaints of junior staff in energy companies is the seemingly endless process of getting a decision from executives. Ideas and project proposals get worked on constantly. There are time-bound constraints: there is always a rush to get the plans done by a certain time; review committees meet only at certain times; managers are measured on projects completed, so there is time urgency within the operations of energy companies. But when it comes to getting a final go/no go decision from the top of the company, often it seems to take forever. Weeks extend into months; months can actually become years; years can add up to a decade or more before final decisions are made.

The final investment decision on multibillion-dollar projects, new country entries, new technologies, new products, new facilities is labored on by staff and examined by managers, senior executives, executive committees, and boards of directors. Until there is agreement that the decision to move forward is the right one, time is generally an ally. Sometimes it is such an ally that a decision not to go forward is the better choice. Execution is like that as well. Projects with a particular completion date can be rolled into the future for any number of reasons, ranging from funding issues, to demand uncertainties, to technological barriers. The energy executive is focused on completing the world's greatest novel during the period of his or her tenure and leaving a strong legacy of opportunities for successors to work on.

■　■　■　■　■

Politics is like water churning through rapids; energy is like a river flowing silently through time. Neither can relate to the other. They are two completely different realities. The people in politics and the people running energy companies are like oil and water in a pipeline. They may share the same space from time to time, they may rub up against one another in the course of public engagement or public policy debate, but their molecules are incompatible and time is the root cause of their incompatibility.

What a politician does to get elected every two or four years is whatever it takes. He or she runs on a platform of pleasing as many voters as possible, confounds tough questions by taking middle ground or equivocating in the moment, runs to the right or left—whichever the bent of the electorate, while returning to party discipline once elected—uses people in transitory ways when helpful. What an energy executive does through his or her tenure is plan, analyze, consider options, evaluate alternatives, and ultimately make a decision that will impact the company for decades into the future. It is not an elected position; he or she doesn't serve the happiness quotient of the stakeholder community. Energy executives do what they consider the right thing over the time period they can imagine. The risk to the politician of delaying or waiting too long to respond to issues is that the opposition grabs the advantage and all is lost. The risk to the energy official of not taking the appropriate time to deliberate and de-risk a project is to put the company in jeopardy. The decision process, time to act, preparation, and deliberation that occurs among politicians versus energy officials is night-and-day different.

A politician who can't rely on his or her gut serves a short tenure. An energy executive who relies on his or her gut is a short-lived executive. What we have to contend with in the setting of national energy policy is "political time," the two- and four-year cycles between elections that define an elected official's priorities, attention span, and policy preferences, together with the party interests of those officials; and "energy time," the decades-long decision and implementation cycles that define major energy initiatives. The timing differences and DNA incompatibility of the principals, elected officials and energy executives, is a serious, ongoing, and possibly never-ending problem for America's energy security future.

When it comes to the nation's energy security, the authority to make policy belongs to government, populated with politicians in both the executive and legislative branches. Because they operate in election cycles, they have limited time to get things done before they are once again held accountable. "Let's get it done" is a phrase that echoes through the chambers, hallways, and offices across Capitol Hill. Executive branch offices work day and night to help evaluate and propose alternatives for legislative branch policy considerations. Public policy decisions are shaped and formed by what elected officials in the majority party believe will work best with and for their electorate in time for the next election cycle. This means they are taking advantage of what their electorate views as being in their best interests in the current election cycle. Meanwhile, elected officials in the minority party are working to dispel or cast doubt on the policy proposals of the majority party, believing that they are representing their constituents' best interests to prevent such policy from moving forward, or proposing alternatives to such policy to, in their minds, make it better.

■　■　■　■　■

Beginning in 2005, with the second inauguration of President George W. Bush and with the Republicans continuing in the majority in both houses of Congress, it was clear to everyone that energy policy was important. The nation was in an era of higher energy prices. Crude oil prices were increasing due to sustained demand from around the world and also within the United States. Geopolitical uncertainties were impacting the predictability of secure future oil supplies. Supply uncertainties in the Middle East, Venezuela, Russia, Iraq, Iran, and Nigeria were prominent in the face of demand growth from the United States, China, India, and the developing world. No one knew how high oil prices might go; what was clear was that their rise was certain.

On the strength of the 2004 Republican election victories, congressional leadership went to work on the 2005 energy bill. Led in large measure by relevant committee chairs—Congressman

Joe Barton (R-TX) in the House and Senator Pete Domenici (R-NM) in the Senate, both advocates of comprehensive energy reform—the two committees, in conjunction with priorities emanating from the White House and various cabinet departments, were hard at work framing the issues to be addressed and the directions to be taken. Energy companies and their associations were actively engaged in ongoing conversations with members and executive branch officials.

By midyear, bills were taking shape in both houses. There were issues on the table that had not been addressed for years. The energy industry had high hopes that 2005 would be the year to make major progress on a range of energy opportunities. Oil, gas, coal, nuclear companies, biofuel, wind, solar and hydrogen interests, renewable energy venture capitalists, electricity producers, along with pipeline and transmission firms, traders, and retailers—they were all there, pitching for their particular priorities.

In late June 2005, there was a huge row as the House Energy and Commerce Committee was getting ready to vote on its version of a bill. The row was symptomatic of "political time" coming smack up against "energy time." Looking ahead to the next election cycle, the House bill included language on biofuels, intending to address the availability and supply of these fuels as an offset to high-cost oil imports. There was "political time" concern that the United States needed to demonstrate its willingness and ability to diminish its reliance on foreign imports. The bill was shaping up to include major subsidies for biofuel producers to begin to impact future liquid fuel supplies.

Oil industry participants considered the "political time" priority in the bill a major negative impact on important and serious "energy time" requirements. From their perspective, the extraordinary focus on biofuels was, if anything, too little and too late to make a material difference on liquid fuel supplies not only before the next election cycle but over the next decade of election cycles. These participants believed that the nation needed an "energy time" decision to finally and fully deal with future access to abundant, off-limits oil and gas resources in the outer continental shelf and federal lands.

The industry's argument was that 30 years of congressional and presidential moratoria on exploration and production of U.S. domestic natural resources was the primary cause of high crude oil prices, impacting U.S. retail fuel costs. Focusing on biofuels was a trifling matter; if volumes of energy were required, there was no better resource than untapped oil resources, which could be developed over the next decades, leading to far greater energy security than dithering around with biofuels would ever deliver. So the industry resisted for "energy time" reasons the biofuels mandates that were being built into the bill for "political time" reasons.

The conflict came to a head after a mark-up session on the bill. Chairman Barton, not known for his patience and frustrated by the single-mindedness of the oil lobbyists, had heard enough resistance from oil companies. In an explosive and accusatory manner, he essentially told the oil companies that he and his committee had had enough of what he considered their nonsensical obstructionism. He gave them until the next day to either get their act together in support of what he was trying to do or get out of the process. The oil companies were divided. Several were actually working on their own biofuels initiatives, seeing the impending change in the energy landscape, and were willing to work with the chairman. Other companies had no interest in biofuels and were prepared to resist to the end. Challenged to work together, the industry backed down. "Political time" considerations with regard to biofuel ruled the day.

The energy bill that ultimately worked its way through the political process nonetheless fell short of the president's "political time" objectives, although he signed it. President Bush, closely advised by economic advisor Al Hubbard, remained unhappy with the efforts of the House and Senate. He felt they did not go far enough to bring enough biofuel to the market. In the president's judgment, it would be important to match or exceed proposals that the Democrats had been articulating. So he threw down the gauntlet in his 2006 State of the Union speech, with an eye toward November elections, and committed the nation and his party to legislate a renewable fuel mandate to deliver some 36 billion gallons per year of biofuels within a certain time frame. The oil industry watched "political time" trump "energy time" again as there was limited mention in the speech of lifting presidential or congressional moratoria on offshore and federal land exploration and drilling rights. Congress proceeded to pass another energy bill in 2006 and included the renewable fuel standard. As a sop to the oil industry, the bill also included a relatively postage stamp–sized new offshore opportunity in the Gulf of Mexico, known as Lease Area 181.

■   ■   ■   ■   ■

With their congressional wins in 2006, the Democrats became the new majority. New "political time" priorities started flying through both houses right away. Immediate efforts were undertaken to reverse, undermine, or stop various initiatives that the Democratic Party had taken exception to in the Republican energy bills of 2005 and 2006. New energy bills in 2007 and 2008 focused on the new majority's "political time" priorities: alternative forms of energy, including extended tax incentives for wind and solar investments; efficiency initiatives including building, lighting, and appliance efficiency programs. None of the bills included more access to offshore oil and gas resources. Declining domestic supplies would continue to be offset by increased foreign imports.

Nowhere in any of the "political time" bills from 2005 through 2009 are serious "energy time" needs, as identified in this book, addressed. As a nation, the United States has been essentially toying with new energy and efficiency prospects. The politicians are frittering at the edges, appearing to do a lot while actually doing very little to produce material new energy. By promoting new energy supplies from renewable sources, increasing energy marginally by using biofuels, wind, and solar energy, we're impacting 2 percent of our energy supply. Yet throughout this period, in a nation that consumes most of its energy—some 93 percent—from hydrocarbon and nuclear sources, no significant legislation promoting the future development of these important and abundant sources has passed into law. The risk to the nation is that the marginal increases in new energy resources do not offset the predictable declines in traditional energy production. No new "political time" policy has ever suggested that biofuels could exceed roughly 15 to 20 percent of the nation's liquid fuel supply. Similarly, there has never been an assertion that wind, solar, and other renewables could exceed 20 percent of the nation's future electricity supply. There has never been a proposal suggesting that the nation could improve its overall efficient use of energy by more than 20 percent. The combined efforts that marginally impact the nation's energy system, with its growing population, fall short of securing the nation's energy future.

For the past five years, the nation's political leadership on both sides of the aisle has dallied on the edges and made the easy, not the hard, decisions about the nation's energy supply requirements. Politicians have ignored our base energy supply for too long. "Political time" policies are making our energy future insecure. Public policy is at best fractionally or marginally addressing energy supply and demand. "Energy time" options that secure the nation's base energy load and provide future long-term, large-quantity energy needs are essentially off the table.

■   ■   ■   ■   ■

If we were serious about energy reform, wouldn't we also be building the manufacturing infrastructure to construct the entire new energy system? We import solar panels and wind turbines from Europe and China, wind turbine blades from India, and traditional electrical products such as transformers and switchgear that used to be built here. Meanwhile we watch Japan and Germany build a totally new hydrogen infrastructure to support introduction of the fuel cell technology they are developing to replace the internal combustion engine. A sustained build-out of a new energy system warrants a comprehensive "energy time" manufacturing and production system across the entire range of energy sources. From the 1930s to 1970s America built its energy infrastructure and manufactured its energy products. Today we import more energy products than we make. To me, that's wrong. Where are our leaders taking us? Investors worry that we're in another flavor-of-the-day public policy period and that by ignoring our base energy sources, our current policies offer little promise of real energy security—certainly not enough to invest private-money billions in manufacturing plants and other infrastructure. Yet the idea of renewables is highly popular because it sounds so good, so promising, so independently American. Is it not understandable that "energy time" executives, who have done and continue to want to do the nation's heavy lifting for future energy supplies, are not only frustrated but deeply worried about America's energy future?

Energy executives know that the existing supply capacity from traditional sources is about tapped out. It is functioning now, but without public policy support to extend, renew, and expand it, we face potential negative consequences in the years ahead that impact the 93 percent base of our energy supply. With rapidly aging coal plants (more than half of which are over 38 years old), postponement or cancellation of more than a hundred new coal plants in the past five years, declining domestic oil production, avoidance of the tough decisions on coal gasification and carbon capture and sequestration, and an aging nuclear electricity fleet, there is a huge pent-up need for renewal and expansion of these forms of energy that the nation relies on for its economic competitiveness and lifestyles. And it's not happening. We fritter with renewables when we need so much more.

"Energy time" decisions are not easy. Only a small constituency understands the risks to future energy supplies the nation is facing by deferring hard decisions on unpopular topics. There's nothing inherently wrong with the energy bills of the period from 2005 to 2009, except that they simply do not go far enough to provide the energy security that the people of America deserve. By failing to make "energy time" decisions on expanded oil production, new safe nuclear plants, and the ultimate direction for cleaner coal-fired electricity production with sequestration of carbon dioxide, and by threatening new restrictions on expanded development of natural gas reserves using horizontal drilling and fracturing technology, "political time" priorities are putting the nation at ever-greater risk of sustained high prices and supply insecurity.

The risks we face are not likely to be evident in the next election cycle. The real risks begin in the later years of this decade. The recession of 2008–2009 contributed a false sense of security and affordability to the underlying problem when energy prices receded from their peaks and supplies were in surplus. It made it that much easier to make "political time" choices that fed the frittering-on-the-edges energy policies. With no meaningful constituency other than unpopular executives from major energy companies and a few associations and learned individuals who follow energy closely, neither Congress nor the president have been willing to tackle the problems we face.

And it will get worse before it gets better. With the backdrop of the recession and the need for jobs, especially popular so-called green jobs, coupled with the "political time" efforts on climate change and global warming, the die is cast for the next several years. Anyone who speaks differently from the political currency of the day (renewable and alternative energy, bio-fuels, wind, solar, green jobs, and energy efficiency) sounds like a creature from a former time and is hushed. For example, hundreds of thousands of "brown" jobs could be created with sizable expansion of offshore drilling and new nuclear plant construction. Yet brown jobs are heralded with silence. Nuclear plant loan guarantees do nothing to reduce the costs of building new plants or treating nuclear waste.

We're facing a "political time" reality that hydrocarbons and nuclear are considered essentially historic, not present, energy supply sources. We're governed by a new crowd, the anything-but-hydrocarbons-and-nuclear people, led by populist and progressive thinkers from the Center for American Progress and Repower America, who have never worked in core energy although they have analyzed and criticized it for decades. We're declaring a new form of "national energy independence" predicated on developing new additions to 2 to 3 percent of our current energy supply. We hear pronouncements from the administration and Congress that we will double renewable energy supplies and double them again. Let's hope that we do. It would mean that we're getting to a high-single-digit percentage of our energy supply. Biofuels may move from 7 percent to 15 percent of our liquid fuel supply within a decade. However, that amount is unlikely to either meet

growth requirements for liquid fuels or offset declines in gasoline production that may be prompted by carbon management
requirements; it may also further inflate the nation's fuel prices
(because of the higher cost of biofuels) and budget deficit (because
of the subsidies that underwrite biofuels production and without
which no one would be producing biofuels in this country).

It is now politically correct to tell the American people that
we can have energy security in our time by concentrating on
wind, solar, biofuels, efficiency efforts, and green jobs. What a
great sound bite. But the renewables efforts alone can't satisfy
the needs of the future, and such unreal prognostications will not
last. Remember, great "political time" sound bites only deliver
results in "political time." High-cost gasoline, gas lines, brownouts and blackouts of electricity will become reminders of what
the energy system requires in "energy," not "political time."

When "energy time" decisions on more hydrocarbons and
more nuclear are deferred for "political time" reasons, there will
come a time to pay the piper. Political accountability occurs every
two and four years. The current Democratic majority leadership
and the president are gambling that the future of energy security and affordability will not have to be seriously confronted
on their watch. They are gambling that the frittering, because
it has proven popular, will carry them through the 2010 and
2012 elections. But if they have gambled wrong, they will be
held accountable by an electorate that is both energy poorer and
more insecure. If they gambled right, they'll make it through
2012, but by 2014 and 2016, the consequences will be clearer
and the accountabilities more obvious.

By not making "energy time" decisions—which would mean
decades' worth of new investments and developments for
nuclear electricity production renewal, coal (ideally, clean coal)
projects, and major new oil supplies for liquid fuels—within the
next decade the nation will come up short on its energy supply
requirements. Carbon management without clean coal investments, serious and large, will result in the demise of first dozens
and then later hundreds of coal plants. Failure to address nuclear
renewal will lead to the decommissioning of dozens of nuclear
facilities due to expiring licenses at a time when we should be

constructing more. Failure to open up more domestic resources for oil exploration and production will lead to either sky-high gas prices and shortages or much higher dependence on foreign imports at the same time that China and India want more. In just a few years, the crude oil price could be back at its previous $147 record high by $50 to $100 more per barrel.

Failure to make decisions now on these critical energy sources defers supply increases from these sources by at least another decade. We don't ramp up quickly an infrastructure that took the past century to build. We don't replace decommissioned nuclear plants, coal plants, and oil fields by doubling and doubling again wind and solar electricity production and biofuels. If our current leaders' terms are up by the time the aging energy base infrastructure goes into decline, they may escape immediate accountability. But their legacy will be a decade or more of energy shortages and record prices because they deferred the hard choices, making the easy choices in "political time" when the nation needed them to lead in "energy time."

■   ■   ■   ■   ■

The problem with democracy is that it is messy. We Americans also complicated it with multiple checks and balances, including an independent judiciary. In the context of "political time" and "energy time," we need to say a bit about how the third branch of government fits into this formula.

The simple answer: it doesn't. It stands separate and apart, which can be good or not. The federal judiciary is agnostic toward elections, since appointments are for life. It is uninvolved in energy issues, except when a case is brought to the bench. But never underestimate the potential of the judiciary to rule on a case that may or may not benefit "political time" or "energy time" advocates.

Earlier we looked at the impact of the Federal Court of Appeals for the Ninth Circuit decision on the environmental impact statements that Shell had relied on to develop an exploration plan off the coast of Alaska. The court ruled that the government failed to provide adequately for marine mammal and other protections in its original Environment Impact Statement, requiring a complete redo, which will take years (if the administration even chooses to redo them). Then the statements will be subject to more court challenge by parties who continue to resist the opening up of oil exploration and development off the Arctic coasts of Alaska.

Other court rulings are also driving energy policy:

- The Supreme Court ruled that carbon dioxide is governed by the Clean Air Act and therefore the Environmental Protection Agency (EPA) must determine the implications regarding this greenhouse gas. Although the Court's ruling occurred during the Bush administration, the EPA's decision was extended into the Obama administration, resulting ultimately in a finding by EPA that carbon dioxide is a threat to public health.
- In the *Exxon Valdez* oil spill case that went on literally for decades, the Supreme Court decided the amount of punitive damages that ExxonMobil was required to pay plaintiffs.
- Royal Dutch Shell settled a case in 2009 in the New York District Court brought by a Canadian citizen, accusing it of complicity in the death in Nigeria of the plaintiff's father, Ken Saro Wiwa, a Nigerian political activist in the early 1990s who was put to death under a corrupt military dictatorship. Shell made the decision to settle rather than face the potential of a ruling by a U.S. court on a death in Nigeria predicated on a two-century-old maritime law that was passed during the period of piracy in the Barbary Straits.

The judiciary decides cases brought before it based on the law of the land. Whether the law is new or old, relevant to energy security and affordability or not, passed by Democratic or Republican majorities in Congress and signed by Republican or Democratic presidents, it matters not. The "political time" exigencies and the "energy time" requirements are irrelevant to the courts. What matters is who did what based on the law. And although cases can be appealed for years all the way to the Supreme Court, ultimately, that Court's word is final.

Why is this important?

The economic vitality and energy security, the lifestyles of Americans, are at greater risk today than at any time since the

United States became the world's economic leader. As I have mentioned, America's twentieth-century economic leadership, comfortable way of life, and its ability to lead its allies to victory in two world wars and to conduct national security operations in subsequent wars were based on the availability and afford-ability of energy.

America's energy future is at greater risk today of not keep-ing up with requirements and expectations than at any time in its modern history. Nearly 40 years of "political time" public policy, starting with President Nixon's fallacious commitment to "energy independence in seven years" and continuing up to the present "political time" decisions affecting only the edges of future energy supplies, ignoring our aging base infrastructure, bring us closer to the time when we simply will not have enough of what we need.

We have failed to make sound "energy time" decisions since the 1970s. We've tied the hands of the nuclear energy industry; we've declared massive supplies of domestic oil and gas off limits for decades; we're toying with natural gas restrictions that may constrict an otherwise abundant new source of hydrocarbon energy; we've consciously failed to develop oil shale commer-cial prospects in the Rockies; we're approaching carbon man-agement in a manner that will greatly reduce the availability of traditional coal-fired electricity production. We are investing in alternative and renewable fuels that will only marginally add future supply sources. We do little more than watch as Asia and Europe prepare for new technology platforms to replace the internal combustion engine by building infrastructure and manufacturing capacity.

The independent judiciary does not care about and cannot decide cases based on concerns regarding our economic well-being, quality of life, and energy security. We don't have laws that govern those essential elements of what it means to be an American. They are outcomes of a healthy system of democratic capitalism and pluralistic representative democracy. Yet when energy and the environment are subject to more proactive legisla-tion than at any other time in recent memory, is there any doubt that innumerable court cases will be brought by individuals, special interests, associations, corporations, and possibly various levels of governments, testing the limits on either side of whatever legislation is at issue? It's a foregone conclusion. The courts will be called on to judge these issues.

As the nation faces its self-imposed insecurity, the importance of the judiciary is paramount to getting things right. If we continue to postpone addressing the supply-side requirements of our base infrastructure, impose regressive new carbon management policies without considering the implications, and continue to implement intrusive industrial intervention policies that frighten away investors, the courts may be the inadvertent but ultimate adjudicators of America's economic strength and well-being. There may be no other alternative.

It is critical to dive deeper into the consequences of "political time" reality and how that manifests itself by examining how government actually works on energy policy. The next chapter considers the obstacles that must be understood if they are to be overcome.

11

OUR GOVERNMENT IS BROKEN

When addressing energy and the environment, the federal government is paralyzed by partisanship and stymied by dysfunction. "Political time" makes it worse.

My worst moment as a taxpayer, citizen, corporate executive, and believer in the American system came during a visit to Capitol Hill not too long after Hurricane Katrina stunned the nation by ravaging New Orleans in August 2005. This was an extraordinarily difficult and stressful time for Shell as my colleagues and I wrestled with the devastation of both Katrina and Hurricane Rita, which hit three weeks later. The storms had damaged our facilities, displaced employees and their families, and caused us to suspend some operations and expend both funds and management attention to bring our businesses back on line and support our staff and hard-hit communities. The damage also caused energy shortages and high prices across much of the nation.

In this period of constrained supplies, 48 state attorneys general had written letters to me or Shell's general counsel accusing Shell of anti-competitive price fixing and other collusive actions to withhold product from the market. My picture had just appeared on the front page of the *New York Times* as part of a "rogue's gallery" of oil company executives testifying at the joint Senate Commerce and Energy committees hearing early in November. There industry executives were collectively accused of harming the American people due to high prices and high profits; "pain at the pump" was filling the news headlines; and interview requests on supplies, prices, and hurricane recovery status were flooding our media relations office. Meanwhile, there was reality. Outside the suffering Gulf Coast region, the rest of Shell Oil and its stakeholders expected business as usual.

Surprising, then, that the moment that caused me the most doubt about our governmental system had nothing to do with hurricanes, "gotcha" hearings, or current gas prices. My visit to Capitol Hill on this occasion was part of my ongoing effort to meet with elected officials on public policy issues that were impacting our industry's productivity and/or international competitiveness. This visit was to discuss tax policies, which I believed were harmful to the industry's international competitiveness, future capital investments in the United States, future oil production, and ultimately jobs and gas prices. As usual, my plan was to call on both the chairman and ranking member of various committees in both the House and the Senate.

That day I went to Capitol Hill with an aide from Shell's government affairs office, an individual well known in the Capitol. We went to the office of California representative Bill Thomas (R-CA), then the House Ways and Means Committee chairman, to talk about specific tax policies I viewed as hurtful to the country and what might be done about them. Thomas received us in businesslike fashion, acknowledged my colleague, whom he had known for some time, and then proceeded to tell us the problems he faced on the issue we wanted to discuss. He rattled off a litany of obscenities with derogatory descriptions of personal ineptitude and lack of integrity—directed at another person, his same-party counterpart in the Senate—and issued his position on the major tax issue we wanted to discuss: a flat-out rejection. He declined to deal with the substance of the issue not because of its merits or lack thereof but because he refused to take up the matter with the other person in the Senate with whom he would have to deal. He simply would not do so. This was followed by a general description of what he considered to be the complete degeneration of the Senate and a warning that its continuing incompetence and arrogance threatened America's future. This was the viewpoint of one chairman in one house regarding the other house, led by the same political party. He also indicated he was retiring at the end of this term and said that perhaps our issue would be seen differently by his successor, whoever that might be. Apart from the diatribe, he wished us a good day.

Ouch. With everything else going on in my corporate life, I thought, "What is the value of our political leadership today? And isn't it clear what the problem will be for the Republicans in November 2006?" This was my personal political low point for the period: dysfunctional behavior in what we will discuss as a dysfunctional system.

Other meetings that day went more smoothly but were a total waste of time under the circumstances. When a committee chairman, with absolute authority to determine what business his committee will entertain, and at what time and in which order, determines he's not going to do something, hell will freeze over before that something is dealt with. My take on this particular meeting was that I was not singled out for his diatribe, and my company and industry were not his issue. His issues were pent-up frustration, dysfunctional personal relationships, the arrogance of power, intraparty conflicts, House versus Senate incompatibilities, and probably too long in the job. More profoundly it was the lack of accountability that long-serving elected officials from essentially one-party districts enjoy to the detriment of the people of this country. It was a bad day for me as I witnessed the inner workings of a sausage machine called Congress.

That meeting was a low point for me also because, although I had heard about examples of political self-interest overcoming national interest, it was the first time I experienced and saw the raw and visceral form it takes. The acting out was unforgettable and a symptom of why citizens get angry at nonresponsive government: too much power for too long in an individual's unaccounted remit. My colleague shrugged it off, saying, "This

is Washington. It happens." I couldn't let go so easily. It stays
with me.

■ ■ ■ ■

On another occasion, in 2008 at a hearing of the House Select
Committee on Energy Independence and Global Warming, where
I was testifying, I noticed a House member who was not on the
committee observing the proceedings. At an appropriate moment,
the committee chairman, Representative Ed Markey (D-MA),
introduced the visitor, Representative Bart Stupak (D-MI), and
suggested he might be invited to say a few words after all the
committee members had had the opportunity to speak or question the witnesses. Markey runs a tight hearing, but nonetheless
the hours passed. The guest member sat patiently and silently
throughout the hearing. After the final comments and last questions from the least senior Republican member, which is the
normal order of protocol at a hearing, the chairman requested
"unanimous consent" so that Stupak, who had a particular
interest in gas prices and their relationship to oil company profitability, might query the witnesses. Unanimous consent is normally a fairly standard practice, enabling considerable informal
business to be conducted in committee hearings, and is rarely
challenged. However, the ranking member, Congressman Jim
Sensenbrenner (R-WI), a stickler on protocol when he chooses
to be, instantly declared there would be no unanimous consent. As the ranking member, he determined that the minority
party would not agree to hear Stupak's questions since he had
no formal role in the committee's proceedings. Markey looked
dumbfounded and turned to Sensenbrenner, sitting right next to
him, saying he couldn't believe what he was hearing and asking
why he was refusing such a basic request. Back and forth the
discussion went, Markey explaining the normal practical protocol on unanimous consent for visiting members to committees, Sensenbrenner reiterating his refusal to explain his lack of
cooperation.

Finally, Stupak spoke up, out of order, protesting Sensenbrenner's refusal to agree to unanimous consent, remarking on

the waste of time that his inability to speak meant to him as he had sat through the entire proceedings, and predicting that as the minority party plays out such behaviors, it should expect such treatment in kind from the majority party, under the rules of committee proceedings.

Relieved to be out of the line of fire for the moment, I and the other oil company executives who had been testifying watched, bemused, as our political leaders turned the heat on one other instead of us. It was obviously embarrassing to the committee members, especially to the chairman, who, as I said, runs a tight and orderly hearing. It played to the stereotype of what by this time I had come to expect of interaction in both the House and Senate: partisanship played out for partisanship's sake, regardless of the consequences. Sensenbrenner had simply heard enough for the day. He had no interest in what Stupak might have to say. He used his prerogative to deny unanimous consent and didn't think twice about it. He owed nothing and expected nothing in return. He had the authority to do what he did, unchallenged. And so I never did learn what Stupak wanted to ask or say. He wasted the better part of a day, and when he pointed that out to the ranking member, he got a simple shrug of the shoulders in reply.

■　■　■　■　■

Partisanship is one of two root cause issues preventing this country from securing our future energy security and affordability. Partisanship is ugly. When you look into the face of normal, intelligent, motivated, normally service-oriented elected officials and explain your point of view logically and rationally and they tell you unblinkingly, honestly, and without pause that they will not agree to or support your position because as much as they might individually agree with you and know that you are right, they are upholding the party line and that is the way it is going to be, you think to yourself, What planet am I on? Where is common sense? Where is decency? Where is the interest of the average citizen? Where is America headed? We're falling apart here on energy's future and the environment, and the response is the party line? What kind of pluralistic democracy is it when a few individuals at the top of a party—either party—determine the agenda, the priorities, the tactics, and the playbook, control the choices of their party members, and that's the end of it?

In my view, partisanship has run amok. When intelligent members of Congress and executive branch appointees are required to adhere to a party position under penalty of threats, such as the loss of party financial support, removal from earned office and/or preferred committees, or assignment to a backwater committee that has nothing to do with a member's constituents, you have to wonder whether your vote as a citizen means anything and whether representative democracy is being practiced according to the Constitution. In my opinion, the period from 1963 to 1972, marked by extremism and conflict—from political assassinations and civil rights murders and riots, to the divisive Vietnam War and far right and left presidential candidates like Barry Goldwater and George McGovern, and a corrupt president, Richard Nixon—buried bipartisanship in America.

The decades since then have continued to promote ever-more rabid partisanship in the American political process. We have had not just candidates but presidents such as Ronald Reagan and Barack Obama representing far right and left perspectives, impeachment hearings, ethical breaches, extreme capitalism and religious extremism creating further political divides, and the widening spread between the haves and have-nots in a country that promotes equality of opportunity. We have seen the same trend on a global scale with oil embargoes, the rise of religious and political fundamentalism here and abroad, the September 11 attacks, and interminable wars.

Domestically, America's great middle is pulled and torn by its extreme right and left politicians and activists who react to these challenges from very different positions. There is no talking space left for centrists, no reward for bipartisan leaders. They are ripped to political shreds by both extremes.

What this means when it comes to energy and the environment is that we're left with two extremes: more hydrocarbons and ignore their environmental effects, or no hydrocarbons and save the planet from overheating by making energy too expensive for people to use. What kinds of choices are these? They are partisan and extreme choices, neither of which meets the requirements of the nation's future sovereign, economic, energy, and lifestyle security.

Partisanship is eroding America's reputation, credibility, and ability to act, both internally and externally. "A house divided cannot stand." Where have we heard that before? A divided house is where the nation is headed if we continue on our current course. The right and left are driving us there. We could end up in either hell; or worse, alternate between them.

Disrespect of current government is revealed in favorability rankings of major industries. Earlier I noted that the oil and gas industry continuously ranks in twenty-fourth place out of 24 industries. The U.S. federal government consistently ranked twenty-third, except for 2009, when the shenanigans pulled by the real estate industry pushed the government's favorability up to twenty-second place, by default rather than improved performance. Ask yourself: whom do you trust more, your real estate agent or your elected official?

The race to the bottom is self-inflicted, I argue, on the part of the oil and gas industry, which chooses to live under a rock or in a bunker most of the time and doesn't tell its story. In the case of real estate, it frankly screwed up big time and is getting its just desserts. But government? That's a big problem. We hear, feel, see, touch, and are surrounded by it all day every day. We think we know what it does, but it rarely does anything we consider productive. It taxes us, employs a lot of people, gives a lot of speeches, but does it solve our problems? By consuming itself with partisanship, it is our house divided and can't solve our problems. We disrespect and disregard it. Unfortunately, the rest of the world is coming to that view as well. Ask yourself: How much help is America actually getting from its allies in the ongoing wars? How much respect is there for the dollar? Who is really with us on the intractable problems of today, including energy and the environment?

Partisanship is self-perpetuating. If you are a centrist, a pragmatic problem-solving service-oriented citizen who hankers after public office so that you can do good things for your fellow citizens, what is the likelihood that you will run for office, stand up against partisan extremists, get elected, and serve your constituents as you intended? It's not impossible, but it is unlikely. Try to get reelected on a record that did not support and promote your party's agenda! I've talked to many candidates. They see how partisanship works: you're "one of us," in which case we'll help you; or you're not, in which case you're on your own. Translated, it means you won't last. Ultimately you have to go along to get along.

Have you heard or read the conversations that take place between party leaders and members as legislation moves in Congress? Unlikely. In the unwritten code of conduct in the legislature, what is said between party leaders and members stays between them. Whether it's an offer of prime committee assignments for compliance or banishment for noncompliance, it's all part of the process. And the pressure is not simply to ensure Republicans and Democrats stay on their own sides of the aisle. There is pressure for intraparty compliance as well.

For example, Congressman Gene Green (D-TX) from Houston professed his continuing support for Congressman John Dingell's (D-MI) leadership of the House Energy and Commerce Committee after the 2008 elections. Dingell was the longest-serving member of the House and the committee chairman from time immemorial; Green believed in both the seniority system and the capability of the chairman. At the time Congressman Henry Waxman (D-CA), who wanted the chairman's role for himself and had the support of House Speaker Nancy Pelosi (D-CA), challenged Dingell and won. Waxman's victory was public. Less public was the retribution delivered to Congressman Green, a respected, honorable, and committed public servant. Waxman's retaliation included the dissolution of the subcommittee Green chaired and the lasting public stigma of what happens to you when you cross Waxman.

With no end in sight to partisanship in national government, it is imperative for both parties to seek supermajority status to govern. The Democratic Party is essentially there for now, but for how long is uncertain. The divisiveness and animosity that roiled the Democrats when the Republicans were in the majority is now roiling the Republicans. They will organize themselves, get their messages straight, and go right at the opposition as hard as they can as soon as they can. They will chip away at the majority and work on achieving their own supermajority, just as the Democrats did during their terms in the minority.

In the meantime, what outcomes will the nation experience in response to the serious problems we face? Representative of the sentiments that characterize partisan behavior, I recall a meeting with the Senate majority leader, Senator Harry Reid (D-NV), and members of the board of the American Manufacturers Association in the spring of 2008. He was feeling pretty good about the Senate's track record under his leadership and was preparing for a busy fall election season where he had aspirations of achieving a 60-seat, cloture-proof margin of majority.

Throughout the meeting, he talked about issues between the Congress and the White House, clearly signaling that the Democrats would be running against the Bush agenda as hard as they could. Disconcerting to a roomful of business leaders in his office Reid never referred to the president once as "the president." He repeatedly used the derogatory phrase "that man," pointing his finger in the direction of the White House, as he denigrated Bush's decisions or programs and promoted his own. I have no doubt that the feelings were mutual. But it reminded me of the juvenile behavior I used to see in my early career as junior managers politically fought one another for dominance on the way up the hierarchy. My impression is that those in the political hierarchy cling to the juvenile behaviors that enabled them to climb the ladders of authority. They can't let them go. They must have their partisan way. Partisanship is deeply, emotionally personal. Partisanship is not just extreme, it is juvenile acting-out behavior; people who act like juveniles run our country. Even worse, they run a country with broken governing structures and processes.

■　■　■　■　■

If partisanship is one of the root causes of broken government, it is and will continue to prevent the nation from achieving energy security and environmental sustainability. Just as bad, if not worse, is the second root cause of broken government: structural and process dysfunction. This dysfunction has been going on for years with no end in sight. Vice President Al Gore was the last senior executive branch official to try to tackle the problem of governmental structure and process efficiency and effectiveness in the early years of the Clinton administration. His list of 1,200 corrective actions announced in 1994 essentially fell into the dust bin of history when the Republicans took over the House in 1995 to implement their *Contract with America*. We're now led by our eighth president and eighteenth Congress since President Nixon declared energy independence in 1973. We're getting less secure, not more secure, by the day because the process by which work is done and the structures within which it should be done can't fix the problems we face.

The bad news is that the federal government has become so large and dysfunctional, it can't work. The good news, however, is that within the government, there are many hardworking, knowledgeable, committed professionals who do their best to try to get it to work. Among this number are tens of thousands of civil servants and thousands of appointees who spend careers or long parts of their careers doing their best for their country and fellow citizens.

Karen Harbert is a prime example of the dedicated professional who has committed years of her life to public service and to her country. She was appointed to a key role, assistant secretary for policy and international affairs in the Department of Energy (DOE), by President George W. Bush. She served him and energy secretary Sam Bodman well. She is top flight in everything she does. Well educated and poised for whatever challenges come her way, she was up to the tasks at hand and did a good job—at least as good as she could do in the structures and with the processes available to her.

I met Harbert on several occasions and came to understand that she had the very difficult task of working on international energy matters in the interests of the country. She was the ongoing and prime interface between the U.S. government and many state-owned oil companies. She was frequently called on by

Congress to testify on what the DOE was doing to encourage
the Organization of Petroleum Exporting Countries (OPEC) to
increase its oil production so that crude oil prices could moderate. She fully understood the unwillingness of Congress to budge
on the issues of increasing domestic production of oil and natural
gas by opening up land to America's own offshore exploration
and production but dutifully responded to members' questions
about how hard the DOE was pushing OPEC to meet America's
oil needs.

Harbert now runs the Institute for Twenty-first Century
America's Energy at the U.S. National Chamber of Commerce,
where she remains committed to the cause of energy security.
She shared with me her views as to what problems she had faced
in advancing the president's agenda on energy. In addition to the
White House and its political and policy leadership on energy,
she noted that an additional 13 executive branch agencies simultaneously have governance responsibility and authority for
energy and environment policy development and execution.

Many Americans might logically think that with a name like
Department of Energy, the DOE is the cabinet office that sets
and guides the nation's energy pathways. The situation isn't that
rational or logical. Over the years, multiple cabinet offices have
taken on energy responsibilities for several reasons. Just a few
examples: Homeland Security sets policies on energy facility
security and access; the Department of State addresses international energy agreements and issues; the Department of the
Interior manages the Bureau of Land Management, which governs environmental impact statements and permits for onshore
drilling; the Department of Agriculture oversees biofuels policies; the Environmental Protection Agency regulates waste management; and another half-dozen or so executive branch agencies
manage and govern every other aspect of energy production and
delivery.

The energy efforts by the government are as massive as they
are complex. Adding to the difficulty of knowing which agency
governs what responsibilities across the executive branch structures is also the need to figure out the process for how work gets
done, first in respective agencies and then across the agencies

in cases where interagency cooperation is required. The process of internal agency cooperation is challenging enough; the interagency process is not only convoluted, due to agency prerogatives, but it is mostly voluntary because there are few mandatory interagency requirements for cooperation.

Inherent in the fragmentation of energy governance is the explicit desire by Congress to ensure that the executive branch has its own checks and balances on itself. No department has the unilateral authority to grant, permit, assign, or regulate an energy initiative to the exclusion of other departments. Energy companies spend not days or weeks but months and years interacting with multiple executive branch agencies on virtually everything that they do and anything they want to initiate. Some Americans might believe that companies have offices in Washington to lobby on policy. Well, most Washington corporate offices do lobby regarding proposed legislation. But the primary work of those corporate offices is simply to figure out how to get work done with and through the executive and legislative branches under existing legislation and regulations.

Energy and the environment are sensitive areas that involve licenses and permits for everything that is done. I once dove deeply into the status and process of obtaining a particular permit that Shell needed to shoot seismic images and prepare for drilling operations in the Beaumont and Chukchi seas off the coast of Alaska. Under the law, Shell needed the Minerals Management Service (MMS), another agency within the Interior Department that looks after offshore permits, to create an environmental impact statement, which then needed approval from the National Oceanic and Atmospheric Administration (NOAA), under the Department of Commerce (DOC), to obtain a permit to shoot the seismic picture of the subsea drilling opportunity. The MMS and NOAA had a legal maximum of 120 days, under the authorizing legislation, to complete the environmental study, then consider and grant a permit, ensuring that all necessary information was in order. Timing for the permit was critical because of the short ice-free season in these geographies in which seismic operations could be conducted. Shell worked in earnest a year ahead of time to provide the needed information and had good working relationships with the people in the MMS, but despite everything being in order, no permit was forthcoming. We kept hearing that the staff was "still working" on the environmental impact statement.

The 120-day statutory due date for the permit to be released was in early June 2006. The earliest ice-free operations could commence was July, so we felt we had a month's grace period. July came and went; so did August. No permit. I had multiple conversations with top executives in NOAA and the DOC. They assured me everyone was working as hard and effectively as they could and indicated that there had been some work interruption in order to prepare environmental impact statements for certain military operations, which took priority over commercial requests. I accepted that. August gave way to September; the permit was still not ready. There were four weeks of potential ice-free waters left. I asked again when the permit would be ready. The commitment was two weeks hence. It actually did arrive on October 15. With two weeks before ice returned to the area and with a dismal weather forecast, Shell canceled the work plan for the year. A year of preparation and activity was lost due to a late permit. Tens of millions of dollars of logistical planning and preparation and hundreds of jobs were literally lost at sea.

Wanting to better understand what went wrong with the work process, I asked Vice Admiral Conrad Lautenbaucher, head of NOAA and arbiter of the permit, if it might be a good idea for me to visit the MMS to learn about the flow of work that goes on behind the scenes in the process of license granting. He was supportive and arranged a visit early the next year. I had the pleasure of meeting a small group of professional staff, experts in their field, who were motivated and eager to achieve results for their clients. They explained step by step what they do. What I, along with my Shell colleagues, had failed to understand were the preparatory activities the MMS went through to put a permit together. When they showed me the final permit and the 800-plus pages of materials, data, analysis, and projections that supported it, I came to see that a permit was not a simple piece of paper with a signature on it. It was months and months of work.

I asked about the 120-day statutory limit on permit granting. Common sense told me that no one could put an 800-page
permit together in four months. They acknowledged as much,
knew what the law said, and admitted they were in violation.
They also said that if they delivered what they could do in 120
days, no permit would be granted by NOAA because it would
be incomplete. I asked why they operated in sustained violation of the statue, or illegally, and why they had not sought
to change the law so common sense might guide a legally permissible permit granting period. They said they had tried on
numerous occasions to have the law changed. In every instance,
the recommended statutory change was not accepted because
Congress, as was explained to them, could not be seen to have
made an error. So an erroneous bill remains the law because
congressional leadership is unwilling to acknowledge that at
some point in the past a mistake had been made in the craft-
ing of the bill requiring environmental permits for offshore oil
exploration.

Shell was making business decisions on flawed law that could
not be corrected because the legislative branch is not required
to accept advice or input from the executive branch, due to the
separation of powers. The executive branch flagrantly violates
the law of the land by arbitrarily extending the time to grant
a license due to the physical impossibility of working legally.
Common sense rests with the MMS. But when this is a nation
of laws, doesn't Congress have a responsibility to get the law
right? Will a nation that has a government so flawed ever own
up to the important issue of energy security and do what it takes
to provide for its citizens? (Four years later Shell Oil, I'm told, is
still determined to move forward in Alaska, requesting permits
to shoot seismic and drill test wells, while facing lawsuits aimed
at preventing the activities from going forward.)

Thus, we have an executive branch that is fragmented,
together with confused work processes that are unique to each
agency and that may or may not be compatible with interagency
cooperative efforts. As a corporate executive who has spent
the better part of 35 years streamlining and simplifying global
organizations in multibillion-dollar companies with hundreds of

thousands of employees around the world, I assert the following: The executive branch of the federal government is dysfunctional in its structures and work processes. Given the congressional mandates that have been imposed, it is also not fixable in its current form.

■　■　■　■　■

The use of White House czars to consolidate and simplify cross-agency work has been tried again and again. The Obama administration is to be credited for once again trying to make government work effectively. It will not happen, as it hasn't happened before. The complexity, structures, processes, and people are too much to deal with. The system has existed for too long, with too much history, with too many competing departments to make over in the short time in which a single administration is in office, even if for two terms. And major changes would require congressional approval, which is generally unlikely, especially without supermajority control. By the time an administration has figured out what it would take to fix the problems, it's too late to get it done. Every modern administration that has set out to do so has failed. This one will too. Congress, with its two houses, committee structures, large staffs, short election cycles, seniority systems, and long-held practices and protocols is unable to legislate the functional structures and work processes that the executive branch could deploy to get work done in any way that is different from the way it has done heretofore. The problem is unfixable. "Political time" is too short to fix "energy time" needs.

I asked Karen Harbert about energy and environmental governance in the legislative branch. She smiled and asked if I really wanted the answer. I said, "Please, even if the truth hurts." She said that at last count during her tenure at the DOE, between the Senate and the House there were 26 congressional committees and subcommittees with jurisdiction over energy and the environment.

It would be simple to react with derision at such a ludicrous congressional structure for two policy areas. But that would miss the even more fundamental problem the nation faces than the proliferation of energy and environmental governance across 26 committees and subcommittees. Think about how Congress works, not how it is organized. Congress works on two-year cycles! Every two years the members of Congress are put to the test of accountability, election day. Every two years House leadership is subject to recall by the voters. The majority could become the minority and vice versa. Every two years there is an ever-present probability that committee and subcommittee chairs will be voted out of office, or returned to office but in the minority instead of the majority, which means they lose their chairmanships. Every time the Congress turns from Republican to Democratic or the reverse, all the committee and subcommittee chairs change. And even if the majorities don't reverse, chairmanships are up to party leaders and members and therefore still subject to change, as in the case of Dingell/Waxman.

The same dynamic applies to the Senate, where a third of all seats are up for election every two years. In any given two-year period, the Senate and/or the House could change parties, change chairs, reorder priorities, and reorganize committees and subcommittees.

Energy and environment policies are determined in the arbitrary and sometimes powerfully arrogant ways described in this chapter. Combine this with two-year governing cycles, and it is clear that this dysfunctional reality of so much churn and constantly changing priorities, subject to fragmented and dysfunctional administration and excruciating partisanship, is indeed the enemy of the energy and environmental good. There is a problem when it comes to congressional legislative leadership and execution of the nation's energy and environmental future. While constitutionally brilliant for the overall governance of the nation perhaps, both branches, separate and equal, are structurally dysfunctional, don't work, can't work, and won't work for energy and the environment. As discussed, these areas require decisions in "energy time," where lead times between initiation and completion of a single project can be a decade or more.

The nation can't go on like this. No president can lead us to energy and environmental security. No Congress can get us there either. If partisanship doesn't shoot down every potentially sound policy, executive and legislative branch structural and process dysfunction will. And even if there was unprecedented bipartisanship (which there isn't and won't be), the frequency of elections will change key players whose support is necessary for bipartisan policy continuity. The nation's energy and environmental future is adrift at sea with a storm brewing, surrounded by sailors who might want to but can't save it because they destroyed their own paddles, rudders, and sails fighting one another to save themselves.

And let us not forget judicial review. Every act of Congress and every policy put forward by an administration is subject to the review and decision of another separate and equal branch, the independent judiciary that has (theoretically) not one iota of interest in either partisan politics or government dysfunction. It simply rules on the law as written based on the facts of a case as presented. Whatever Congress or the administration does in the course of its terms may or may not last, depending on judicial review. The courts' decisions are the waves crashing over the energy and environmental policies adrift at sea.

With partisanship and dysfunctional structures and processes at the federal level, a fragmented industry and a disconnect between the time perspectives of the two, what can be done to ensure the nation's energy and environmental future? Let's move from what's broken to how America can successfully reform its structures and processes and set an example for the world of how to govern toward a secure energy and environmental future.

12

HERE'S HOW WE FIX IT!

*We need an intervention to put the nation on the
right course to deliver energy security and
environmental protection.*

For nearly five decades after the Civil War, America was in
turmoil. Chronic economic instability and monetary stress
accompanied the traumatic process of adjusting the social structure from slavery to freedom. Booms, busts, bank failures, pan-
ics, inflation, deflation, unemployment, extreme wealth, and
extreme poverty roiled the nation. In 1907 financial collapse
was prevented only by the personal and corporate funds provided by J. P. Morgan and his friends to essentially float the U.S.
Treasury. In 1912 the nation experienced another near-fiscal
failure. It was in the context of these crises that Congress and
the president created the Federal Reserve System in 1913 to provide monetary stability and financial security for the country.

It was a successful strategy. Although the Federal Reserve is
not perfect (witness the challenges of the 1930s and the past few
years), it has created order in the place of disorder, professionalism and knowledge instead of politics of the day, and experience
and judgment capable of swaying presidents and Congress over
nearly a hundred years, during which time the United States
became the largest, most successful, most stable economic pow-
erhouse in the world. The independent and regulatory powers
of the Fed, which include determining the money supply, setting
interest rates, setting the federal funds target rate (which drives

the cost of overnight bank borrowing), and market intervention when needed, have made the difference. Since the Federal
Reserve came into existence no nation has experienced greater
financial security and stability than the United States.

Today America needs an equivalent body to independently
regulate the future of energy security and environmental
protection.

■   ■   ■   ■   ■

The Federal Reserve Bank is a bridge to the future, a shock
absorber for the nation. It is not subject to the vagaries of election cycles, temporarily larger-than-life political personalities, or
issue-of-the-day fanaticism. Frankly I don't know anyone who
loves the Fed; but I also don't know anyone who doesn't understand that it must continue to govern U.S. monetary stability
and financial order. The Federal Reserve Bank was democratically established; its governors are selected by the president, with
the advice and consent of the Senate, for 14-year terms; its chairman is likewise selected, but for a 4-year term. The nonpolitical nature of the Fed is evidenced by the tenure of its chairmen
and board governors across multiple administrations under both
parties. Over its history, human beings may have failed the Fed,
but the Fed has not otherwise failed the nation.

Congress or the president can propose legislation to modify
or change the Fed at any time. The fact that this rarely happens
is an indication of broad satisfaction with the fit-for-purpose
design and the successful management of its tasks and responsibilities. Because the Fed is not taxpayer funded, Congress
does not approve or control its budget; it is supported by fees
from member banks, borne as part of the cost of doing banking under the protection and support of the system. Consumers
ultimately pay such fees, but the amounts are so minuscule at
the individual level that no one notices. Under the Fed system
the banking industry operates profitably within "big rules"
that provide predictability, degrees of certainty, and stability.
Consumers, companies, the economy, society and the nation are
the beneficiaries.

It is time, given everything we know about the volatility and uncertainties of our energy and environmental past, present, and future, to take a similar path to "big rule" management of these sectors as well. Now is the time for Congress to legislate and the president to sign a bill to create and implement an independent regulatory agency, the Federal Energy Resources System, to manage the nation's energy and energy-related environmental footprint. The American people, our economy, international competitiveness, national security, and social harmony would be better served by governing energy and its environmental implications via the charter and responsible administration of an independent board of governors whose sole purpose is the enabling and support of the nation's future energy system. By creating such a governing body, the United States could lead by example the rest of the world's nations, which could in their own time follow suit if they choose.

How would this system be structured, and what would it do? Ultimately Congress would decide, but here are some suggestions.

■ ■ ■ ■ ■

The structure and governance of the Federal Reserve Bank is a good model to start with, but it would need to be adjusted to cope with very different responsibilities and accountabilities in entirely different sectors of the economy and society where costs, science, and technology are critical variables.

A national board of governors with a number of regional boards makes as much sense for energy as it does for money. The nation is large and its regions have unique and exceptional characteristics that require local modifications. For example:

- The Southwest has lots of wind and sun but limited water.
- The Rockies have lots of wind and considerable sun as well as coal and unconventional oil, called oil shale, and gas.
- Appalachia has lots of coal, natural gas and wind.
- Alaska and the Gulf Coast have a lot of oil and gas.
- There are vast swaths of undeveloped agricultural land in the Midwest, although these regions also host very large cities.

- The Northeast and Mid-Atlantic states are densely populated, with considerable air quality challenges and few energy resources.
- The Southeast is increasingly populated but with limited energy resources other than considerable agriculture and forestry.
- Most of the nation's population lives in states closer to the nation's coasts and Great Lakes.

All these regional characteristics need to be taken into account. Thus, a single federal board seated in Washington, DC, would need the assistance of a number of regional boards organized by natural common or shared interests from geographies across the nation to determine policy that fits a regulatory framework.

The national board and the regional boards should be populated by people who know the subject matter on which they govern. But unlike the Fed, whose members are primarily bankers and economists, the Federal Energy Resources Board and its regional boards should not consist solely of energy producers. Instead, members should include knowledgeable leaders who understand energy production, consumption, technology, economics, transportation, science, nature, and the environment. Members could include accomplished experts from energy, academia, industry, agriculture, consumer, labor, and environmental groups. Like the Fed, the board will require support staff in adequate numbers and with competencies to professionalize subject matter, prepare materials for consideration, analyze issues, review available research, and put forward reasonable alternatives based on science, economics, and achievability for the boards' policy considerations.

The costs of the federal and regional boards should be funded independently of taxpayer general funds to protect their separation from executive and legislative branches. They could be funded by a small fee on the production and import of energy, measured by British thermal unit (Btu) of energy or kilowatt of electricity produced. The fraction-of-a-cent fee, multiplied by the quads of energy produced in this country, would be essentially not impactful to the consumer yet produce sufficient funds to support the work of the board. No one really asks how much

the Fed spends. I suspect it would be the same for the Federal
Energy Resources Board.

■   ■   ■   ■   ■

What will the board regulate? Regulatory authorities across four
distinct high-impact areas are essential to address the whole of
energy and the environment. These areas are energy supply,
technology choices, environmental protection, and infrastructure choices.

ENERGY SUPPLY

The Federal Energy Resources Board should determine the
amounts and relative percentages of the future supply sources of
America's energy. As I have explained, the nation has abundant
natural resources to produce all the energy it needs, forever. It
is important for a regulatory board to determine what sources
of energy are right for what time in America's future and to
govern production capacity accordingly to assure ample supplies
of affordable energy. Thus, it could determine how much of our
energy comes from hydrocarbons (oil, gas, coal, and liquefied
natural gas), nuclear, renewables (including wind, solar, wave,
and biofuels), hydrogen, hydropower, and geothermal and in
what periods of time over many decades.

Until now, the nation generally has been haphazard about
what sources and amounts of energy supply we produce, and we
have relied to an extent on so-called market forces and prices to
determine what we use. That system has worked only because
of the historic abundance of hydrocarbons and the relative lack
of environmental considerations. In recent decades, this near-
Darwinian supply system has brought us volatile prices; environmental damage; uncertain future domestic supplies; the
Organization of Petroleum Exporting Countries (OPEC), an
international cartel led by sovereign nations focused on their
self-interests; a near-national "fight to the finish" over the future
of coal; the near abandonment of new nuclear energy resources;

unreliable promises of "anything but hydrocarbons"; and politically motivated on-again, off-again environmental initiatives.
How many more so-called "free market" benefits do we want?

Going forward, the nation should move beyond the haphazard and the political to implement deliberate, sound energy supply strategies based on the sources the Federal Energy Resources
Board recommends, considering availability, affordability, and
environmental sustainability. The industries and companies that
produce such energy from different sources will, as today, compete vigorously for their shares of production capacity by continuing to create value for customers and using the tools they
have available to sustain their unique competitive advantages.

What might such a supply system look like?

A comprehensive and coherent energy supply plan would be
created to take into account the nation's short-, medium-, and
long-term energy and environmental future, defined in the years
and decades of energy time. In reality, we are still in a hydrocarbon age and are likely to be in it for some time to come.
In view of ongoing declines in known hydrocarbon basins, an
orderly short-term plan would require the nation to produce
more of its native, domestic hydrocarbons to feed the infrastructure that we've constructed over these past hundred-plus years.
Doing so would enable us to meet the known demand over the
coming decades without relying even more intensely on foreign
supplies.

There is nothing shameful about using hydrocarbons. The world
will continue to use them for decades to come, regardless of what
we do in the United States. What the Federal Energy Resources
Board can do, however, is to make their production possible and
encourage use in cleaner and more sustainable ways.

Looking toward the medium term, the Federal Energy
Resources Board can regulate the planning and construction
of more clean nuclear electricity production and finally determine the nuclear waste management plan that has been politically elusive for decades. It can plan and implement a clean coal
strategy that utilizes and pays for the technology that we know
works: coal gasification with carbon capture and sequestration.
Meanwhile, the board can also move forward with wind, solar,

and biofuels in a thoughtful, planned manner rather than the boom/bust exercise we've seen launched and retrenched and reinvigorated in recent years. It could also consider the role of hydrogen for both stationary power and for transportation.

In the longer range future, the board can decide major increases of supplies of energy from alternative sources, such as more nuclear, solar thermal, wave, and possibly geothermal, moving us toward de-carbonizing our entire energy supply system. Such decisions not only lead us to more, cleaner sources of energy; they also deliberately diminish the use of dirtier hydrocarbons based on reliable technological change. This approach combines continued affordability with environmental improvements. The timing can be managed so that the economic disruption and social impact of change are minor and regionally adapted so as to balance the effects of change on affected populations and employment.

The supply system may well require a plan that stretches out in "energy time" from now to 2060. Such a five-decade plan is impossible to conceive in "political time" because it would span at least 25 Congresses and as many as 6 to 12 presidents.

Will supply-side energy management work? Today the Fed balances its regulatory authority with the business and competitive needs of banking to address the national monetary supply-side interests. There is no reason to believe that the Federal Energy Resources Board could not balance its regulatory authority with the business and competitive needs of energy production and environmental protection to address the national energy supply-side interests.

TECHNOLOGY CHOICES

Technology has two roles in our energy future: unleash undiscovered or undeveloped new energy supplies and enable far more efficient and clean consumption of energy.

On the supply side, I am confident that technology advances will allow us to increase yields from existing hydrocarbon sources, extract resources from previously unreachable or seemingly impossible geologies, develop ever-safer operating processes and procedures for nuclear electricity production, examine the molecular structures of biomass to extract energy from current agricultural production or waste materials, expand the potential capture of energy from wind and sun, utilize Earth's core waste heat for electricity production, and use nanotechnology solutions across the range of energy sources that have yet to reveal themselves.

On the efficiency side, the future will see different power sources for personal mobility, new materials used to construct buildings and homes, new methods by which electricity turns motors that are designed with ever-more-efficient materials, new more efficient electronic devices from computers to servers to personal electronics, new materials and designs used for lighting, and new intelligence built into the transmission grid to manage an array of local, distant, or central sources.

With respect to the environment, technology will safeguard the manner in which energy is produced, assist in cleaning the water that energy requires, and provide the tools to reduce and manage our gaseous wastes.

In other words, technology will unleash new energy from both traditional and new sources; it will help clean our environment; and it will diminish the amount of energy we need on a per-capita basis to support competitive enterprises, national security, and an affordable and comfortable lifestyle.

How do we know what technology choices are best? Who makes such choices?

Some would say, "Let the market choose." I understand that logic. Many people fundamentally believe that consumers should ultimately have the final say about what products and technologies they can buy to satisfy their interests and tastes. And I agree with that logic as far as consumer choice is concerned. But energy and the environment are more than consumer products; they are the engine of the nation's economy; are dependent on available national resources; impact the land, water, and air that humans depend on; and are critical to our national security. Technology decisions that significantly impact the production, consumption, distribution, and environmental effects of energy are not really consumer choices.

Such technology choices should fall within the domain of an independent regulatory agency. Consumers will continue to choose the energy-using products they purchase, from lighting, appliances, electronics, and vehicles to the homes they live in. What the Federal Energy Resources Board will make are the broad technology decisions: the scope and key components of an electricity smart grid; the common design and construction elements and technologies for nuclear plants; the range of carbon capture and sequestration technologies for coal plants; the methods and technology to expand wind, solar, and geothermal energy production; the most suitable biomass and production technologies for biofuels; and the range of batteries for electric vehicles. The board will also be tasked with the big decision on whether and when hydrogen fuel cells will finally replace the internal combustion engine as the primary power system for long distance personal mobility.

There will continue to be private and venture capital–funded research and development and academic research and development, as we know it today. The new independent regulatory agency will rely on existing research and development sources, such as the Department of Energy, major corporations, universities, laboratories, and entrepreneurs. Technology decisions will be debated based on professional science, economics, and industry knowledge, not politics of the day. In my mind, there is no difference between NASA deciding what technologies are used for space research and travel, relying on industry and science wherever it can be found, and the Federal Energy Resources Board deciding what technologies are most appropriate for the nation's energy and environmental security, relying on all available sources. The regional boards may serve as entry points and filtering systems for locally developed technology initiatives that otherwise might struggle to find access directly at the national level.

ENVIRONMENTAL PROTECTION

Some may question why my proposed Federal Energy Resources Board should have environmental regulatory responsibility when there is a functioning Environmental Protection Agency (EPA) already in existence. One overriding reason: to fundamentally depoliticize the work of the new agency on environmental protection related to energy. If anyone wishes to argue that the current EPA is not politicized, consider this. On January 19, 2009, the EPA's official position was that carbon dioxide was not an endangering pollutant that warranted national regulation. Six weeks later, based on no new studies, no new information, no scientific breakthroughs, but with the confirmation and swearing in of a new administrator, the EPA ruled that carbon dioxide was a harmful pollutant and set about seeking public comment so that it could enter into a rulemaking exercise on endangerment as it is chartered to do.

What changed? A Republican administration that viewed carbon dioxide one way was replaced by a Democratic administration that viewed carbon dioxide another way. If that is not a political decision, I don't know what is. Going forward, it makes no sense to mix politics into the critically important decision-making process for the environmental protections the nation needs with respect to future energy choices. The safety and health of the nation should not be politicized.

As I see it, the EPA would continue to have primary regulatory authority for its other major current areas of responsibility, protecting land, water, and air resources outside the energy system, together with national enforcement authority for all violations. But the Federal Energy Resources Board would address rulemaking, standards and procedures, and best practices for the environmental impacts of the production, transportation, distribution, storage, and consumption of energy.

This would shift some responsibilities from the EPA to the new agency. It would be advisory to the EPA in some respects and an authority beyond the EPA in other respects, but in all cases it would be limited to energy-related environmental oversight. It would be responsible for setting the nation's carbon or greenhouse gas footprint and for establishing the nation's plan for reducing that footprint over time, particularly through its regulatory impact on future energy supplies. It would set the standards and rules for the environmental impacts of energy production from all forms of energy, including hydrocarbons, nuclear, biofuels, wind, solar, geothermal, and any new form of energy that might emerge in the future. It would be the entity charged with daily interactions with international energy and environmental organizations, such as the International Energy Agency, a data collection, analysis, and forecasting group based in Paris, OPEC, and any agencies that are established as a result of climate change negotiations. It would also absorb the data collection and forecasting roles currently held by the Energy Information Agency within the Department of Energy.

The technologies associated with environmental protection; the costs of introducing, monitoring, and enforcing such protection; and the impact of such protection on the availability and affordability of supply would all come together under the board's regulatory oversight. The board would be informed by science, sound engineering, and risk management. And just as the chairman of the Fed is selected and reappointed or removed based on the president's assessment of the soundness and effectiveness of the administration of the Fed's policies, so, too, would the chairman of the new agency be held accountable for the effective implementation of the environmental protection plan.

INFRASTRUCTURE CHOICES

Today's energy infrastructure is creaking. It is in large measure old, tired, in need of maintenance or replacement. It is certainly not adequate to satisfy the anticipated energy demands of the future. Most of the infrastructure in the country is governed by local or state authorities. There is a minimal amount of regional infrastructure and essentially no national infrastructure. Yet the nation's economic competitiveness, energy security, national security, and quality of life depend on a robust, efficient, contemporary, and environmentally sound infrastructure that covers the nation.

Creating new infrastructure is one of the most difficult of all energy initiatives to undertake. In principle, everyone agrees it is needed; no one tolerates outages of energy caused by broken, outdated, or worn-out infrastructure. Yet the process of going from concept, to siting of new infrastructure, to construction and commissioning is fraught with opposition. Even renewable energy projects meet with objections. NIMBY-ism, not-in-my-backyard resistance, is a serious problem in America and is only getting worse.

When infrastructure decisions are not made, the nation, a region, or a locale stands still. We cannot depend on politicians to make infrastructure decisions. When asked to support or oppose infrastructure initiatives, my experience is that they are easy to persuade to oppose and very difficult to persuade to support, regardless of local or regional need. Nor can we afford to tie ourselves up in extended litigation over critical infrastructure decisions in the future the way we have in the past four decades.

Therefore, it is essential that future infrastructure decisions that impact interstate, regional, or national energy supplies be made by an entity such as the Federal Energy Resources Board, advised by its regional boards and professional staff, taking into account the appropriate analysis of alternatives, environmental impacts, and economies of scale. The board can also be advised by public hearings and local, state, and regional input. In some situations it may conclude that remunerative relief is warranted for impositions that would otherwise be made on local populations. Once decisions are made, they should not be subject to tort claims on behalf of individuals and special interests but should be subject only to appeal and review within the confines of the board itself. In extreme situations, an act of Congress could obviously override the independent regulatory agency, but such situations would be hard to imagine. The national good should supersede individual preferences.

It is not without precedence that individual lawsuits are subordinated to national priorities. The infrastructure authority of the new independent regulatory agency should be defined by law so that the board can make the decisions in the best interests of the nation.

Making and implementing sound decisions in these four distinct realms will position the country for economic growth and sustained international competitiveness, sound national security, a sustainable environment, and an affordable, and socially just and ample supply of energy for centuries to come.

■ ■ ■ ■ ■

The time to begin deliberations on the creation of a new federal independent regulatory agency is now—sooner, not later—before the United States is in dire crisis, before endemic shortages and unprecedented price spikes have further poisoned the national dialogue, before more so-called oil wars or geopolitical rivalries arbitrarily reduce energy supplies and more seriously divide the nation into energy "haves" and "have-nots."

During the campaign of 2008, I discussed with several of the presidential candidates the creation of a National Energy Commission, as a precursor to an independent regulatory agency, to consider the nation's energy and environmental future and to draft plans to meet those demands. Although some of the candidates I spoke to were intrigued by the idea, and two (in opposing parties) supported it in principle, neither of the final party nominees was interested. Today I believe we do not have the time for a commission to study the problem. We need to get on with fixing the future with new structures and processes.

There is no question but that the agency's design, structure, set of authorities, and definition of tasks, responsibilities, and accountabilities will need expertise and champions to move it forward. I understand how Washington works. Any structural proposal that rewrites political authorities and responsibilities is problematic. Some would say such a proposal contains its own death wish, because it asks elected officials to consider shedding some of their current political authority—the same prerogatives that have aided many of them in their election and reelection campaigns—for an abstract promise of reform.

Why would an incumbent choose to assume a passive role in a part of our national life that brings consumers to hotlines and talk shows, citizens to town hall meetings, voters to the ballot box? Why give up the opportunity to drag oil company executives, the ones we love to hate, through a periodic circus of public hearing humiliation?

It is possible that no sitting elected official, from the president to the newest freshman representative, will touch this proposal today. But such a response is simply not good enough for the world's leading economy and only superpower that has had a 40-year energy history fraught with inadequate or nonexistent solutions. The future economic competitiveness, energy security, national security, environmental protection, and affordability and quality of life of America's citizens should not be risked by the status quo bias of incumbent politicians. If the nation's current leaders choose not to undertake the necessary corrections to establish the mechanisms to protect the country from the partisanship and dysfunction of a government that has failed its citizens on energy and the environment for the past 40 years, then it is time to take another route.

If we stay on our current path, the partisan politics that we have seen from the extremes on the right and left will continue to prompt the electorate to zig and zag, with each political swing undoing what's been done before. In between election cycles, the three branches will continuously check and balance one another into inertia. Meanwhile shortages and price spikes will become more frequent, last longer, and cause deeper harm. Democrats will blame Republicans, Republicans will blame Democrats, and both will blame the energy companies while citizens lose out on energy affordability and availability.

By now, skeptics of big government might be choking on this proposal. It's true that change is hard to contemplate and even harder to do. But the status quo is neither credible nor sustainable. We're never going back to the day when the United States could produce all of its own oil and enough to fight a world war besides. We're not going to replace our road fleet of 250 million internal combustion engine vehicles, the ships on the sea, and the planes in the sky, and use less liquid fuel and produce less pollution, within several decades. We can't turn off 600 coal plants in the next ten years to clean our air as some propose. We can't continue to postpone action on nuclear power because of irrational fears.

So to skeptics I offer this: We already have big government; it doesn't work. It can't solve these intractable problems. We will have a democratic solution if and when Congress and the president pass and sign a bill that creates the Federal Energy Resources Board and populate it with presidential appointees with the advice and consent of the Senate. We have precedent for solving the nation's biggest challenges. It's called an independent regulatory agency. Let's be pragmatic as well as visionary. Let's create a new one.

And if Congress and the president won't take the required actions, let's do what we citizens have done effectively in the past. Let's use our grassroots authority to get it done.

13

EVERY VOICE COUNTS

*Governments will create independent regulatory bodies
to govern energy security and the environment only if
grassroots citizens demand them.*

The first time that I spoke publicly about the opportunity to
create a Federal Energy Resources Board was in fall 2008
at the Commonwealth Club of San Francisco. I discussed why
it was needed, what it might do, and how it could improve our
future economic competitiveness, energy and national security,
protect our quality of life, and provide environmental sustainability. The audience was engaged and curious. They asked
questions and offered spontaneous support for such a dramatic
intervention to address our energy needs for the future. It should
not be lost on anyone that the remarks were made in the congressional district represented by Nancy Pelosi (D-CA), Speaker
of the House of Representatives. Many of those in attendance
were her constituents.

Several months later, I had the opportunity to deliver the
Malcolm Wiener Lecture at the John F. Kennedy School of Public
Policy at Harvard University. The same topic; the same response.
A number of audience members asked why such a move had not
already taken place. In this home of distinguished public policy
debate, the concept was well received and stimulated a number
of long-running e-mail conversations.

In addition to these two major events, I have spoken on
the subject literally all over the nation, from the University of

South Florida to the University of California at Berkeley, from an audience of public utility regulators in the upper Midwest to multiple hydrocarbon and renewable energy conferences in the West, Southwest, Midwest, and Southeast. Across a wide range of audiences in dozens of states, after the events I have encountered curiosity, interest, lots of questions, and sustained, ongoing dialogue.

The first time that I spoke publicly about the Federal Energy Resources Board idea in Washington, DC, was as part of a panel at the International Association of Political Consultants annual meeting late in 2008. Afterward, one of my fellow panelists told the audience that such an idea would be "dead on arrival in this town" and would never see the light of day—regardless of its merits. When, several months later, I spoke on the same subject again in Washington at the Energy Marketers Association meeting, there were no questions, no follow-up discussion. It was indeed a dead-on-arrival experience.

What a disconnect between the reactions of grassroots Americans across the country, who worry every day about energy price and availability, and the response of policy and political experts inside the Beltway! The few elected officials with whom I've discussed the board have been uniformly tolerant of me and uniformly uninterested in pursuing the notion, unlike the two (unsuccessful) primary presidential candidates, who were at least receptive to my concepts. When I met with then-candidate Obama in mid-2007, we never even got to the topic. Once he realized that I did not see bio-fuels as the answer to high gas prices and renewables as the solution for energy independence, the discussion was over. His opponent chose not to discuss energy with me at all.

Former elected officials with whom I've discussed the concept have frankly warned me off. I've been encouraged to make better use of my time than to propose this intervention. It's not surprising to me at all. It's disappointing, certainly, but this is not the first time that a disruption of the government status quo has met resistance from incumbent elected officials.

Affordable energy is more than the issue of high pump prices for gas and diesel. Affordable and sustainable energy from all sources is an essential enabler of our unique American form of democratic capitalism, our comfortable lifestyles, our international competitiveness, and the legacy we leave to future generations. If we don't get this right, the nation's economic leadership and superpower status in the world is threatened, as is our pluralistic form of democratic social and economic justice.

How sad it is to see one of the root causes of America's potential decline tied directly to costly energy prices that are headed artificially higher by design of our own government. How upsetting it is that so many policy makers prefer the structural dysfunction of the status quo to the enabling change that can create a better energy future. Public policy choices that make energy more expensive by playing favorites among various forms of energy, depending on the party and special interests in power at the time, is a gross injustice to every American who likes to bathe with hot water, cook a family meal, heat or cool a home, drive a car or truck, earn a living, take a vacation, raise children, attend church, or go to school.

The political status quo raises energy costs and threatens energy security for all of us. Zigzag politics have been self-perpetuating for almost 40 years, and elected officials have failed to come to grips with an increasingly uncertain future. In a country that has more energy than we will ever need, in an increasingly complex urbanized society, affordable energy is not just a privilege; it is a basic human right. Few can live without affordable energy; no one can live without clean air.

The failure of 8 presidents and 18 Congresses to deliver the public policies that provide affordable energy and environmental sustainability to the people of America needs to be addressed. It seems to me that our constitutional rights to life, liberty, and the pursuit of happiness link directly to affordable and available energy in a complex twenty-first-century society that requires energy to live and has available more energy resources than it will ever need. It also follows, for the same reasons, that we have a right to a sustainable environment. Government's failure to provide both affordable energy and a sustainable environment is nothing short of a violation of these rights. As such, it creates an obligation for correction. If the representatives of the people choose to do nothing but perpetuate these denials of rights, it is incumbent on the people who choose the representatives to take action by making their voices heard and choosing other representatives who will make the necessary corrections. If some people have difficulty with the rights argument, then let's call energy and environmental security the "privileges" of citizenship. In either case elected officials are chosen by the people; the failure of political leadership to respond to their constituents' necessary "privileges" is just as unacceptable.

The most effective way to address such failure is by taking the issue to where it matters most: grassroots America, where ultimate power and authority reside.

■   ■   ■   ■   ■

The notion of a grassroots movement is hardly unprecedented in our history. Time and time again, when government has failed to act or has acted in ways that were seen as detrimental to the interests of the people, grassroots movements have surfaced. Time and time again, they have successfully argued for and pressured for change.

I've personally been at least tangentially part of four major grassroots movements that have made a difference in public policy: the civil rights movement, the original Earth Day observances that moved President Nixon to propose the creation of the Environmental Protection Agency, the anti–Vietnam war movement, and the anti–Iraq war movement. None has been easy; each has taken longer than anyone would care to imagine. But the proof is there: When the American people come together to put forward a collective interest, when they organize their messages, confront the wrong they perceive, behave in legal and reasonable but determined and unshakable ways, they move mountains. Even more remarkable, they move representatives who otherwise would prefer the status quo to change their positions in the face of such insistence and recruit and elect new representatives who will help make change happen. Most importantly they move vast numbers of people to join together and align efforts to say in numerous ways: "We've had enough. It's time for a change."

The civil rights movement is a prime example. For too many decades, elected officials failed to address the harm and evils of American apartheid. When millions of Americans from all races and economic strata finally told elected officials "Enough is enough," and the landslide election of 1964 made the inevitable possible, a movement of, by, and for the people went to work to structurally undo institutional racism. It took many more years of hard work by dedicated individuals and organizations, engaging more and more citizens from within ethnic minorities and across the wide spectrum of society, to create an ever-widening definition of civil rights and inclusion across society. The lion's share of credit for civil rights in America belongs to the nation's grassroots population. Many elected officials resisted civil rights changes for far too long. Many political careers went bust over incumbents' reluctance to accept the inevitability of grassroots pressure for justice and social equality.

And so it goes. Grassroots America can be a heartland of participatory democracy, a great strength of our independence and freedom, an inspiration to the world, just as grassroots efforts in other parts of the world have stirred Americans' hearts. Recall elsewhere when a new generation of China's youth stood up for their rights in Tiananmen Square in 1989 and, more recently, when millions of Iranians protested what they believed was a stolen election. Although these two events ended tragically, they are drivers of change and a testament to the power of grassroots initiatives to inspire action. In America, grassroots democracy is part and parcel of who we are.

It is time, therefore, for grassroots America to recognize that affordable energy and environmental sustainability are within our reach now and for the long-term future. It is time to embrace the fact that the nation has more energy than it will ever need; has the technology to deliver more energy and enable more efficient use of energy; has the ability to regulate gaseous wastes and ensure cleaner land, water, and air while producing more energy; and has the knowledge to build infrastructure that is smarter, more efficient, and more powerful. Although many people recognize these concepts, their representatives within the polarized American government have been and currently are unable to work together to implement policy or strategy to secure and deliver our energy future. Rather than tolerating our government standing in the way of energy and environmental security and risking our economic and lifestyle future, grassroots citizens can seize the opportunity to shape the nation's destiny by supporting fundamental change over energy and environmental governance and demand that our representatives create the Federal Energy Resources System.

■   ■   ■   ■   ■

What I am proposing is to invite more than 300 million Americans to take charge of their economic futures, national and energy security, environmental sustainability, and quality of life by informing their elected officials that the way forward must be different from the past. It is a call to the great bell curve of the American people to take pragmatic action for themselves, their families, and their communities in the way that participative pluralism was meant to function. All Americans who have the right to vote have the right, and some would say the obligation, to speak to their elected representatives on the issues that concern them. In this case it is to address the issues of affordable and available energy and a sustainable environment.

If affordable energy and environmental sustainability do not concern you, I am not calling on you to act. But to everyone who is concerned, this is the call to get the facts, understand the implications, look behind the political demagoguery of both parties that only serves to disinform and misinform the uninformed, and let our government know we citizens want and need a new path forward.

We have the opportunity to say to our elected officials that the time has come to intervene, upset the status quo, and create an independent regulatory agency, a Federal Energy Resources System, that can serve the needs of the country and society for now and for the future. To those elected officials who object, who prefer the partisan acrimony and reliance on today's continuing dysfunctional structures and processes, who choose the arrogance of power over the needs of constituents, all that is needed is a reminder that forty years of failed efforts and the prospect of more years of the same failure to act, decide, deliver, and be accountable is not acceptable. They may need an explanation of what the proposed solution is; they may need time to get their heads around it. And this is where you, as a citizen and a voter, can be very useful to them. It's okay to say that what you are suggesting is pure pragmatism, common sense without either a Republican or Democratic Party label on it. It is stamped instead with "Made in America for America by Americans." It is also replicable around the world. If they remain confused or obstinate, they need to be told in no uncertain terms that you will not provide financial support to their political future and instead will work to recall them at the next ballot for their resistance to do what their citizens need. That is the most effective way to get their attention.

There are many local organizations whose purpose is to tell government officials that the status quo is not working. Find out which are pragmatic, not political, and centrist, not left or right wing, and offer them your support. When I did not find a national organization that met these criteria, I started Citizens for Affordable Energy (www.citizensforaffordableenergy.org). It is pragmatic, nonpolitical, and straightforward in what it is attempting to do. It welcomes all Americans who want affordable energy and a sustainable environment to become a part of its efforts.

Change is possible if we confront the partisan politics and structural dysfunction of the status quo. Incumbent congressional members and executive branch officials who are wedded to their peculiar, partisan energy ideologies and who tolerate, allow, or encourage higher energy costs to protect their ideological prerogatives need to hear from grassroots Americans who are not prepared to sacrifice their economic futures and national security to narrow political interests and uninterested incumbents.

Companies in the energy industry have figured out how to succeed in their respective niches within the system. They generally prefer the difficulties of the status quo to the challenges of tackling the government or educating the public on the consequences of failing to develop a holistic energy strategy. With a few exceptions they have essentially given up on comprehensive energy education for the public, trying to find common cause with nongovernmental organizations to reach reasonable compromises or proposing sensible, holistic policy alternatives for debate. They need to hear from you as well.

Environmental special interests have gone for whatever progress they can make, using whatever tools are available to them—including the threat of global warming—and sacrificing social or economic justice and environmental justice to achieve their selfish aims. They have become expert in using the legal system to plant disruptive suits in courts with strong bias in their favor, just as personal injury lawyers shopped their class action suits around the courts in recent decades. That their efforts ultimately might price average Americans out of economic security and quality of life is not their problem. These special interests also need to hear from you.

Elected officials have gone out of their way to promote disinformation and misinformation, with industry and special-interest support on both sides of the political spectrum, to allow the American people to remain essentially uninformed. This has gone on for so long that it has become, of all things, normal. They need to hear you loudly and clearly.

It's unusual for an industry to voluntarily move past its comfort zone. It's not easy to rein in special interests from what they do best—influence selfish outcomes. It's difficult for incumbent elected officials and appointees to make decisions that might be unpopular in the short term—by which I mean the next election. We can understand why we are where we are and how we got here. But we can't stay here. We *must* move on.

We can draw on remedies that have worked for other crises in our past—grassroots involvement to mandate change and creation of an independent regulatory agency—in this crisis to create an affordable energy and environmental future. I'm not appealing to Americans at the extremes of the political spectrum to join the next "big movement." I am not proposing another emotion-laden "Drill, baby, drill" or "No more coal" chant. This proposal is not about shouting; it is about doing.

It's about delivering *affordable energy* because it is available and it is within our democratic reach. It's about producing *energy from all sources* in order to provide enough supply to make energy affordable. It's about selecting *sound technology* to bring supplies of energy to the market and to use energy more efficiently. It's about providing more *environmental protection* to protect our land, water, and air and in particular to reduce harmful gaseous wastes. It's about building *adequate infrastructure* to bring energy safely and efficiently from where it is produced to where it is consumed. What it's not about is continuation of the status quo of zigzag politics as usual, partisan paralysis, and government structural and process dysfunction on energy and environmental public policy.

To make this happen, grassroots Americans need the energy companies, from oil and gas producers and electric utilities, to renewable and alternative energy providers, to recognize that they are participants in solving the challenge of America's energy future, as accountable to the nation for their cooperation as to their shareholders to make a return on investment. They need the special interests to recognize that a *national* interest supersedes their narrow agendas and to get out of the way, stop impeding sound, coherent, responsible short-, medium-, and long-range plans that deliver affordable energy from all appropriate and available resources with responsible care for the environment. They need elected and appointed members of government in both executive and legislative branches to shed their polarizing partisan politics long enough to address the nation's dysfunctional structures and processes by creating an independent regulatory agency, a new Federal Energy Resources System, to take on the responsibility of delivering affordable energy and environmental sustainability to America.

The citizens of the nation need it now, not later. We cannot afford unaffordable energy, as individuals or as a nation. As individuals, we learned hard lessons in 2006, 2007, and 2008 as energy prices made too many Americans choose between paying for gas and electricity or buying medicine, food, and other necessities. As a nation, we saw our national wealth transferred to oil-exporting nations because of the failure of our government to provide for our energy future.

No more.

As citizens we ask our democratically elected government representatives to listen to the grassroots of America and to respond to what we want and need. If our representatives think they know better; if they are more inclined to adhere to the platforms of their party than to the voices of their constituents; if they are so entrenched in their ideologies that they cannot be pragmatic; if they are so personally wealthy that they cannot feel the effects of high-cost energy on the day-to-day lives of average Americans; if they are so arrogant as to dismiss the needs and wants of the electorate; if they are so beholden to their current political prerogatives and authorities that they cannot agree to change the system that has worked against America's best energy and environmental interests for nearly 40 years, they should know they can and will be recalled at the first opportunity. If the current incumbents can't or won't do what is needed, grassroots Americans can ensure there won't be a ninth president or a nineteenth Congress that ignores their best interests. Affordable energy and environmental sustainability are not just needed but demanded by everyday Americans.

The way forward is clear. We citizens just need to make it happen. Failure to act now jeopardizes our future.

14

WHERE DO WE GO FROM HERE?

Independent regulatory leadership could launch nations toward multi-decade journeys of unprecedented economic and environmental renewal. Its absence will take many nations, in particular the United States, to an unprecedented energy abyss.

If you remain skeptical about the prospects of a nationwide grassroots movement that focuses on energy, the environment, and the creation of an independent regulatory agency to guide the nation to energy security and affordability, such as the Federal Energy Resources System, you are not alone. As the ideas expressed in this book were tested over many months across the country, there was a prevailing refrain. "Every time gas prices go way up, when they come back down, everyone soon forgets there was a problem. People go back to their old habits." It's just like when there are gasoline shortages. "When gas lines disappear, everything goes back to normal."

I've heard these statements from industry experts, business leaders, economists, elected officials, and everyday people all over the country. And historically, there is certainly truth in what they say. We've been through crises of one sort or another since the 1973 Arab oil embargo, and every time there is a shortage or a price spike, history repeats itself. Because of that cycle, we have failed to address energy security and affordability.

We've chased after every manner of new energy silver bullet for decades, without ever finding one, and we're running after even more. We've taken climate change and global warming arguments both seriously and not so seriously for years and continue to emit more gaseous wastes than ever. We've watched as our crude oil imports went from 30 percent of consumption in 1973 to 65 percent in 2008 and continued to prevent U.S. oil companies from exploring for more domestic resources, yet we can still fill our tanks whenever we need to. We've now stopped or shelved over a hundred proposed new pulverized-coal-burning electricity plants in the last five years, and the lights are still on. We've been arguing over nuclear waste and whether we should or shouldn't build new nuclear electricity plants for decades, and the air conditioning still works. We've been hearing about an aging infrastructure and transmission grid for so long, we're growing old hearing about it, but the refrigerator still runs.

Why should anyone believe that the future might be different than the past? Isn't the United States the largest economy in the world, the only superpower, and isn't affordable energy its mainstay? Isn't the rest of the world following in its footsteps? Won't the oil and gas and electrical utility industries, motivated by profit, take care of us? Won't it be always so?

The nation's competitiveness, economic growth, security, quality of life, and environmental protection is premised on our ability to supply ourselves with available and affordable energy. In the twentieth century, the United States was the only nation that could both become the world's largest economy and defend the world's freedom because it had affordable energy to do both. We've lived off that strength for nearly 40 years, ever grateful for the prior 40 years of infrastructure investment, power plant construction, and natural resource development, which made it all possible. The brilliant innovations and sustained investments of the period from the 1930s through the 1970s built the world's largest energy infrastructure. From the massive hydropower build-out, to the similarly huge hydrocarbon infrastructure, to the offshore crude oil and natural gas technology developments, to the commissioning of over a hundred nuclear plants, virtually all that we rely on today for 98 percent of our base energy is traceable to that grand

and great period of America's economic expansion. Only recently have we tinkered at the edges of alternative and renewable energy and environmental improvements.

But it's essentially over. Ten years on from now, those glory days will be well behind us. With the exception of a few well-endowed states, ten years from now, the nation—absent the creation of a new governance over energy, the Federal Energy Resources Board—will have relied for 50 years on an aged energy infrastructure and will begin a period of energy suffering that it has never known. As a nation, we will enter the energy abyss. There won't be enough energy. It will cost too much. People will be scared and angry. The abyss will come in the form of much higher prices, brownouts, blackouts, and shortages of liquid fuels. We'll feel like we are living in a third-world nation. It won't be a post-hurricane gasoline supply hiccup. It won't be a particular ice storm or heat wave that precipitates a short-lived brownout or blackout. It won't be an abuse of electricity or crude oil trading. It won't be a temporary price spike due to some international geopolitical upset. Rather it will be a sustained period lasting years in which the continuing high prices and frustrating shortages will impact the overall economy. There will be a multiyear drain on disposable income, changing all buying habits, from housing, to fuel, to food, to medicine. Outages, especially in extreme summer and winter weather, could play havoc with civil order and provoke disturbing consequences.

Not only the price at the pump but also the sky-high monthly electricity or natural gas bill will hit the wallet, credit card, and checkbook like never before. Household after household will hold both heated and frigid discussions about how much to adjust the thermostat in the house or apartment to try to impact next month's bill. Parents will lecture teens on how much gas they can use on a date; trips to see parents, children, and grandchildren will be postponed or canceled because of both high cost and refueling risks. Businesses and families will be hit simultaneously. Energy-intensive businesses, such as manufacturing and food processing, will see their costs soar. The economy will slide into recession; unemployment will rise inexorably. Green jobs will fail to materialize because the government will not be able to afford the required subsidies.

Government at state and federal levels will be powerless in the short term to respond. Local, state, regional, and then national anger will arise when after not months but years of the combination of shortages, outages, and high prices we ask ourselves, "What kind of a twenty-first-century country is this? How did we ever descend to this sorry state? Who did this to us?" We essentially will have done it to ourselves by not acting now to shift governance gears to a new direction.

If the nation enters the energy abyss, it also faces the slippery slope of systemic, sustained economic decline. The energy abyss is all but inevitable, unless we change our governance quickly. The pending slippery slope is avoidable if we do so. It still is possible to convert the expected downward slope to an ascendable incline if persistent grassroots efforts materialize now. In a crisis, everyday Americans respond; people will participate in solutions. The key is to avoid the crisis by acting more quickly. Just as the people of the nation said "Enough is enough" when it came to civil rights for all citizens, the people can and I hope will say "Enough is enough" when it comes to energy affordability and availability now, not later.

If the abyss happens, skeptics and critics will still believe that every price spike and gas line will be remedied by a traditional and historic return to normal. Policy makers will point fingers in every direction but at themselves. Mostly they will blame the last group in charge, whoever was the president or congressional leadership, or the energy industry. No way will they take collective responsibility. Energy companies will sing the old told-you-so tune. Right-wing and left-wing commentators will blame their opposite numbers. Special interests will demand more of their unique special interest.

Unless we act now, the new normal will be scarcity and high energy costs for a long time to come. And if we fail to act now, an increasingly committed, much less patient, national grassroots movement will inevitably arise using far more activist participatory democracy to remind the nation's representatives who is in charge of whom. They will demand that their representatives and their president solve the nation's energy and environmental challenges by doing what they could have and should have done much sooner—or face loss of office, except that the tactics will inevitably be more demonstrative. Grassroots America will insist that for the good of the nation and its future, whoever is running Congress, whoever holds the White House, turn over the future of energy and the environment to an independent regulatory agency and rid the nation of their incumbent incompetence and political arrogance.

By failing to act now, politics will have created the energy abyss. More politics will not end it. The grassroots movement will demand that elected officials give up their "political time" prerogatives to pass a new law through Congress, signed by the president that creates the "energy time" Federal Energy Resources System. The law will establish a group of presidentially appointed, Senate-confirmed governors with 14-year terms, accountable and responsible for the nation's energy and environmental well-being and security, with authority to make directional decisions. The board will then bring this nation back to centrist common sense, energy pragmatism, environmental balance, and coherent, comprehensive planning and deliver affordable energy and environmental security for the nation's short-, medium-, and long-term future. This board will bring to an end the partisan paralysis that led to the energy abyss. As the Fed has delivered financial stability for the past 97 years, the Federal Energy Resources Board (FERB) will launch the process to do the same for energy and the environment. Why wait for an energy abyss to push us in the right direction? The country can fix itself now, if it chooses to do so.

■   ■   ■   ■   ■

The United States has never had a sustained shortage of energy or a prolonged period of high prices such as will occur during the energy abyss. What will cause it, and how can I be so certain it will happen by the end of the next decade?

It will happen because 10 years on, we will have neglected the nation's base energy supplies for 50 years. The system will fail to

produce the demand we require and it will not be quickly remedied. The natural resource base and infrastructure diminished
by prohibitions on finding, developing, and building materially
more energy supplies and infrastructure from the 1980s to the
2010s, especially from 2000 to 2016 because of partisan paralysis and government dysfunction will finally be unable to supply the nation's needs. The era of reliable dependence on foreign
imports will also come to an end as the rest of the world follows
China's lead in direct contracting for their essential crude oil
supplies, shrinking the global trading market. Closer to home,
the impending restrictions on the United States importing oil
sands crude from Canada, because it is perceived by special
interests as "too dirty" for America, will result in those supplies
being shifted to Asia.

The major oil companies and major utilities will have become
so boxed into their respective niches that whatever they can do
will not be enough to meet demand. The combination of carbon management rules, decades of resistance to more domestic
crude oil access, comprehensive restrictions on tight gas shale
expansion, effective prohibitions on further expansion of coal
production, failure to invest in new nuclear plants and to resolve
nuclear waste management will combine to undermine the supply side of energy that supports today some 93 percent of our
energy needs. The 5 percent additional energy we make from
hydropower will drop as the big dams gather more silt.

Efforts to increase wind, solar, and biofuels will make progress over the next 10 years. But their net new supply contribution to the overall demand growth, coupled with their high costs
and sustained taxpayer subsidies, will contribute to the rising
price of energy without providing sufficient new supply. We'll be
squeezed by the elimination of old dirty coal plants, decommissioned nuclear plants, declining oil production, much-reduced
refinery capacity, lack of new pipelines, aging transmission lines,
lack of liquid natural gas regasification terminals, and worn out
storage infrastructure that requires ever more decommissioning
because of health and safety concerns.

The plan to reduce carbon in the atmosphere (as currently
promoted) serves to prevent companies from making otherwise

necessary hydrocarbon investments to increase supplies. It also encourages companies to take facilities, like refineries and other facilities, off-line rather than pay for emission credits, essentially a tax on pollution, under the proposed legislation. In addition to lost jobs the consequence is that the base shrinks while new high cost alternative energy supplies can't come close to meeting both demand growth and base shrinkage. The mythical notion that more efficiency and new renewable energy will satisfy the nation's future energy security will be seen as a bankrupted, ill-conceived strategy driven by an ideological cadre of anti-hydrocarbon, anti-nuclear, postindustrial special interests, helped along by venture capitalists out to make a quick buck on renewables and supported by politicians who believed popular, new, clean anything-but-oil-and-coal-and-nuclear energy would deliver them to power and incumbency.

From the special interests to the politicians, none ever understood "energy time" and the materiality and scalability of production required to sustain the nation's energy availability against our aging, depleting base energy. Looking back, we will see that their ideas and aspirations were created in "political time" and overrode the warnings and advice they received from their political and business friends and adversaries. They believed there was enough core strength in the underlying system to get them through their terms in office. Let the next group deal with the consequences. Polls said people liked green and renewable. Yes, that's true. More than that, however, people needed available and affordable. Politicians won; the nation lost.

■　■　■　■　■

As carbon management rules bite into the supplies of coal-fired electricity production, the first coal plants to go off-line will be the oldest and dirtiest because it makes no economic sense for utilities to invest new money into these facilities. Such facilities exist all over the nation, but predominantly east of the Mississippi, in the upper Midwest, Northeast, Middle Atlantic, and southeastern states. New solar facilities in the

Southwest and wind farms on the eastern slope of the Rockies are thousands of miles from where the coal plants will be taken off-line. The transmission systems that might carry such new power to serve old power customers will not have been built in time, will not carry sufficient power, and will lose dramatic amounts of power due to normal transmission inefficiency. Whatever power finally moves to old markets from new sources will be very expensive. The weather demands of summer and winter will jeopardize the stability and reliability of base-load and peak-load power generation. Just when people need power the most, it will become increasingly unreliable and expensive.

The sustained public policy debate over the costs of nuclear plants and nuclear waste storage will remain mostly unresolved as we fritter away another decade of our nation's energy future. As a result, dozens of nuclear plants will approach or pass the expirations of their licenses to operate and must be decommissioned, or at best recommissioned, a process that takes years of plant shutdown to achieve. Some states will attempt to extend licenses, but at increased risks to populations that live near or around facilities with aging reactors and unprecedented amounts of local nuclear waste storage.

New supplies of natural gas using advanced technology, which might have enabled the construction of many dozens, even hundreds, of new gas-fired electricity plants, will be constrained by restrictions on the fracturing process because of its assumed potential impact on both water movement and subsidence. The increased supplies of gas will not be sufficient to embark on a major building program of new gas plants to handle a switch from coal to gas in the upcoming next ten years. In part, this tightening of gas production through regulation was prompted by the coal industry's efforts to prevent gas from replacing coal as the low-cost energy source of choice. Because policy makers went along with the coal industry's objections, the nation will suffer from both loss of coal-fired production capacity and the lack of new gas-fired production capacity.

Sustained resistance to new domestic crude oil production on the outer continental shelf that has essentially been off limits for more than 40 years, coupled with the anticipated public policy prohibition on new offshore production within 100 miles of shore, will cause the nation's crude oil production to fall from its current 7 million barrels to 4 million per day. The increasing demands from China, India, and other developing countries for crude oil will reduce global crude exports to the United States.

Refinery closures due to carbon constraints will reduce domestic production of gasoline, diesel, and aviation fuel. Prices will rise dramatically. Taxpayer-subsidized biofuels, while taking up some of the slack, will not replace the millions of barrels per day in lost crude and oil products. The U.S. car fleet and other uses of crude oil will continue to demand some 20-plus million barrels per day of liquid fuels. We won't have the 20 million barrels to go around. Our liquid fuel supplies could drop to as low as 15 million barrels per day, leaving much of America short or just plain out of gas, or having to pay a price so high that few people can afford it. Agriculture will be hit hard, increasing food prices. Also hard-hit will be the highest population centers on the East and West coasts, the heart of the anti–offshore crude oil production contingent. All the work done to promote hybrids and electric vehicles will benefit those few who can afford such expensive cars. Ten years from now, there will be no more substantive mass transit to benefit large population centers than we have today. Buses will be crowded! Population will have grown to about 350 million Americans, and we will have about 25 percent less liquid fuel to burn among us.

Americans will be flat-out outraged. The promises of energy efficiency, wind, solar, biofuels, higher-mile-per-gallon vehicles, and battery vehicles were such sure things. Thousands of green jobs were created; hundreds of billions of dollars of taxpayer subsidies were handed over to new energy producers and new energy-efficiency initiatives, which did what they could but could not keep up. The scale of demand was far greater than anyone in policy positions ever understood. Carbon management was considered the right thing to do; and the promises of a new green economy represented the new "contract with America." Failing to comprehend the important roles of nuclear and hydrocarbon energy took us to the abyss.

We were promised we would have the energy we needed to compete, the fuel we needed to sustain our mobile lifestyles, and the affordability we expected to sustain the American way of life. Now the energy abyss will jeopardize what we could always count on: energy availability and affordability. A precious historic entitlement, affordable energy, will have been lost. Even worse, the less well-to-do in America will be reduced to an impoverished and in fact unhealthy and potentially dangerous lifestyle as a result.

Marches, name-calling, protests of every imaginable type, attacks on energy company assets, and finally urban riots on hot summer nights will bring the reality home. The nation will not have enough energy to support its economy, secure its borders, maintain its superpower status, compete internationally, and sustain our lifestyles. How could we ever have gotten into this fix? What do we do about it? How do we begin?

It should not be lost on the nation that several states will be less impacted by the energy abyss. Because of a unique combination of circumstances, Arkansas, Colorado, Louisiana, Mississippi, Montana, New Mexico, North Dakota, Oklahoma, Texas, and Wyoming will be less hurt by the energy abyss. They will suffer the same high prices but face fewer actual shortages. There are three reasons for this: The states are not densely populated, they have huge natural resources, and they have energy policies that combine old energy and new energy in ways that work for their citizens. They have invested in traditional energy resources as part of their core mix while also concentrating on new energy resources. They have crude oil, biofuels, and many have refineries; they have coal mines, natural gas, wind and solar production. They promote energy efficiency and have begun to build out a national transmission grid. Because of this, they face a potential migration of millions of Americans seeking jobs, energy security, and the chance to get lives back on track from energy shortages elsewhere. Many of these states are water and infrastructure short and cannot handle a denser population. The energy abyss at its worst will have taken the nation to a society of energy haves and have-nots. Unfortunately, it will also have diminished national self-respect, impacting social cohesion and human dignity.

■ ■ ■ ■ ■

Let's jump forward to the early years of the 2020s. We are in the thick of the energy abyss because our emerging grassroots movement ten years ago was too little too late and failed to change energy governance sooner. The latest iteration of the now-huge, angry and motivated grassroots movement turns the pain of the energy abyss to positive public policy outcomes in an effort to reverse energy shortages and the economic slippery slope. By 2022, if not sooner, when people are finally convinced that the old ways are never coming back, the Congress and president pass into law the creation of the Federal Energy Resources System. What will it do? How will it turn the slippery slope into a manageable incline, back to energy availability and affordability in a country that, as we saw earlier, has no shortage of natural resources for energy production? Can it ultimately deliver energy security and environmental sustainability?

Here's the roadmap. It starts with a short-, medium- and long-term plan that covers the next 10, then the next 15, then the next 25 years: 50 years in all during this first tranche of the new independent regulatory agency's history. The FERB's first order of business is to create a comprehensive, coherent energy plan for the nation from 2023 to 2075. Expert staff from a range of disciplines will analyze the physical, economic, social, political, technical, demographic, and environmental implications of bringing the nation back from the energy abyss. A series of engagements will take place with regional boards discussing the issues that each faces. The regional boards, on behalf of the board of governors, will consult regarding options and alternatives with leading institutions across the country from industry, academia, government, community interests, consumers, and environmentalists. A plan will be developed and finalized with key parameters laid out that includes energy supplies from all sources to meet demand, key technology decisions timed to take advantage of energy advances; management of the nation's gaseous waste and carbon footprint, and renewed infrastructure encompassing multiple states and regions.

The plan will take decades to implement and incentives and subsidies to accomplish. It will require massive education and training, capital investment, construction and engineering resources. Congress, the White House, industry, labor, environmentalists, and consumers will be informed. Legal requirements will be identified. Congress, the president and the ongoing grassroots movement will be motivated to seek consensus rapidly. Appropriate laws will be enacted, signed, and implemented. The laws will be written such that judicial review is simplified, accelerated, denying lucrative financial awards to defendants or plaintiffs in the national interest and requiring that all parties to a lawsuit pay their own way regardless of outcomes. Regulatory bodies will retain authority to hold states, companies, municipalities, unions and other organizations, and individuals accountable under respective laws and regulations. Financial reporting to eliminate fraud, waste, and abuse of funds will have clear transparency requirements. Appropriate agencies will be staffed to govern the inevitable human or systemic failures, given the massive public and private capital investments in rebuilding the nation's energy and environmental capacity.

SHORT-TERM PLANS

Public health and safety requires stabilization of electricity supplies and demand. Basic living means personal transportation needs must be balanced. In the first few years, let's face it, the nation will have to adopt a rationing system of rolling electricity availability to cover the most people as fairly as possible. Likewise, a system of liquid fuel rationing will be required to balance transportation availability across the country. The have and have-not inequities must be addressed in the interests of national social cohesion, economic justice, and respect for fellow citizens. It took decades of flawed, special-interest politics to get to the energy abyss. It will take a few years of public endurance to better balance demand and supply to meet constitutional guarantees of life, liberty, and the pursuit of happiness for all. Is it socialism or communism? No more than rationing was during World War II. The problem is bigger than the individual. Government's role is to manage outcomes in the interests of society. The market remains free; it is temporarily constrained in its effects due to regulatory requirements. The urgency of the situation demands national and state equalization of distribution of supply and demand.

In the first ten years, the most correctible problems are addressed first. Carbon emission regulations are suspended due to the economic emergency. They will be reinstated and revised downward to even lower emission levels over the life of the total plan. Hydrocarbon resources are opened for development in a planned manner. It's not "Drill, baby, drill!" Instead, it is a reasoned plan that raises hydrocarbon production of coal, natural gas, and crude oil from domestic resources to achieve equilibrium of supply and demand based on expectations of fleet needs over the short and medium term.

The plan requires extraordinary environmental safeguards to enable both protection and restoration of land and water resources. Biofuels remain an important part of the mix. Plans will be brought forward, however, ultimately to transition completely away from the internal combustion engine for most personal mobility and to replace it with battery electric and hydrogen fuel cell vehicles over the medium term. Doing this requires a comprehensive transition of hundreds of millions of vehicles over 25 years, the production capacity to build them, the infrastructure to fuel them, and the carbon management plans to virtually eliminate both hydrocarbon and biofuel liquids as a primary source of energy for personal mobility. Thus, while the outcome is medium term, actions must begin in the short term, building on where the nation is at the time. All major municipalities will be required to develop mass transit plans along select transportation corridors; ultimately, this mass transit will be electric-powered systems.

Electricity supply in the short term will be assisted by recommissioning, where possible, recently decommissioned production facilities. Safety, reliability, and infrastructure standards and requirements are demanding for recommissioning, whether they are coal or nuclear facilities. Natural gas drilling will be expanded, and rapid construction of combined cycle gas plants will be encouraged. Such expansion will take into account the role of gas in balancing output from solar and wind energy expansions at the same time. New generation solar technologies will be tested for their long-term potential impact on the energy system. Coal gasification with carbon capture and sequestration will be encouraged for new coal facilities of 1,000 megawatts or larger. Coal, utility, oil, pipeline, and construction companies will be granted authority to work together to develop regional sequestration infrastructure plans in a timely manner. Liability legislation will protect society's interests and enable utilities to proceed.

New nuclear plants and expansions, utilizing common designs, yielding economies of scale due to the replication of structures, technology and equipment, siting, security, liability, and environmental protection plans, will be promoted. Rate-setting mechanisms at state levels will be redesigned to pay for front-end construction and engineering costs through to commissioning of the new plants. Accelerated depreciation allowances will enable consumers to benefit from ultimate rate reductions, enabling the costs of nuclear energy to match more closely the costs from traditional hydrocarbon sources. Nuclear waste management will be resolved in principle, including nuclear waste reprocessing, and the plans for storage, more than likely a final build-out of Yucca Mountain, will be implemented over the medium term.

MEDIUM-TERM PLANS

The urgency of the short-term energy abyss crisis will lead to a national reconciliation of sorts where the extreme left and right discover the futility of holding out against the centrist middle of America. The nation's U-shaped curve inverts back to its historic bell shape. Partisanship will now mostly be punished at the polls, even while the political parties offer programs and priorities that distinguish choices for the electorate to consider. Free speech

will still exist but the public will find little value in the coun-
terproductive ranting of fringe right- and left-wing radio, television, and web-based hucksters. Free market economics within
the context of the overall FERB plan will replace the rationing
and heavy management of draconian, crisis-based plans, which
are soon forgotten because of the sustained economic expansion
under way across the nation that positively impacts every sector
of society.

The transition away from internal combustion engines and
the build-out of the new American manufacturing infrastructure
and new car fleet, relying on battery electric and hydrogen fuel
cell vehicles, will gain momentum. Infrastructure will be well
on its way to providing both ubiquity and homogeneity of new
supply while subsidies are offered to local retailers to sustain traditional supplies for the remaining fleet of older-technology vehicles. Hydrogen and electricity, initially supplied from any source
available, including coal, natural gas, and crude oil, will begin
a long-term shift to lower-carbon sources. Eventually hydrogen
will be produced from the electrolysis of water using nuclear and
renewable energy, and batteries are recharged from such sources.
Crude oil production, together with biofuels, begins to retrench
as market demand declines based on new transportation technologies. However, both forms of liquid fuels will continue to be
required in the FERB's long-term plans because of transportation requirements for off-road and on-road heavy transportation, agriculture, aviation and marine uses, and support of the
petrochemicals industry. As part of the industry retrenchment,
social plans will be required to provide for the employability and
resettlement of impacted workers.

A major electricity production and transmission build-out will
be under way across the nation. The FERB plan to double the
2025 fleet of nuclear plants and then to double it again in the
long-term plan will be executed. Manpower, financial capital,
and construction and engineering will be scarce resources, but
meeting the demand adds to the economic recovery. Large coal
gasification and carbon capture and sequestration build-outs will
be progressing in more than a hundred sites around the nation.
New solar technology, which delivers up to a record 50 percent

efficiency based on advances in nanotechnology and materials science, will be delivering both residential and commercial distributed power generation at kilowatt-hour rates that compete with utility-provided power from nuclear and clean coal sources. Transmission technology improvements and new transmission line build-outs will enable solar, wind, nuclear, and clean coal electricity production to move literally coast to coast by the end of the medium term. Supply and demand will re-achieve equilibrium; reserve capacity will be available to ensure energy security regardless of regional weather events. Affordability will be directly related to the supply availability, which now rivals the best experiences of the late twentieth century but without the carbon emissions.

LONG-TERM PLANS

The United States will take international center stage for energy availability, affordability, and environmental sustainability. It will have recaptured leadership for innovation, technology, manufacturing, economic, energy, and social security. No other nation on Earth will enjoy the benefits of affordable, clean, virtually carbon-free energy for both electric power and transportation to the degree America will have reached. During the 2060s, because of the comprehensive and coordinated efforts of the FERB, the United States will achieve carbon emission reductions that will bring it to 80 percent below 2010 levels. It will be the first large nation in the Organisation for Economic Co-operation and Development (OECD), the organization that links developed countries to one another, to achieve the objective that dates back to that time period.

The FERB will be studied, analyzed, replicated, and implemented across the Group of Twenty countries. An international cooperation will emerge that interconnects planning and implementation, capital financing, manpower development, and environmental stewardship best practices across these countries.

Oil and the Organization of Petroleum Exporting Countries (OPEC) will not have disappeared from modern geopolitics and economic reality. However, the roles that both will play are minor among countries that have emulated the strategy and planning of the U.S. FERB. The world will always need oil for certain applications. However, the supply/demand balance issues that used to drive nations, societies, companies, and consumers to desperation will have receded. OPEC countries actually will say they saw it coming. The mature societies will have adapted; the ideologically extreme countries will be in local distress. As an example, Saudi Arabia will become a prosperous information-based economy balancing a combination of industries that supply an ever-increasing population with intellectually challenging but purposeful careers and a promising long-term transitional future. Iran will regress, despite its intelligentsia and long history of social and cultural leadership, to an Afghanistan-like Stone Age existence where extremism will be a way of life and the migration of people out of the repressive and immutable society will be irreversible.

■ ■ ■ ■ ■

With "energy time" planning and implementation, there is every opportunity to evolve our economy and infrastructure over the next 50 to 60 years to a virtually carbon-free energy supply system that meets essentially any level of demand. If grassroots America begins now and helps change the nation's energy and environmental governance to an independent regulatory agency, it will happen sooner; if we can't get it together and instead enter the energy abyss and implement the Federal Energy Resources Board when we are more deeply mired in energy problems, it will be later. "Political time" energy decisions are dangerous to our economy, competitiveness, security, lifestyles, and social cohesion. We must reform our structures and processes to vastly reduce energy and environmental risks, as we did for our financial system nearly a hundred years ago. The United States is on a path to learn this the hard way. Unfortunately I'm of the view that we will not act sooner and will only act later. Thus within ten years we will experience the energy abyss. Companies, special interests, and incumbent politicians will reject the arguments this book makes and convince themselves that they know better. Grassroots efforts will fall short in the near term and be unable to overcome the entrenched establishment. But there should be no doubt, we will need a grassroots effort to restore the equanimity and economic security that the energy time requirements of our society warrant to offset the unfortunate but real political time consequences of partisan paralysis and government dysfunction in effect for too many decades.

This grassroots effort is not about incriminating individuals for what the system and process created. America's energy and environmental future went off the rails a long time ago. This is not a 2000 or 2010 issue alone. This has been a systemic, long-term, aberrant, politically selfish, special-interest-driven function of too much prosperity, inherited without merit, from predecessors who exploited nature and the environment to create an unsustainable energy bubble that eventually received insufficient reinvestment and lacked the natural capacity to carry on to future generations.

Unfortunately for today's U.S. population, the problems are larger and more intractable than the current political system can resolve. We have resorted to extraordinary extremism on the right and the left and allowed info-tainers to define the terms of debate. So we are now suffering and will suffer further the consequences of the misinformation, disinformation, and lack of energy information that characterizes our society today. We will pay a huge price ten years out and even before then.

Why do we hate the oil companies? Because politicians have taught us to by using them as scapegoats for their own inability to lead and because the oil companies have been content, along with utilities, to sit it out under a rock, making money all the while. In fact, the energy companies and special interests are party to the whole mess, given their fealty to the extraordinary fragmentation that our system has created and thus deserve some of our disdain. However, they are not the root cause of our coming descent into the energy abyss. The root cause is our dysfunctional, myopic political system, and its elected leadership, that fails over and over again to address national energy planning for the short, medium, and long term in a rational, economic way.

But all is not lost. We are a democracy. We are participants in the world's oldest and most successful experiment in self-managing our society and its future. Like all nations, we have the opportunity to decide to change. Our system may be messier and clumsier than others, but in the end we can make it work. Our system is not without setbacks, including self-imposed, own-goal-line calamities. We will emerge from the energy abyss crisis with a renewed understanding of the importance of participatory democracy, a renewed sense of nation, and a new commitment to social cohesion and the importance of looking out for our fellow citizens. And finally we will emerge from the energy abyss with a secure, economically competitive, socially just society that thrives on growth and purpose fueled by energy availability and affordability, and we will hand on to future generations a legacy of environmental sustainability that will last for all ages.

ACKNOWLEDGMENTS

My wife, Karen (Otazo), first brought authorship and exemplary hard work, deep, probing insights, and the passion to finish her books into our London home several years ago. So for her example and accomplishments I thank her first and foremost for showing me the way to bring this book across the finish line. Her background in energy (many years at Arco) and executive leadership assisted me in framing and cataloguing the multitude of issues an energy solutions book requires. My appreciation is ongoing. My love is hers. My entire family, my daughters, granddaughters and grandson, their dads, parents, brothers and sisters and their families, has assisted by shaping my perspectives and bringing joy to life. I hope my support, seriousness, and humor have returned in kind.

Politics and political behavior have fascinated me since the day my parents put a television in their home. It was August 1952 and the only shows I remember were the Republican and Democratic conventions, along with the *Howdy Doody Show*. Somehow their simultaneity (or do I mean similarity?) triggered my life-long fascination with the content and process of politics. Later my decision to study political science brought me into contact with a number of brilliant mentors who helped me build the foundations and frameworks for a lifetime of learning. Michael Suleiman, K. Erik Solem, and Louis Douglas, among others, all at Kansas State University, patiently and personally stoked my curiosity and provided the fusion of ideas and thinking that has sewn participatory democracy and government to my heart and mind.

Business and economics are to me what arts and sciences are to others. Essentially they create value and purpose for individuals to sustain careers while enabling whole societies to become whatever they will become. I thank hundreds of colleagues who helped me along the way at GE, Nortel, AlliedSignal (now Honeywell International), and Royal Dutch Shell. After university I can't imagine a more sustainable learning journey than to have participated in the work life and executive leadership of these organizations. I would especially thank Al Hill, Bob Gosser, Carmen Romeo, Howard Pollock, Nel Wieland, Sumner Kibbe, Dave Momot, Don Bussick, Dave Berges, David Genever-Watling, Dennis Rocheleau, Bronson Hindle, Frank Doyle, Larry Bossidy, and Jack Welch from GE for hundreds of lessons over many years. Dan Burnham, Don Redlinger, Gwen Payne, Lou Sears, Pete Mercer, and again, Larry Bossidy, at AlliedSignal provided me the gateway to an international curriculum and career. Gary Donahee, Kate Donnelly, Jewell Weatherly, Kerry Bessey, Dennis Melton, Phil Randall, and Tim Williams were part of an extraordinary team at an unusual pre-dot.com growth surge at Nortel. We learned to paddle hard and fast together in the new digital age.

Royal Dutch Shell leaders are life-long students of global energy and the environment. With lessons learned in science and "hard knocks," their willingness to share what they know is a gift to the world at large. Hundreds of scientists, engineers and technologists, risk-takers, entrepreneurs and business leaders were kind enough to take me around the world from the depths of the earth to the heights of the atmosphere for my final corporate learning journey. In particular I appreciated the wisdom and insights of Mark Moody-Stuart, Phil Watts, Jeroen van der Veer, Maarten van den Bergh, Steve Miller, Malcolm Brinded, Linda Cook, Aarnout Loudon, Lodewijk van Wachem, Beat Hess, Peter Voser, Garmt Louw, Michael Reiff, Lee Patterson, Mike Wilkinson, Hugh Mitchell, Govert Boeles, Rick Brown, James Smith, Clive Mather, Leslie Mays, Jan Schaapsmeerders, Nick Turner, Peter Otten, Liz Morrish, Ellen Middendorp, Roxanne Decyk, Sharon Rapp, Randy Braud, Cathy Lamboley, Marvin Odum, Julian Dalzell, John Jefferson, Phil Metzler, Francene Young, Albert Myres, Kevin Ilges, Brian Malnak, Kim Paisley, Chris Bozman, Mary Monaco, and Dick Francis, and so many more colleagues, each of whom was generous with their time, patient with understanding and committed to getting things done.

I've benefited over many years from bigger-than-life advisors and friends whose counsel and challenge have helped to sharpen my focus and round my edges, including Rodger Martin, whose wise counsel helped guide me since grade school; Rick Day, who worked with me from the outside looking in throughout my corporate career; Senator Chuck Hagel, Senator John Breaux, Ron Liebman, Secretary of State Hillary Clinton, Secretary of Agriculture Tom Vilsack, Secretary of Energy Sam Bodman, Deputy Energy Secretary Clay Sell, Assistant Energy Secretary Andy Karsner, Assistant Energy Secretary Karen Harbert, General Jim Jones, Congressmen Robert Walker, Ken Brady, Al Green, Gene Green and Congresswoman Sheila Jackson Lee, Alan Lloyd, Ken Smith and Red Cavaney, whose wise counsel and guidance helped open the doors and windows of the nation's capital to me; Marc Morial, Alexis Herman, Mike Critelli, Robert Taylor, and Charles Hamilton, and other colleagues from the National Urban League Trustee Board, who never allow one another to forget social justice and why we are here and to help our fellow citizens with whatever needs they bring with them. Walter Ulrich, Conrad Lautenbacher, Harvey Lunenfeld, Jane Roberts, Brenda McDuffie, and Stephen White, Diana Espitia, and Arlene McCarthy, who helped to launch the grass roots efforts to provide enduring solutions for energy and the environment via Citizens for Affordable Energy, Inc.; Jeff Moseley, Tracye McDaniel, Dan Wolterman, Jodie Giles, Chip Carlisle, Dan Bellows, Pat Oxford, and Jeff Love, gifted colleagues from the Greater Houston Partnership who while outside the energy industry know its inherent value to society; James Calloway, Gene Vaughan, and Catherine Mosbacher, who care deeply about our society's future and the relationship of energy and the environment to that future through their work at the Center for Houston's Future; Noel Lateef, brilliant CEO of the Foreign Policy Association, who links the world together through study and engagement; Napier Collyns, Peter Schwartz, Barbara Heinzen, and Art Kleiner, longtime friends from Global Business Partnership who network the world and link us to the future through realistic scenarios; John Boudreau, Pam Stepp, and Pat Wright, dedicated professionals who helped me back into the United States after a decade abroad; my Houston friends who challenge and deepen my thinking and commitment to the needs of energy, environment, and society, Mayor Bill White, Howard Jefferson, Lane Sloan, Peter Brown, Christopher Ross, Marcus Davis, Jerry Davis, Marty McVey; Aquil Busrai, whose faith and cultural understanding remain forever a beacon of integrity; Eliot Jacques, who guided my thinking about organization and how work gets done; and Dale and Allyson Brian, friends who keep me grounded in the hard work of sustainability while nurturing Karen's and my family farm and preserving Lime Valley Mill.

My special thanks are extended to the community of persons who have helped me bring this book to you. The insights and support that Jim Levine and Kerry Evans from Levine Greenberg Literary Agency, Inc., and Alessandra Bastagli, Michelle Fitzgerald, Sarah Thomas, Donna Cherry, Jake Klisivitch, and Colleen Lawrie from Palgrave Macmillan have provided me are truly special. In addition Alice Brink, who assisted me with ideas, structure, and text for speeches across the nation, as well as Congressional testimony, on so many occasions during my final years at Shell, also critiqued my writing, and helped me build the chapters and complete the book. I cannot thank her enough. While doing my best to write on difficult and challenging topics, I'll no doubt fall short of perfection. For any mistakes, I apologize to the reader and all interested parties.

John Hofmeister

NOTES

INTRODUCTION

1. The Harris Poll, Harris Interactive. In 2005, only 3 percent of respondents considered the oil industry "honest and trustworthy." In a 2009 poll, more than 60 percent of respondents believed that oil companies were doing a bad job.
2. *Meet the Press,* June 11, 2006.

CHAPTER 1

1. David M. Dickson, "Former Oil Exec: Gas Rationing Needed," *Washington Times,* September 15, 2008.
2. Daniel Sperling and Deborah Gordon, *Two Billion Cars: Driving Toward Sustainability* (New York: Oxford University Press, 2009).

CHAPTER 3

1. William Tucker, *Terrestrial Energy: How Nuclear Energy Will Lead the Green Revolution and End America's Energy Odyssey* (Bartleby Press, 2008).
2. Elizabeth Shogren, "Windmills Called Threat to Condors," *San Francisco Chronicle,* September 14, 1999.
3. U.S. Energy Information Administration, "Energy in Brief," http://tonto. eia.doe.gov/energy_in_brief/energy_subsidies.cfm

CHAPTER 4

1. A speech by HRH the Prince of Wales to launch the Legal Sector Alliance, London, December 10, 2008, www.princeofwales.gov.uk.
2. Steve Cohen, "Recycling Street Waste," *The New York Observer,* July 10, 2008.

CHAPTER 5

1. H.R. 3089: No More Excuses Energy Act of 2007, www.govtrack.us.
2. Congressman John Culberson mailer to constituents, 2008.

3. George F. Will, "Dark Green Doomsayers," *Washington Post,* February 15, 2009.
4. "Gore Issues Challenge to Repower America: 100% Clean Energy in 10 Years," posted on July 17, 2008, www.repoweramerica.com.
5. Kent Garber, "Obama Stops Short of Adopting Gore's Ambitious Climate Goal," *U.S. News & World Report,* July 17, 2008.
6. Daniel Whitten and Catherine Dodge, "Bush Lifts Ban on U.S. Offshore Oil, Gas Drilling," www.bloomberg.com, July 14, 2008.
7. Alex Kaplun, "Coal Industry Group Linked to a Dozen Forged Cap-and-Trade Letters," *New York Times,* August 4, 2009.

CHAPTER 6

1. Transcript, U.S. House Committee on the Judiciary Antitrust Task Force and Competition Policy, May 22, 2008.

CHAPTER 8

1. Business and Industry Sector Ratings, www.gallup.com, 2009.

BIBLIOGRAPHY

Beckjord, Eric S., ed. *The Future of Nuclear Power: An Interdisciplinary MIT Study*. Cambridge: Massachusetts Institute of Technology, 2003.

Burrough, Bryan. *The Big Rich: The Rise and Fall of the Greatest Texas Oil Fortunes*. New York: The Penguin Press, 2009.

Carter, Luther J. *Nuclear Imperatives and Public Trust: Dealing With Radioactive Waste*. Washington, DC: Resources for the Future, Inc., 1987.

Committee on Alternatives and Strategies for Future Hydrogen Production and Use, Board on Energy and Environmental Systems, Division on Engineering and Physical Sciences, National Research Council and National Academy of Engineering of the National Academies. *The Hydrogen Economy: Opportunities, Costs, Barriers, and R&D Needs*. Washington, DC: The National Academies Press, 2004.

Committee on Global Oil and Gas, National Petroleum Council. *Hard Truths: Facing the Hard Truths about Energy*. Washington, DC: National Petroleum Council, 2007.

Committee on Review of the FreedomCar and Fuel Research Program, Phase 1, Board on Energy and Environmental Systems, Division on Engineering and Physical Sciences, Transportation Research Board, National Research Council of the National Academies. *Review of the research program of the FreedomCar and fuel partnership*. Washington, DC: National Academies Press, 2005.

Deutch, John and James R. Schlesinger, chairs. *National Security Consequences of U.S. Oil Dependency: Independent Task Force Report No. 58*. Washington, DC: Council on Foreign Relations, 2006.

Energy Security Leadership Council. *A National Strategy for Energy Security: Recommendations to the Nation on Reducing U.S. Oil Dependence*. Washington, DC: Securing America's Energy Future, 2008.

Friedman, Thomas L. *Hot, Flat, and Crowded: Why We Need A Green Revolution—and How It Can Renew America*. New York: Farrar, Straus and Giroux, 2008.

Gelbspan, Ross. *Boiling Point: How Politicians, Big Oil and Coal, Journalists, and Activists Are Fueling the Climate Crisis—and What We Can Do to Avert Disaster*. New York: Basic Books. 2004.

Goodell, Jeff. *Big Coal: The Dirty Secret Behind America's Energy Future*. New York: Mariner Books, 2007.

Gore, Al. *An Inconvenient Truth: The Planetary Emergency of Global Warming and What We Can Do About It*. New York: Rodale, 2006.

Greenspan, Alan. *The Age of Turbulence: Adventures in a New World*. New York: Penguin Books, 2007.

Greider, William. *Secrets of the Temple: How the Federal Reserve Runs the Country.* New York: Simon & Schuster Paperbacks, 1987.

Heinberg, Richard. *The Party's Over: Oil, War and the Fate of Industrial Societies.* Gabriola Island, BC, Canada: New Society Publishers, 2003.

Hoffman, Andrew J. *Carbon Strategies: How Leading Companies Are Reducing Their Climate Change Footprint.* Ann Arbor: The University of Michigan Press, 2007.

Holbrook, Don A. *Who Moved My Smokestack? America's Failure to Protect Our Jobs and Stop the Erosion of the American Dream.* Xlibris, 2008.

Horner, Christopher C. *The Politically Incorrect Guide to Global Warming and Environmentalism.* Washington, DC: Regnery Publishing, Inc., 2007.

———. *Red Hot Lies: How Global Warming Alarmists Use Threats, Fraud, and Deception to Keep You Misinformed.* Washington, DC: Regnery Publishing Inc., 2008.

Inslee, Jay and Bracken Hendricks. *Apollo's Fire: Igniting America's Clean Energy Economy.* Washington, DC: Island Press, 2008.

Jet Stream Contexts to 2025: Global Scenarios and Mapping Tools. London: Shell International Limited, 2004.

Khosla, Vinod. *Biofuels: Think Outside the Barrel.* PowerPoint presentation, Khosla Ventures, August 2006.

———. *Is Ethanol Controversial? Should it be?* White paper, September 2006.

———. *Imagining the Future of Gasoline: Separating Reality from Blue-sky Dreaming?* White paper, September, 2006.

———. *A Near Term Energy Solution.* White paper, September 2006.

Klaus, Vaclav. *Blue Planet in Green Shackles: What Is Endangered: Climate or Freedom?* Washington, DC: Competitive Enterprise Institute, 2007.

Kunstler, James Howard. *The Long Emergency, Surviving the End of Oil, Climate Change, and Other Converging Catastrophes of the Twenty-first Century.* New York: Grove Press, 2005.

McKinsey & Company. *Reducing U.S. Greenhouse Gas Emissions: How Much at What Cost?* McKinsey & Co. and The Conference Board, December, 2007.

National Petroleum Council. *Balancing Natural Gas Policy: Fueling the Demands of a Growing Economy, Volume II, Integrated Report.* Washington, DC: National Petroleum Council, 2003.

Pickens, T. Boone. *The First Billion Is the Hardest: Reflections on a Life of Comebacks and America's Energy Future.* New York: Crown Publishing, 2008

Reed, Alan. *Precious Air: The Kyoto Protocol and Profit in the Global Warming Game.* Albuquerque, NM: Green Fields America, 2003.

Reisner, Marc. *Cadillac Desert: The American West and Its Disappearing Water.* New York: Viking, 1986.

Ross, Christopher E. H. and Lane E. Sloan. *Terra Incognita: A Navigation Aid for Energy Leaders.* Tulsa, OK: Pennwell Books, 2007.

Shuster, Joseph M. *Beyond Fossil Fools: The Roadmap to Energy Independence by 2040.* Edina, MN: Beaver's Pond Press, 2008.

Simmons, Matthew R. *Twilight in the Desert: The Coming Saudi Oil Shock and the World Economy.* Hoboken, NJ: John Wiley and Sons, Inc., 2005.

Sperling, Daniel and Deborah Gordon. *Two Billion Cars: Driving toward Sustainability.* New York: Oxford University Press, 2009.

Spiegel, Eric and Neil McArthur with Rob Norton. *Energy Shift*. New York: McGraw-Hill, 2009.

Stoel Rives Biofuels Team, *The Law Of Biofuels: A Guide to Business and Legal Issues*. Stoel Rives, LLP, 2006.

Tertzakian, Peter. *The End of Energy Obesity: Breaking Today's Energy Addiction for a Prosperous and Secure Tomorrow*. Hoboken, NJ: John Wiley & Sons Inc., 2009.

Tucker, William. *Terrestrial Energy: How Nuclear Power Will Lead the Green Revolution and End America's Energy Odyssey*. Savage, MD: Bartleby Press, 2008.

United States Senate, Permanent Subcommittee on Investigations, Committee on Governmental Affairs. *Gas Prices: How Are They Really Set?* Washington, DC: 2002.

U.S. Department of Energy, Energy Efficiency and Renewable Energy. *Hydrogen, Fuel Cells and Infrastructure Technologies Program Multi-Year Research, Development and Demonstration Plan*. Washington, DC: rev. 2007.

U.S. Federal Trade Commission, Bureau of Economics. *The Petroleum Industry: Mergers, Structural Change, and Antitrust Enforcement*. Federal Trade Commission staff study. Washington DC: 2004.

White, R. Stephen. *Energy for the Public: The Case for Increased Nuclear Fission Energy*. BookSurge Publishing, 2005.

Winston, Andrew S. *Green Recovery: Get Lean, Get Smart, and Emerge From the Downturn on Top*. Boston: Harvard Business Press, 2009.

Yergin, Daniel. *The Prize: The Epic Quest for Oil, Money and Power*. New York: Free Press, 1991, rev. 2008.

Zoellner, Tom. *Uranium: War, Energy, and the Rock That Shaped the World*. New York, Viking Penguin, 2009.

INDEX

AB32, 147
American Petroleum Institute (API),
    6, 17, 82, 119, 130, 132
anti-trust laws, 118–20, 123
Arctic National Wildlife Refuge, 77
Aviation Industries of China
    (AVIC), 61

Barton, Joe, 64, 164, 165
"big rules," 194–95
  biofuels
  climate change and, 66
  energy demand and, 20
  energy independence and, 24,
    29–30
  as energy source, 35, 49–53,
    56–58, 197, 199
  environmental protection and,
    203
  free market and, 100–1, 109–10
  future of, 224, 227–28, 231, 233
  government and, 185
  oil industry and, 117, 119, 121–22
  politics and, 78, 81, 164–67,
    169–71
  technology and, 201
Bloomberg, Michael, 91, 92
Blumenthal, Richard, 91
Bodman, Sam, 184
British Petroleum (BP), 52, 99, 116,
    118
Broadwater, 89, 91–92, 93
Bush, George W., 51, 57, 81, 84, 92,
    115, 119–20, 122, 136, 163,
    165, 172, 183–84

Cadillac Desert (Reisner), 154
cap-and-trade, 72, 74, 82
Carter, Jimmy, 2

Cavaney, Red, 120
Center for American Progress,
    78, 169
Chernobyl, 89
Chevron, 3, 6, 99, 118
Chu, Stephen, 40, 57, 101
Citizens for Affordable Energy,
    7, 64, 215
clean coal, 37, 78, 104, 107, 121,
    170, 198, 234
  see also coal
clean energy, 7, 35, 48, 76, 78, 100,
    102, 105, 122–23
Clean Skies internet television, 122
Clinton, Bill, 113–15, 184
coal, 36–37
  see also clean coal
Committee on the Judiciary
    Anti-Trust Task Force and
    Competition Policy, 97
competition, 120–24
ConocoPhillips, 3, 6, 99, 116, 118
Contract with America, 184, 227
Copenhagen climate conference, 64
Culberson, John, 76
Curb Hopper, 34

DeLay, Tom, 155–56
Department of Commerce (DOC),
    186–87
Department of Energy (DOE),
    184–85, 189
Dingell, John, 182, 190
Domenici, Pete, 164

Eco-Marathon, 33
electric power, sources for, 36–47
  coal, 36–37
  geothermal energy, 45

hydrogen fuel cells, 45–46
hydropower, 44–45
natural gas, 39
nuclear power, 39–41
solar energy, 43–44
subsidies for, 46–47
wind power, 41–42
energy independence, 7–8, 21,
    23–32, 75, 77–78, 81, 93–94,
    108, 113, 117, 119, 121,
    124, 156, 164, 169, 173,
    210, 215, 222
energy supply, 197–99
environmental justice, 86–87, 216
environmental protection, 201–3
Environmental Protection Agency
    (EPA), 87, 155, 172, 185,
    201–3, 212
ethanol, 49–52, 59
ExxonMobil, 6, 52, 82, 99, 113–14,
    116, 118, 172
Exxon Valdez, 4, 129, 138, 172

Federal Energy Resources Board,
    196–99, 201–2, 204, 207,
    209–10, 221, 223, 235
Federal Energy Resources System,
    195, 214, 219, 223, 229
Federal Reserve, 193–95
fossil fuels, 47–49

gasification, 15, 38, 89–90, 168,
    198, 224, 232, 233
General Electric, 1, 119, 146
geothermal energy, 35, 36, 45, 117,
    197, 199, 201, 203
Gingrich, Newt, 76
Goldwater, Barry, 160
Gore, Al, 77–78, 81, 184
Green, Gene, 182
greenhouse gases, 62, 64, 76, 147,
    172, 202
Gulf of Mexico, 29, 50,
    113–14, 166
Gulf War, 2

Harbert, Karen, 184–85, 189
Hastert, Dennis, 132
Houston Technology Center, 145
Hubbard, Al, 119–20, 122, 165

hurricanes, 26, 29, 43, 58, 131,
    175–76, 221
    Gustave, 16
    Ike, 13, 16
    Katrina, 3, 115, 129, 138, 175
    Rita, 3, 115
hybrid and electric engines, 53–55
hydrogen fuel cells, 21, 45–46,
    56–57, 58, 59, 199, 201,
    231, 233
hydropower, 35–36, 44–47

immigration, 95, 145, 148
infrastructure, 203–5
Iran, 163, 213, 235
Iraq, 5, 163, 212
Issa, Darrell, 115

J.P. Morgan, 193

Kunstler, James, 144
Kuwait Oil, 118

land use
    development and, 151–52
    population density and, 154–57
    sustainability and, 152–54
Lautenbaucher, Conrad, 187
Limbaugh, Rush, 69, 80
liquefied natural gas (LNG), 90
Long Emergency, The
    (Kunstler), 144

manifest destiny, 145–46, 149–50,
    157–58
Markey, Ed, 73, 178
Kerr McGee, 116
McGovern, George, 180
Minerals Management Service
    (MMS), 86, 186–88
Mulva, Jim, 3
Murkowski, Frank, 85
Murkowski, Lisa, 85

NASCAR, 33, 125, 135
National Association of
    Manufacturing (NAM), 95
National Oceanic and Atmospheric
    Administration (NOAA),
    186–87

natural gas, 11, 14–15, 39, 57–58
Natural Resources Defense Council
    (NRDC), 91
Nixon, Richard, 1, 25, 58, 110, 173,
    180, 184, 212
No More Excuses Energy Act
    (2007), 76
nuclear power
    energy industry and, 117,
        120–22
    as energy source, 34–36, 39–41,
        46–47, 59
    free market and, 102, 104–9
    future of, 197–201, 203, 206,
        220, 224–26, 228, 232–34
    growing demand for, 9, 11, 15,
        19, 21
    land use and, 145
    politics and, 76, 78, 89, 164, 166,
        168–71, 173
    public perception of, 137

Obama, Barack, 26–27, 40, 57, 81,
    92, 101, 110, 122, 172, 180,
    189, 210
offshore drilling, 4, 15, 29, 32, 42,
    48, 76, 81, 83, 85, 89, 96,
    99, 166, 169, 185–86,
    188, 220, 227
Organization of Petroleum
    Exporting Countries (OPEC),
    27–28, 98–101, 185, 197, 203,
    234–35
O'Reilly, Dave, 3

Palin, Sarah, 75, 77, 84
particulate waste, 37–38, 48, 62, 71
Paterson, David, 91–92
Pelosi, Nancy, 182, 209
Petrobras, 118
Petronas, 118
Pickens, T. Boone, 39, 100
population density, 154–57
public utility commissions (PUCs),
    102–5, 140

Reagan, Ronald, 180
Reid, Harry, 40–41, 183
Reisner, Marc, 154
Repower America, 78–79, 169

Rockefeller, John D., 136
Russert, Tim, 3
Russia, 88, 99, 163

Saro Wiwa, Ken 172
Saudi Aramco, 118, 139
Sensenbrenner, Jim, 178–79
Shell Oil Company
    author's experiences with, 1–7
    conservation and, 143, 147
    consumers and, 125–30, 133,
        135–36, 138–39
    Eco-Marathon event, 33
    energy industry and, 114, 116, 118
    environment and, 186–88
    ethanol and, 52
    free market and, 99–100
    gasification technology, 38
    government and, 175–76
    Hurricane Ike and, 16
    hydrogen fuel cell technology and,
        56
    politics and, 82–90, 92–93,
        171–72
    solar panel manufacturing, 43
solar energy, 43–44
Specter, Arlen, 3
Spitzer, Eliot, 91
Standard Oil, 4, 118, 136, 141
Stephens, Ted, 85
Stupak, Bart, 178–79
subsidies, 46–47
synthetic gas, 2, 38

Tarbell, Ida, 136
tax credits, 76
technology choices, 199–201
Thomas, Bill, 176
Three Mile Island, 40, 89
Total, 99
TransCanada, 89–90
transportation, energy for, 47–58
    biofuels, 49–53
    fossil fuels, 47–49
    hybrid and electric engines,
        53–55
    hydrogen fuel cell vehicles,
        56–57
    natural gas, 57–58
Tucker, William, 39–40

Valero Energy, 82
Venezuela, 26, 48, 98, 163
Vietnam War, 7, 180, 212

waste management
    gaseous, 70, 71–74
    liquid, 66–67
    physical, 70
Waste Management (company), 66
Waters, Maxine, 97–98
Waxman, Henry, 69, 73, 182, 190
Welch, Jack, 146
Will, George, 76
wind power
    consumers and, 128
    energy independence and, 32

energy industry and, 116–17,
    121, 123
as energy source, 34–36, 39,
    41–42
free market and, 104, 106–7,
    109–10
future of, 195, 197–98, 200–1,
    203, 224, 226–28,
    232, 234
growing demand for, 11, 14–15,
    20–21
politics and, 76, 78, 81, 164,
    166–67, 170–71
"windfall profits" tax, 116

Young, Don, 85